MALICE IN
WONDERLAND

Robert Maxwell

v.

PRIVATE EYE

Court 11: High Court of Justice. As imagined by Charles Griffin.

MALICE IN
WONDERLAND

Robert Maxwell
v.
PRIVATE EYE

REPORTED BY JOHN JACKSON

**INTRODUCED AND WITH AN EPILOGUE BY
ROBERT MAXWELL**

EDITED BY JOE HAINES AND PETER DONNELLY

CARTOONS BY CHARLES GRIFFIN AND DAVID LANGDON

Macdonald

A Macdonald Book

Copyright © 1986 Robert Maxwell

Copyright in the transcripts © 1986
by Beverley F. Nunnery & Co.

First published in Great Britain in 1986
by Macdonald & Co (Publishers) Ltd
London & Sydney

ISBN 0-356-14616-2

Reproduced, printed and bound in Great Britain by
Hazell Watson & Viney Limited,
Member of the BPCC Group,
Aylesbury, Bucks

Macdonald & Co (Publishers) Ltd
Greater London House
Hampstead Road
London NW1 7QX

A BPCC plc Company

Contents

INTRODUCTION
The Case, by Robert Maxwell   10

CHAPTER 1
Day 1   38

CHAPTER 2
Day 2   48

CHAPTER 3
Day 3   52

CHAPTER 4
Day 4   61

CHAPTER 5
Day 5   65

CHAPTER 6
Day 6   70

CHAPTER 7
Day 7   72

CHAPTER 8
Day 8   74

CHAPTER 9
Day 9   78

CHAPTER 10
Day 10   85

CHAPTER 11
The Court of Appeal   86

CHAPTER 12
Mr Bateson for the Defence   98

CHAPTER 13
Mr Hartley for the Plaintiff   110

CHAPTER 14
The Judge Sums Up   132

CHAPTER 15
Day 15   167

CHAPTER 16
Epilogue   173

APPENDIX 1
The 'Litany of Lies'   177

APPENDIX 2
Mr Maxwell's Diary   187

APPENDIX 3
The *Eye*   189

IN THE HIGH COURT OF JUSTICE, QUEEN'S BENCH DIVISION

ROYAL COURTS OF JUSTICE
MONDAY, 3rd NOVEMBER 1986

Before:

MR JUSTICE SIMON BROWN
(and a Jury)

Between:

MAXWELL *Plaintiff*

and

PRESSDRAM LIMITED & Anor *Defendants**

MR R HARTLEY, Q.C. and MR T SHIELDS
(instructed by Messrs Nicholson Graham and
Jones) appeared on behalf of the plaintiff.

MR A BATESON, Q.C. and MR D BROWNE
(instructed by Messrs Wright Webb and Syrett)
appeared on behalf of the defendants.

(Transcribed by Beverley F. Nunnery & Co.,
Official Shorthand Writers and Tape Transcribers,
25 Dulverton Mansions, Gray's Inn Road, London
WC1X 8EJ. Telephone: 01 278–7047/0975)

*Richard Ingrams and *Private Eye*.

PROCEEDINGS

Judge	**MR JUSTICE SIMON BROWN** Appointed a Judge in the Queen's Bench Division of the High Court in 1984; aged 49; educated at Stowe School and Worcester College, Oxford; First Junior Treasury Counsel 1979–84; recreations: golf, skiing, theatre.
Counsel for Robert Maxwell	**RICHARD HARTLEY, Q.C.** Queen's Counel since 1976; aged 54; educated at Marlborough College and Sidney Sussex College, Cambridge; recreations: golf, tennis. THOMAS SHIELDS — Junior counsel.
Counsel for *Private Eye* and Richard Ingrams	**ANDREW BATESON, Q.C.** Queen's Counsel since 1971; aged 61; educated at Eton; recreations: shooting, fishing, gardening. DESMOND BROWNE — Junior Counsel.
Witnesses for Plaintiff (in order of appearance)	Alex Kitson Henry Timpson Rt. Hon. Michael Foot Rt. Hon. Michael Cocks Richard Clements Nick Grant Robert Maxwell, M.C. Alex Kitson (recalled) Rt. Hon. Lord Elwyn Jones Mark Young
Witnesses for Defendants (in order of appearance)	Christopher Silvester Richard Ingrams Christopher Hird John Walker
The Jury	Six men and six women drawn from the panel called the jury service at the Old Bailey but switched at the last moment to the High Court. A middle aged man, the tenth to be called, was excused because of a dental appointment for an abscess on a tooth. He was replaced by a younger man. The jury was told the case had been set down for ten days, certainly not longer than two weeks. It lasted three full weeks.

MALICE IN WONDERLAND

Robert Maxwell

v.

PRIVATE EYE

The Case, by Robert Maxwell

In its issue of July 12, 1985, the fortnightly satirical magazine, *Private Eye*, published the following:

'Mirror Group publisher Robert Maxwell may not be popular with some sections of the Labour movement, but he is definitely de rigueur with Party Leader, Neil Kinnock.

Patricia Hewitt, Kinnock's once fun-loving press secretary, is shortly to announce a visit by the Welsh windbag to the East African capitals of Dar-es-Salaam and Nairobi, though she won't be revealing that Maxwell is acting as paymaster for the trip.

The dates chosen for Kinnochio's visit are unfortunate, however, since the relevant heads of state will be away attending the Organisation for African Unity's congress in Addis Ababa. A revised plan has been made for Kinnock to stop off in Addis and exchange pleasantries with Nyerere and Arap Moi before whizzing down to their Marie Celeste capitals. An ideal opportunity, you would have thought, for Kinnock to tour the famine-stricken areas of Ethiopia. Not so, say his staff - he would only be accused of cynical exploitation. Never mind that Labour MPs are longing for him to do some exploiting.

Members of Kinnock's kitchen cabinet are fond of boasting how they 'made money out of the Moscow trip' (another Maxwell subsidy) and recall how the Captain picked up the tab for Kinnock's Central American tour after the international charity War on Want backed-off for publicity reasons.

How many more Kinnock freebies will Maxwell have to provide before he is recommended for a peerage?'

As soon as I saw that article, I reacted. On July 15 I wrote to the editor of *Private Eye*, Mr Richard Ingrams, whom I inadvertently described as 'Mr Ingram', a minor error which was to have a considerable bearing on subsequent events. My letter said:

Dear Mr Ingram

There is not a word of truth in the allegations published in the 12th July issue of *Private Eye* alleging that I am acting as paymaster for Mr Kinnock's trip to Moscow, nor that I picked up the tab for Kinnock's Central American tour.

Finally, the disgraceful allegation that I provide Mr Kinnock with 'freebies' (which presumably is intended to mean 'bribes') for the purpose of securing for myself a peerage recommendation is as insulting as it is mendacious. I call upon you, your printers and publishers to withdraw these allegations unreservedly and to publish prominently in the next edition of *Private Eye* a retraction and suitable apology, the draft of which I enclose herewith, and to pay £10,000 to the *Mirror*'s Ethiopia Appeal Fund. Failing which I will issue proceedings for libel and damages against you, Pressdram Ltd and its printers without further notice.

    Yours sincerely,
Robert Maxwell

Neil Kinnock's press secretary, Miss Patricia Hewitt, wrote similarly to *Private Eye*, saying:

    Sir,

    You have got it wrong again.

    Robert Maxwell has nothing whatsoever to do with the financing of Neil Kinnock's visit to Addis Ababa, Tanzania and Kenya. Nor did he have anything to do with the financing of Mr Kinnock's visits to Moscow and Nicaragua. All were paid for in the usual way, by this office.

    I know that you will want to print a correction and apology and I look forward to their being given equal prominence in your next issue.

    Yours faithfully,
Patricia Hewitt

Both letters, including my mis-spelling of Mr Ingrams' name, appeared in the following issue of *Private Eye*, dated July 26, 1985.

But there was no response from the *Eye* to my demand for a retraction and an apology, nor to the call for a substantial donation to the *Mirror*'s Ethiopian Appeal, though the *Mail on Sunday*, which had reprinted the story in a milder form, had immediately agreed to apologise and to donate £5,000 to the Appeal. This donation was later used successfully as a yardstick for the award of damages by *Private Eye*'s counsel, Mr Andrew Bateson, QC, in his final speech to the jury hearing my subsequent libel action against his clients.

But that issue of *Private Eye* also repeated, in truncated form, the allegation in the previous issue. My denial, which I thought forceful enough, was described as 'lame'. In its column about the ways of Fleet Street, 'Street of Shame,' it said:

'The guest list for the glittering, champagne-all-the-way party marking Cap'n Bob's first glorious year at the helm of the *Daily Mirror* was awesome indeed. On it was Prince Charles (who puzzlingly failed to turn up) and, of course, Neil Kinnock.

'On the day, Maxwell ordered political hack Julia Langdon to confirm with Kinnock that he would be coming. Kinnock told her he had no intention of gracing the affair as he was concerned with more important matters of state that evening. The fat man's response was typical. "Tell him," he boomed, "that if he doesn't come to my party the *Mirror* will not be reporting his African tour."

'Kinnock was furious. "You tell him," he stormed, "that I will not be bribed!" Thankfully good sense finally prevailed. Mindful of His Master's Voice, Kinnock duly turned up. Maximum publicity for the African junket, which Maxwell lamely denies financing, was promised. Kinnock and the rest left happily clutching their souvenir of the evening: a mock-up of the *Mirror* featuring the gigantic form of Maxwell on every page.'

To emphasise the allegation it was making, the magazine also printed a cartoon alongside the 'Street of Shame' article.

As soon as I became aware of the further article and cartoon I instructed my legal advisers to try, by injunction, to prevent the distribution of the magazine containing the repetition of the original libel.

Mr David Eady, QC, appearing for *Private Eye* in the Court of Appeal on July 24, 1985, was categoric about the attitude of the magazine:

'They intend to justify in relation to (the allegation of payment for trips to) Moscow and South America.'

In answer to a question from the Master of the Rolls, Sir John Donaldson, Mr Eady added:

'I have probed a little further and I do know the identity of the witnesses and the nature of the evidence they will give in relation to the Moscow and South America trips. But simply because the journalist who wrote it is not available, I have not been in a position to obtain similar evidence in relation to Africa.'

The following exchange then took place:

The Master of the Rolls: 'Let me put it this way. By 10.30 tomorrow you will be able, in the form of an affidavit sworn or, at any rate, in a form that will be sworn, to set out your instructions that there is an intention to justify Moscow and South America, and you would either be able to say, "We are going to justify East Africa or we are not going to justify East Africa", or "We are not in a position to know whether we are or we are not because the journalist concerned is locked up in Beirut and we cannot talk to him."'

On the following day, Lord Campbell, QC, who replaced Mr Eady, appeared for *Private Eye* and said that the affidavit had been sworn.

My counsel, Mr Richard Hartley, QC, who appeared for me when the action was heard some fifteen months later, read to the Court part of that affidavit, sworn by Mr Christopher Silvester, *Private Eye*'s political correspondent:

> 'The sources for the defendants' statements are reliable and highly placed. The defendants also have evidence by which they can identify the method whereby funds from the plaintiff were channelled to Mr Kinnock's private office, the amount of such funds being calculated by reference to expenditure in his overseas trips to Moscow and to Central America.'

Needless to say, no attempt was ever made to justify those allegations, no source was ever produced and no evidence was ever introduced. But because of the affidavit, *Private Eye* was allowed by the Court of Appeal to distribute that edition. My solicitors had sent a lengthy telex to all the main wholesalers, including W.H. Smith and Menzies, warning them that a High Court writ for damages had been issued in respect of the articles in *Private Eye* on July 12 and July 26. It said:

> 'Tomorrow morning the Court of Appeal will decide whether our client is entitled to an injunction preventing publication of any suggestion which appears in the articles and in the cartoon on page 6 of the issue of *Private Eye* dated 26th July. In the meantime we suggest you cease any further distribution.
>
> 'The further purpose of this telex is to put you on notice that, without prejudice to the decision taken by the Court of Appeal tomorrow, our client will institute proceedings for damages for libel if any publication of those allegations takes place. We would draw your attention to page 11 of the issue of *Private Eye* dated 26th July 1985 where letters from our client and Mr Kinnock's press office make clear that these allegations are wholly without foundation.'

Menzies did their best to prevent further distribution. W.H. Smith declined to do so.

Battle against the *Eye* was now inevitable. The allegation, as I saw it, and as the High Court jury eventually saw it, that I was bribing Mr Kinnock for the purpose of obtaining a peerage was, in fact, more than mendacious and insulting. It was an allegation of a criminal offence.

After the Lloyd George-Maundy Gregory scandal over the sale of honours in the 1920s, Parliament passed, in August, 1925, the Honours (Prevention of Abuses) Act. It was short, precise and unmistakeable.

Its principal clause states:

> 'If any person accepts or agrees to accept or attempts to obtain from any person, for himself or for any other person, or for any purpose, any gift, money or valuable consideration as an inducement or reward for procuring or assisting or endeavouring to procure the grant of a dignity or title or honour to any person, or otherwise in connection with such a grant, he shall be guilty of an offence.

'If any person gives, or agrees or proposes to give, or offers to any person any gift, money or valuable consideration as an inducement or reward for procuring or assisting or endeavouring to procure the grant of a dignity or title or honour to any person, or otherwise in connection with such a grant, he shall be guilty of an offence.

'Any person guilty of an offence under this Act shall be liable on conviction on indictment to imprisonment for a term not exceeding two years or to a fine not exceeding five hundred pounds, or to both such imprisonment and such fine, or on summary conviction to imprisonment for a term not exceeding three months or to a fine not exceeding fifty pounds, or to both such imprisonment and such fine, and where the person convicted (whether on indictment or summarily) received any such gift, money or consideration as aforesaid which is capable of forfeiture, he shall in addition to any other punishment be liable to forfeit the same to His Majesty.'

If *Private Eye*'s allegation had been correct, then Neil Kinnock and I would have been guilty of an offence under that Act. That is why I felt I could not ignore, as I had frequently done on other occasions, what the magazine had written about me.

This was not, however, sufficiently brought out during the course of the trial of the action, either by my counsel or by the defendants'. Indeed, Mr Bateson, in his final speech for *Private Eye* said: 'If it is said in a publication that Mr Maxwell pays money to a political party in the hope of a peerage, that is not a libel ...'

As I understand it, recommendations for political honours must be accompanied by a certificate, signed by the Chief Whip or the leader of the political party making the recommendations, to the effect that there was 'no payment or expectation of payment to any party or political fund' by the intended recipient for the purpose of obtaining an honour. I could never see how the suggestion that the payments I was alleged to have made (but which were not made) could have been interpreted other than as an attempt to obtain a corrupt reward.

I had forgotten that in *The Listener* for November 18, 1982, exactly four years earlier, I had reviewed Patrick Marnham's '*The Private Eye Story*'. In it, I said, in words similar to those I was to use in the witness box in November, 1986: '*Private Eye*'s speciality is fiction, disguised as anonymous special knowledge - and the seamier, the more saleable.' I went on: 'Couple that speciality with a callous disregard for the victim's feelings and with prejudices which find expression in queer-bashing, Jew-baiting and besmirching those who give service to the public and you arrive at a policy of publication without respect to any consideration other than the victim's power to retaliate, and of refusal to correct except for the most compelling financial reasons.'

The *Eye* is a phenomenon of our age. I said in *The Listener*: 'There are those who praise *Eye* on the grounds that it has changed the way this generation views its public men, not only by making fun of them, but also by implying that they habitually have their noses in the public trough and act for personal financial or private motives. But is this really a matter for praise? Does it really make a valuable contribution to our society to destroy both in our own eyes, and in those of the world at large, our major national asset of incorruptibility in public life - to replace it by a belief that the instincts of the piggery motivate our public servants and successful entrepreneurs?'

During his evidence on November 7, 1986, Mr Ingrams said: 'Our aim is to be satirical, which involves making fun of public figures and those set in authority over us.'

That is a confession of anarchy, of a motive to destroy, because indiscriminate ridicule is ultimately destructive. It is certainly the case that some public figures do not deserve the renown they enjoy. It does not follow from that that all public figures are destructible merely because they are public figures, or that every man or woman on the public stage has feet of clay, a discreditable private life and unworthy ambition.

I concluded my review in *The Listener* - and I repeat it not for reasons of self-publicity but because it foreshadowed the action of November, 1986 - in these words: 'I cannot help feeling that Mr Ingrams carries within his morose self a death-wish. Sooner or later he will risk everything on a major protracted libel battle in the belief that the best way for him and the *Eye* to go down is with all its malicious guns blazing. It is only a matter of time and of choice of target.'

The *Eye* is so successful that it will not go down as the result of my action against it. It was, however, severely holed. The estimated costs amounted to £250,000, to which must be added the £55,000 damages, including exemplary damages of £50,000, which were awarded by the jury. They were not lethal, but they will, I hope, prove to be a deterrent.

It was the most expensive engagement on which the *Eye* has ever embarked. In one sense, I was lucky. Seeking redress for libel is only open to those who can afford it. It is expensive, uncertain and not covered by the provisions of legal aid. It is a law which can only be invoked by rich men and women or by wealthy corporations. Those who do not have financial resources of their own or the backing of their employers have to grin and bear any assassination of their character. Were that not the case, I doubt if a magazine of *Private Eye*'s type would be able to survive, not least because its editor would spend more time in the High Court than in his editorial chair.

A unique feature of the November, 1986 action was that for the first time the *Eye* issued a counter-claim for libel, taking exception to an article in the Mirror's diary, of July 1985, headed 'Another Whopper'.

It began ... '*Private Eye*, or Public Lie as it ought to be called ...'

On the Wednesday of the second week of the trial, the *Private Eye* counter-claim against the *Daily Mirror*, relating to the article which accused them of 'Another Whopper', was withdrawn in the absence of the jury.

Mr Justice Brown told the jury when they returned that the defendants 'had not thought it right to continue with it'. It was, accordingly, dismissed with costs against the defendants. We had called *Private Eye* liars. They had issued a writ for libel. Now they withdrew it. Whatever gloss on the withdrawal Mr Bateson tried to put, I felt that the jury would be influenced by their failure to contest what we had said about *Private Eye*.

When the trial opened on November 3, my leading counsel, Mr Hartley, recalled that I had once previously - and successfully - sued *Private Eye* for libel, in l975. *Private Eye* apologised unreservedly on that occasion - though some of the most remarkable evidence heard during the course of the action was from Mr Ingrams and Mr Silvester about the worth of the magazine's apologies - and undertook not to publish defamatory statements about me in the future. As Mr Hartley said, that undertaking was hollow.

Mr Hartley's opening statement is set out at length in Chapter 1 of this book. He demonstrated the untruthfulness - to use a word which *Private Eye* would no doubt prefer for its lies - of every allegation by simply pointing out that the *Eye* was not intending to attempt to prove the veracity of any of them. 'We say,' he added, 'they had it in for Mr Maxwell.' He did not suggest I was the only target. Indeed, the list of those admittedly defamed by *Private Eye* reads like a shortened version of Who's Who.

BELOW: *Dec. 12, 1976. Damages for André Previn.*

André Previn, the conductor. Lord Weidenfeld, the publisher. Harold Soref, the former Tory M.P. Harold Evans, former *Sunday Times* editor. Sir James Goldsmith, the businessman. Roddy Llewellyn, the gardener. Lord Goodman, the solicitor. Ian Coulter, the journalist. Penelope Keith, the actress, and her husband. Desmond Wilcox, the TV producer. Lady Havers, wife of the Attorney-General, about whom a particularly foul allegation was made. Jocelyn Stevens, the publisher. Lady Rothermere. Edward Heath. Sara Keays. Clive Jenkins. The list went on and on.

It was, said Mr Hartley, 'a litany of lies'.

The case as it developed was, to me, more disturbing than that. As I have said there was to be no pretence on the part of counsel for *Private Eye* or its witnesses to justify the original allegation that I had financed Mr Kinnock's visits abroad. Instead, they sought to justify them by reference to an issue which had nothing to do with Neil Kinnock and related to a time in 1983 when he was neither leader of the Labour party nor had an immediate prospect of becoming so.

It was alleged that I had had a meeting in 1983 in the Gay Hussar restaurant in Soho - and, incidentally nothing could be more open than meeting there: it is populated each day by politicians, journalists and trade union leaders - with Michael Foot, then Leader of the

BELOW RIGHT: *Mar. 23, 1977. Damages for Lord Weidenfeld.*
BELOW LEFT: *Oct. 23, 1981. Damages for Lord Goodman.*

Opposition, Mr Michael Cocks, then Labour's Chief Whip, Mr Jim Mortimer, then general secretary of the Labour party, and Mr David Hughes, the Party's National Agent.

At that meeting, I was said to have handed over a cheque for £75,000 to pay for the legal costs of litigation in the High Court against proposals by the Boundary Commission for changes in constituency boundaries.

Mr Foot was explicit in his denials. 'I never attended a Gay Hussar lunch, nor did the Chief Whip and the other two parties to the proceedings. That is absolute rubbish.'

The only lunch at that restaurant with me, he said, was on a different matter with different people. No cheque was handed over and Mr Foot paid for the lunch.

What I did do on other occasions, which I freely admitted, was to make contributions, totalling some £38,000, to the costs of that unsuccessful action by Mr Foot and the others (not by the Labour Party), after I had been approached by them to do so. There was nothing improper in that, nor was any suggestion made that it was.

The other issue used to try to justify totally different allegations was that I had paid some £43,000 to the Labour Party at its Blackpool conference in 1984. Here again, I was responding to an approach which

LEFT: *Dec. 4, 1981. Damages for actress Penelope Keith and husband Rodney Timson.*

had been made to me by the Party's treasurer and its chairman. It was publicly announced at the time that I had promised to match, pound for pound, whatever the party could raise at the conference. It was announced to the conference. The money was openly paid over and reported. It had nothing to do with Mr Kinnock or his office. He was not involved in any way.

I went into the witness box on Wednesday, November 5, spending a total of six hours there on that and the following day. A summary of my evidence is in Chapter 3. My counsel took me through the long history of the insults which *Private Eye* had delivered to me, stretching back more than ten years. Appearing in the High Court to give evidence is a strain. Even the former Lord Chancellor, Lord Elwyn-Jones, with his long legal experience, was nervous when he gave evidence in my support towards the end of the trial. I was especially moved, and wept, when Mr Hartley recalled the 'joke' letter, printed in the *Eye* under my wife's name, comparing the Duke of Edinburgh with Adolf Eichmann, the war criminal responsible for destroying most of my family.

I was asked for my reaction to the second article repeating the original libel and the cartoon which accompanied it. I replied: 'It was not only accusing me of bribery of the Leader of the Opposition, but

LEFT: *May 6, 1982. Damages for TV producer Desmond Wilcox.*

this is an allegation, if it is not instantly withdrawn, not only gravely damaging to me and to the Leader of Her Majesty's Opposition, but an allegation of bribery for purposes of buying a peerage is destructive of the body politic of the Government and the country.'

Mr Hartley put to me the allegation that I had wanted a peerage. I told him: 'I have no ambition to be a member of the House of Lords.'

When I was cross-examined by Mr Bateson, he immediately returned to the same question. He asked: 'Mr Maxwell, if you were offered a peerage, would you accept?'

I replied: 'The answer to that I can only say is this: I have been offered it twice before and I have said "no."'

The first of those occasions, I explained, was when an old colleague at Westminster, Lord Goronwy-Roberts, a former deputy leader of the Labour Party in the Lords, approached me in the early 1980s. I refused it on the grounds that I could not accept the defence policies of Labour's then leader, Mr Michael Foot.

More recently, I said, Mr Roy Hattersley, the present deputy leader of the Labour party, had asked me a similar question. Before I gave evidence, I checked this with Mr Hattersley. He has subsequently told me that his remark, along the lines of, 'I suppose you will want to be the next to go to the Lords,' and made at the time when our mutual friend Mr Charles Williams was made a peer, was jocular and not to be taken as an offer of any kind. Naturally I accept that. But I took his words seriously and made a serious answer and that answer remains my position.

Mr Hattersley's spokesman later told newspapermen that Mr Hattersley had not offered me a peerage but that he had discussed with me one or two people who were already peers, during the course of which I had intimated to him that I would never want to be a peer. Whatever Mr Hattersley's recollections are today, at least he remembers that last part.

If I had entertained the desire to go to the Lords, the payment of any monies at all to the Labour Party would, in law, have prevented me from doing so. I know it is commonly said that the law, the one I quoted at length above, is more honoured in the breach than the observance. All I can say is that it has never been proved to be so, and that any man or woman who donates money to any political party in hope of a title or some other coveted honour is taking a risk and committing a criminal offence, as is the party leader in giving it.

Despite my answers, Mr Bateson continued to gnaw at this meatless bone. Three times he put it to me that I desired a place in the House of Lords. When I replied: 'I see no reason why my answer a third time should be any different from what it was twice,' the judge, Mr Justice Simon Brown, intervened: 'I think that is a fair response, Mr Bateson.'

The whole issue led me to say later to Mr Bateson something I have felt for a very long time. I believe that the funding of political parties should be through the public purse. It is undignified and potentially corrupting - though I do not believe such corruption has occurred - for

ABOVE: *Oct. 6, 1980.
Damages for Roddy
Llewellyn, friend of
Princess Margaret.*
LEFT: *Feb. 10, 1984.
Apologies for Lady
Rothermere.*

political leaders, in office and out, to have to seek private money to perform their public duties. Some advance was made in the 1970s when Mr Edward Short, then Leader of the Commons, introduced the scheme whereby Opposition parties are funded, to a limited extent, according to the support they received at the previous general election. But it is not enough. It leads to the circumstance where Labour relies heavily upon the trade unions to carry out its official role as Her Majesty's Opposition, where the Conservative Party seeks substantial assistance from its business and City friends, and where the other parties will seek assistance from wherever it may fall.

But for private individuals to fund a political office ensures the continuance of a practice which I consider to be detrimental to the functioning of our democracy. As I said in evidence, I was once asked to contribute to Mr Harold Wilson's office and I declined. When Mr Bateson asked me if I would be willing to put my hand in my pocket to assist Mr Kinnock to perform his duties, I said 'no.' To alleviate a condition is to perpetuate it. I would prefer a fundamental change to be made in political financing.

At this point, a moment of light relief entered the trial. The judge announced he had received a note from the jury which read: 'Please can we the jury be informed exactly what a peer is and what his compulsory, if any, duties would be?'

A peer, said Mr Justice Simon Brown, was a member of the House of Lords, of either sex, and wasn't compelled to do any work at all, an answer which seems to me to be a perfect summary.

During my cross-examination, Mr Bateson made a remark which seemed to me to go to the heart of *Private Eye*'s defence.

He had been questioning me at length about what the *Eye* maintained was my obsessive self-publicity. He quoted a *Daily Mirror* headline about the Commonwealth Games, saying, "Mirror saves the Games."

'By Mirror you mean Maxwell?' asked Mr Bateson.

'I mean the *Mirror*,' I replied.

'You were identifying yourself with the *Mirror*?' persisted Mr Bateson.

'No,' I said.

Mr Justice Simon Brown intervened again: 'Mr Bateson, is that really fair? If he had said, "Maxwell saves the Games", then really you would have had a field day, would you not?'

'My Lord,' Mr Bateson replied, 'I, with respect, intend to have a field day either way.'

After several hours of cross examination, subjected to questioning in which I was accused of everything from bullying to self-publicity and union-bashing, Mr Hartley rose to object to 'a rolling cross-examination' over every part of my life, saying in conclusion: 'It is because there is no defence that what the defendant has to do is to have this scatter gun and try somehow to get something to stick against Mr Maxwell.'

That ended my first day in the witness box.

By the next morning, Thursday, November 6, relations between counsel on both sides appeared, to the layman, to be deteriorating. At one point, after an interjection from Mr Bateson, Mr Hartley protested: 'I am not saying you are a liar.' Later, Mr Bateson remarked on 'continual complaints' from Mr Hartley. This acerbity was repeated at various stages of the trial.

Much of this morning was taken up by legal argument over Mr Bateson's wish to cross-examine me about my general reputation, which he wanted to establish was bad. The jury was asked to leave the court while the argument went on. The judge told them, I thought wearily, when they returned that one piece of advice should invariably be given to juries and that was to bring "a rattling good book" to court with them.

The rest of my cross-examination, when it resumed, ranged widely, from an interview I had given, but could not recollect, to Anglia Television in which an unnamed senior executive of mine said I was 'as tough as old boots' - apparently, evidence that I was a bully - to a false report in *The People* about the pregnancy of Princess Anne. The one issue which was not covered was the allegation which was the cause of the action, namely that I had bribed Neil Kinnock. Mr Bateson told the jury that 'there is nothing wrong in our modern society about people paying money to a political party in the hope that they will get a peerage.' I still disagree with him.

Mr Bateson sought to defend *Private Eye* from charges that it was actuated by malice, a word which was taken up by my counsel in the final stages of the action when he uttered the phrase which became the title of this book, 'Malice in Wonderland.'

Private Eye's first witness was Mr Christopher Silvester, grandson of the dance band leader to whose rhythms some of the older members of the jury and counsel no doubt danced in their younger days.

Mr Silvester it was who had sworn the affidavit in July, 1985, that the *Eye* would justify its allegations, which it had received from 'reliable and highly placed' sources. He repeated in the witness box the distinguished nature of his source (at this stage he used the singular), stating he was: 'highly respected within the Labour Party. He is a prospective Parliamentary candidate. He was also privy to what went on in Mr Kinnock's private office. In other words, he used occasionally to advise members of the office about various matters.'

Mr Silvester said that he had hoped that the source was going to be a witness and he still maintained that the article about me was 'true in substance'.

What he could not prove was the allegation that I had paid for the overseas trips of Mr Kinnock, which to my mind, by any reasonable interpretation, was the substance.

He repeatedly referred to his 'source' or 'sources', including 'two sources' on the staff of the *Daily Mirror*. They were unnamed, like the prospective Parliamentary candidate, because they were supposedly in fear of their jobs. Said Mr Silvester: 'I would be no more prepared to disclose a source than I would expect Mr Maxwell's journalists to disclose their sources in a court of law, unless the sources wished to be disclosed.'

It was not said in court, but I know it is the case, that Mirror Group Newspaper lawyers will ask a journalist who has written a story containing a high legal risk whether their source or sources would be prepared to give evidence in court. If the answer is 'no,' then the lawyers will normally advise that the story should not be used.

Is your source alive? Mr Silvester was asked. He is, was the answer. So he can come and give evidence? He could if he so wished, said Mr Silvester.

Thus we moved into one of the most contentious issues which was to arise in the case: whether *Private Eye* should be ordered by the court to disclose its sources - if, indeed, those sources existed.

Three witnesses - Alex Kitson, Henry Timpson and Richard Clements - had already given evidence that the assertion I had paid for Mr Kinnock's trips abroad was untrue.

Mr Justice Simon Brown asked Mr Bateson: 'You would not contend that the jury without hearing from or even having identified to them this source, could properly conclude that the evidence that they

BELOW: *July 1, 1983. Damages for Lady Havers, wife of the Attorney-General.*

have heard is perjury?'

Mr Bateson: 'No, my lord.'

Mr Justice Simon Brown: 'The defendants for their part are not contending that there is any truth in the allegation that those payments were made towards overseas trips?'

Mr Bateson: 'I am not so alleging and I cannot!'

That killed that one, though the action was to continue for another two weeks.

My counsel returned to the question of sources.

Mr Silvester said that at the time of swearing his affidavit before the Court of Appeal he 'had every reason to believe this source would appear to give evidence.' A couple of months later, he found he would not.

He was prepared to admit that the article making the original allegation against me was untrue but it was not a lie - a semantic quibble which was to go on and on. He was not prepared to apologise to me at all and accused me of 'emotional blackmail' for having been ready to settle our dispute on the basis of *Private Eye* making a donation of £10,000 to the Ethiopian Appeal Fund.

His source, he said, was 'hiding behind' him. He was not prepared to come to court and give evidence.

LEFT: *Mar. 9, 1984. Apology to Miss Sarah Keays (and Marcus Fox, M. P.)*

Mr Silvester then made the remark which eventually compelled me to seek disclosure of his source or sources under Section 10 of the Contempt of Court Act, 1981, which permits such a ruling, either on grounds of national security or in the interests of justice. His source, he said, had been told by Mr Alex Kitson that I had subsidised Mr Kinnock's visit to Moscow.

Mr Hartley asked him: 'So if your source is correct, Mr Kitson is not only a liar but a perjurer?' and Mr Silvester replied: 'If my source is correct.'

The judge was troubled, he said, that a witness (Alex Kitson), who was not even cross-examined about the truth of his evidence, could in this way be alleged to be a perjurer. He said later that he was not ordering the disclosure of sources, 'though sorely tempted to do so'.

The general cross-examination of Mr Silvester continued, over the Boundary Commission payment and a host of other allegations about me, all of which were admitted not to be true. I thought he wriggled throughout the afternoon. As Mr Hartley said to him: 'The impression you are giving the jury is that *Private Eye* is accident-prone with their witnesses.'

Mr Silvester was followed in the witness box by Richard Ingrams, editor of *Private Eye* when the libellous articles appeared. He has since retired from that post but remains chairman of the company.

Mr Ingrams answered his questions with frankness on the whole, if not always to his own advantage.

The policy of his magazine, he said, was: 'to be satirical, which involves making fun of public figures and attacking those set in authority over us.'

He said that he had considered the article about me 'to be a convincing story'.

An interesting insight into Mr Ingrams' style of editorship appeared in *The Independent* newspaper the week after the jury's verdict. Jane Ellison, an employee of *Private Eye* until she wrote a critical article about it earlier in 1986, said: 'Ingrams has always believed that he has an instinct for the truth of a story, however defamatory and however insubstantial in terms of the facts. If it sounds right, he will print it ...

'Ingrams would study the story and after a few moments of concentration accompanied by a paroxysm of facial contortion, utter the famous reply: 'Put it in.' And sure enough, it would appear.'

No doubt that instinct which Ms Ellison so graphically describes has helped *Private Eye*'s circulation to its level of around 250,000. But it must also have contributed significantly in the past to the annual total of around £300,000 which the magazine has to pay in legal costs, a sum swollen to rather more than that, I imagine, in 1986.

Ms Ellison said that Maxwell v Pressdram would be the last great battle the *Eye* would fight in court because Mr Ian Hislop, who succeeded Mr Ingrams as editor, 'regards libel payments as an unnecessary and expensive waste of money'. We shall see.

One thing which did not emerge nor draw any comment was the fact that as Mr Ingrams approached his retirement from the editor's chair he was engaged to write a fortnightly column in The *Sunday Telegraph*, starting at the beginning of August. His very first column included a sneer at me. At the end of October, the *Sunday Telegraph*'s editor, Mr Peregrine Worsthorne, sacked Mr Ingrams. It was a short life but not a merry one.

Back to Mr Ingrams in the witness box. He was asked for his reaction to my denial that I had paid for Mr Kinnock's overseas trips. He answered - curiously for an editor whose consistent policy has been to mis-spell the names of his victims - 'The first thing I noticed was that my name was mis-spelt'.

Mr Ingrams continued to insist, though I thought the issue had long been abandoned by Mr Silvester and Mr Bateson, that the allegations for which he could introduce no evidence were true. In answer to the judge, Mr Bateson agreed that he would not be inviting the jury to accept the truth of the allegations. 'So far as I am concerned,' he said, 'the concession stands.'

Mr Justice Brown said, 'So far as this jury is concerned ... they, as a matter of law, will have to accept that the statement is untrue and the source, therefore, is unreliable.'

Mr Ingrams was asked repeatedly about the main source for the *Eye*'s allegations. Without dissembling, he refused to give any indication or any clue. Mr Hartley had earlier that day, Monday, November 10, sought to win a ruling from Mr Justice Brown that the source or sources for the *Eye*'s allegations should be named.

Mr Justice Brown said: 'Powerful though in my judgment the arguments are in favour of an order for disclosure, I still on balance have decided to adhere to my earlier ruling' (which was not to compel disclosure).

Mr Hartley, at the conclusion of the day's proceedings, announced that I wished to test the judge's ruling in the Court of Appeal.

The ruling of the Court of Appeal was against me, though there again it was deemed to be a borderline case. Its findings are summarised later in this book.

I realised then, and I realise now, that moving to compel a journalist, under threat of imprisonment, to disclose the sources of his information, rightly sends a shudder of apprehension through every other journalist. It must seem even more sinister to them if the application is made by the publisher of three major national newspapers.

But the position was this: On July 24, 1985, when I sought an injunction to prevent the distribution of *Private Eye* containing the repeated libel against me, the magazine's counsel not only stated that the allegations would be justified but added that he knew the nature of the evidence which the witnesses would give in relation to them.

No attempt was made to justify those allegations when the case came to trial, nor were any witnesses - the sources - called to prove them. We were told that the unnamed sources were highly reliable and respected and that one of them was a prospective Parliamentary candidate with access to Mr Kinnock's office - clearly a person of importance.

This particular source had accused me of behaviour which I considered to be scandalous. Because of his word - not to be produced before the court in first-hand evidence - three of the earlier witnesses were, in effect, being called perjurers. One of them, Alex Kitson, had actually been named as the source of the source. *Private Eye*'s editor had identified him without any evident compunction, which might be thought to reflect a peculiar double standard so far as naming sources is concerned. If he would not name his own source, it hardly seemed ethical to name someone else as the purported source of his source.

Sauce for the goose was not thought to be sauce for the gander, so far as Mr Ingrams was concerned. I was left in the position that a man of considerable public reputation had been named as being responsible for an article which was, at the very least, highly offensive to me - an old friend - or to Neil Kinnock, the leader of the party of which Mr Kitson had been an active and prominent member for many years.

Mr Kitson had later to be recalled to rebut the evidence given. I noticed that some newspapers which had used Mr Ingrams' evidence naming him did not report his evidence in refutation.

Had Mr Kitson not been named, I would not have proceeded to the Court of Appeal. But by being named, it was conceivable that the jury would be influenced against his evidence and that they might have thought that what he had said in the witness box was not to be relied upon. I thought then, and I think now, that that was an intolerable situation. In the event, Mr Kitson had to be recalled at a later stage in the trial to rebut the allegation made against him.

After the Court of Appeal had decided against me, the cross-examination of Mr Ingrams resumed on the afternoon of November 11. He made it clear, I thought to the suprise of the court, that many of the apologies - perhaps a quarter of them - which *Private Eye* tendered to those it had defamed were insincere. That included an earlier apology to me.

I urge you to read, in particular, the chapter dealing with the apology given to Miss Penelope Keith and her husband. It encapsulates the attitude of *Private Eye* towards those whom they malign better than any brief summary I can make.

Mr Ingrams was asked about my letter of denial and asked if he remembered it. He replied: 'I remember vividly getting this letter because I thought, "My name's wrong."'

The reader will recall that I had inadvertently left the 's' off his surname. The following exchange then took place.

Mr Hartley: 'That is what incensed you, is it?'

Mr Ingrams: 'Well, it wasn't a good start.'

Mr Hartley: 'Did that colour your judgment about how to respond to this letter?'

Mr Ingrams: 'I think it does colour your judgment.'

Mr Justice Brown: 'Surely not!'

Mr Ingrams: 'It does!'

Mr Justice Brown said later to Mr Ingrams: 'I am bound to say I find it an astonishing answer that you gave earlier.'

'What was that, my lord?' inquired Mr Ingrams.

'That you have the least interest in whether anybody puts an "s" on your name and that you actually have regard to that when you are evaluating a letter of this sort. Was that a serious answer?'

'Absolutely serious,' replied Mr Ingrams. 'That is why I particularly remember receiving this letter.'

Talk about 'for want of a shoe a battle was lost!' Would Mr Ingrams have persisted in defending his libel through all those months had I spelt his name correctly in the first place? For the editor of a magazine which has wounded so many people so deeply over the years, he showed an astonishing sensitivity to an unintended slight.

Mr Hartley concluded his cross-examination of Mr Ingrams on Thursday, November 13, when he took him through the past apologies made by *Private Eye*, an exercise characterised by Mr Bateson, at one point, as 'a piece of mudslinging'. In the history of the law, there could hardly have been a more classic example of the pot calling the kettle black, for Mr Ingrams was later to describe statements of apology as 'the one form of statements in *Private Eye* which I put in knowing them to be untrue'.

Mr Christopher Hird, who teaches investigative journalism for one day a week at the Journalism Department of the City of London University, was introduced by *Private Eye* to discuss my general reputation. As far as I know, I have never employed him nor met him. The only answer of importance that I could detect in his evidence was his statement; 'It is very important that people check their sources,' which immediately followed his confirmation that he had never taught any of the journalists now working on *Private Eye*.

An attempt by the *Eye*'s junior counsel, Mr Desmond Browne, to compare a few feet of barbed wire placed on the top of a wall at the back of the *Daily Record*'s premises in Glasgow after evidence was found of an intended break-in - the wire was removed after twenty-four hours - with the many thousands of feet of barbed wire surrounding the News International plant at Wapping was dismissed by Mr Justice Brown as 'wholly misconceived' and a 'trifling matter'. He added: 'I am stunned that it is persisted in.'

Mr John Walker, who has written a book, 'The Queen has been Pleased,' about the Honours system, was the *Eye*'s last witness. He sought to demonstrate, as his book does, a correlation between the giving of money to political parties (mainly the Conservative Party) and the award of honours to the donor. But the only reference to me in his book reads: 'No doubt Robert Maxwell's intention as proprietor of the Mirror Group of newspapers is different.'

The former Lord Chancellor, Lord Elwyn-Jones, gave evidence for me. We have known each other for thirty years. My counsel asked:

'Did you speak for Mr Maxwell when he was Labour Parliamentary candidate for the constituency of Buckingham in the general election campaign of 1959?'

Lord Elwyn-Jones replied, drily: 'I think so. I hope that is not why he lost.'

Mr Mark Young, general secretary of the British Airline Pilots' Association, also gave evidence. He recently negotiated with me over the purchase of British Airways' helicopter company by the *Scottish Daily Record* and *Sunday Mail*, Ltd., one of the newspaper groups of which I am publisher.

He said he had found me 'very pro-union' - in contrast to the defendants' attempts to show I was a 'union-basher' - but 'a very, very tough negotiator'. He said he had discussed the take-over with senior trade union figures who advised him 'that he was a tough man to deal with but, on the whole, all the companies he had ever taken over prospered and that in turn provides security of employment for people, and generally they grew and created new employment'.

That was the end of the evidence. Further legal argument before Mr Justice Brown and the Court of Appeal (which the reader will find elsewhere) gave the jury a four-day break - Friday, Saturday, Sunday and Monday. They returned on the Tuesday to hear Mr Bateson make his final submission for the defendants.

In the event, it was Tuesday afternoon before the jury were to hear Mr Bateson, who displayed a gift for knocking his papers, files and books onto the floor. He cloaked his threadbare case, as well as he could, with his engaging personality.

He said: 'We do not contend, on behalf of the defendants, that if the words mean Mr Maxwell bribed Mr Kinnock, that that is true. We say that the words do not mean that and it is nonsense to suggest that they do, but if you decide that they do mean that we do not say that the words are true. We do, of course, accept that Mr Kinnock's trips were not paid for by Mr Maxwell - we have to, we have called no evidence to support the suggestion. However, you may take the view it does not mean bribes but it does mean, in your view, that for somebody to be said to be paying money to a political party with the motive of getting a peerage out of it, brings him into hatred, ridicule and contempt, or lowers him in the estimation of right-thinking people - two tests for whether something is a libel.'

Instead, he returned to the payments I had made over recent years to the Labour Party, half of them before Neil Kinnock became leader and all publicly announced or freely admitted. I was, he said, 'a man, ruthless, vindictive, with a vast ego'. The purpose, of course, was to demonstrate that my general reputation was so low that damages should be derisory. It is one of the risks in our present libel laws that one risks further defamation in court when one seeks to counter defamation outside it. Mr Bateson was also anxious, quite properly, to protect his clients from the danger of exemplary damages in which the repetition of the first libel and the promise to justify it when the case came to trial had placed them.

He tried to give authority to the unnamed source of the articles by saying: 'We know he is a prospective Labour candidate. First of all, if he was revealed as the source - you are twelve ordinary, decent people - what do you think would happen to his political career? He is not prepared to risk that career by coming to give evidence.'

I thought it was an equally pertinent question to ask what kind of political career ought to be available to a man who had told an outrageous lie and then refused to justify it on the grounds that it would affect his public standing, despite the fact that, uncorrected, it damaged my public standing and the public standing of the leader of his own party.

In his final speech, Mr Hartley recalled to the jury the hearing before the Court of Appeal on July 24, 1985, 'when the defendants told the court that they would justify the specific allegations that Mr Maxwell had paid for Mr Kinnock's overseas trips. The defendants at that stage were defiant - rather, you may think, like the roar of a lion. Compare that with their position now. The facts on which they rely, the alleged facts before the Court of Appeal - totally abandoned. The defence of fair comment - gone for evermore. Counter-claim - ignominiously abandoned. All the planks of their defence of justification broken. The roar of the lion ... is now reduced to the squeak of a mouse - admittedly, still quite a vicious little mouse.'

The evidence of Mr Silvester and Mr Ingrams, said Mr Hartley, was 'Malice in Wonderland'. He had, I thought, little difficulty in destroying the defendants' case. Indeed, he said, their defence had collapsed 'like a pack of cards' when Mr Ingrams said he did not suggest I had done anything improper in making payments to the Labour Party or to the Boundary Commission Fighting Fund.

Mr Justice Simon Brown began his summing up on the afternoon of Wednesday, November 19, a little impatient, it seemed, at the time which the case had consumed - an impatience which I wholeheartedly shared.

The case, he said, had been fought out keenly and passionately - from time to time, the jury might have thought, even venomously. The jury had to decide what they believed to be right, without worrying overmuch who won or lost. Unlike a criminal case, the plaintiff has to establish his case not beyond all reasonable doubt but on the balance of probabilities, more likely than not, 51 per cent.

He examined the original article for the benefit of the jury, especially the last paragraph, 'the critical paragraph', as he put it: 'How many more Kinnock freebies will Maxwell have to provide before he is recommended for a peerage?'

He told the jury: 'You can take as absolutely plain and axiomatic the defendants are not asserting that there is any truth in the suggestion that any of these three payments for trips were made or were being made. They recognise that there is absolutely no question of them being able to show that, and you must decide this case on the basis that

RIGHT: *June 14, 1984.*
Apology for former
Prime Minister
Edward Heath.

none of those payments were made or were being made.

'You may think that a freebie does at least connote this: that what is being provided free of charge is being provided as a favour. And so, in its overall context, you may think that the final paragraph may be paraphrased in this way: How many more of these continuing, secret favours will Mr Maxwell have to provide to Mr Kinnock before Mr Kinnock recommends him for a peerage?...

'That last paragraph, you may conclude, must inevitably be read as something of a jibe or dig or comment, not so much upon Mr Kinnock but upon the plaintiff. The words in particular, "have to provide", you may think imply that the plaintiff was himself acting in a calculating fashion, intending some relationship between the payments and the suggested end product of a peerage.'

He was still summing up at the end of the day. He returned the next morning, Thursday, November 20, and continued for the rest of the day.

He took the jury carefully through the labyrinth of possible meanings of the two articles which *Private Eye* had published and the defence of justification: 'The defendants have to show that, first, the plaintiff was ambitious for a peerage and, second, that the plaintiff was improperly seeking to realise that ambition by patronage of the Labour Party.'

The paragraphs of the pleadings, he said, which went to the heart of the plea of justification had 'finally bit the dust - you may think a good deal later than they should have done - after the end of the plaintiff's case. Not one single word of evidence has been called to support the truth of those matters. It is conceded that you are bound to regard them as wholly and utterly untrue.'

Mr Justice Brown turned to my alleged ambition to become a member of the House of Lords.

'Consider this matter. Mr Bateson has asserted repeatedly that this particular plaintiff can take a peerage whenever he wants to. That indeed, Mr Ingrams told you in evidence, was his view. Mr Ingrams supported it by saying: "After all, as the plaintiff himself told you, he has been offered a peerage more than once." So here is somebody, by common consent - and indeed as part of the defendants' case - who is a very obvious candidate for a peerage. He has really got all the right qualifications, you may think. He is a press baron, and as you have seen that very often they go to the House of Lords. He is a benefactor of the Labour Party. Again, it is part of the defendants' case that that eases the journey. He is a Labour Party activist and supporter, and you may well think that he is the sort of person who could in any event properly contribute to the debates and the processes of the upper legislative house, which, as I told you yesterday, is what the House of Lords is. And if all that is so, which you may think is indeed very convincing, well then, you may ask yourselves, "Why on earth should Mr Maxwell have been reduced in July of 1985 to having to continue patronising the Labour

Party with payments and self-publicising himself in order to achieve the ambition that could be achieved at the asking anyway?"'

As for my payments to the Boundary Commission Fighting Fund, he told the jury: 'You may think he merely responded generously to a personal plea.'

When he turned to my counsel's plea for exemplary damages, he warned the jury: 'They are only very, very rarely awarded ... it is only when the defendants have behaved quite disgracefully and in certain narrowly defined circumstances ... it is rather to punish the defendants additionally and to deter them and others like them from behaving so disgracefully in future.'

Mr Justice Brown turned to the £5,000 which had been paid by the *Mail on Sunday* to the *Mirror's* Ethiopian Appeal after Lady Falkender had repeated the *Eye's* original allegation, albeit in milder form, in her column in that paper.

'You may think it would not be right to regard that £5,000 as, so to speak, something which should compensate Mr Maxwell for the quite different injury and the continuing hurt to his feelings that *Private Eye's* more serious libels, if you accept they are libels, have caused.'

In the event, the jury thought that £5,000 was enough in compensatory damages. Mr Bateson had successfully pleaded that.

On the question of aggravated damages, Mr Justice Brown said: 'There was never any apology for the untruths - indeed there still is not. Rather, despite the denials, despite the back-tracking of the source as to his willingness to give evidence, there has been instead a plea of justification persisted in to the very end with a repeated avowal of the truth of the original allegation.'

Mr Justice Brown went over the evidence of the witnesses as to character and reputation called by both sides - he found Lord Elwyn-Jones a man of 'immense distinction and matchless charm' - and asked the jury what it all came to: 'You may think it is plain that the plaintiff does indeed have a driving will and perhaps a fairly relentless ambition to prosper and succeed in life and become a substantial public figure of influence and standing, both in the Labour Party and the affairs of the national generally. No doubt on occasions all that makes him act immodestly, unpleasantly, on occasions ruthlessly and even threateningly.

'On the other side of the coin, as Mr Hartley says, you have got a man who, some may think to his considerable credit, has pulled himself up by his boot straps and has done well not only for himself but his companies and his country, a creator of employment, a creator of profits within British business.'

As for the counter-claim for the *Mirror* Diary article, 'Another Whopper'. Mr Justice Brown commented: 'It was brought, Mr Ingrams accepted, as a tit-for-tat in response to the plaintiff's claim. You would be entitled, members of the jury, to regard it as a thoroughly ill-judged impertinence, and you may think that it was wholly misconceived, based, as it was, on the untenable proposition that because a lie is a deliberate untruth, therefore an article in *Private Eye* is not a lie unless Mr Ingrams himself, or just possibly one of his more regular staff, actually knows it to be untrue. You may have thought, from first to last, that a lie is a lie is a lie, and what starts as a lie is not in some mystical way purified by its appearance in *Private Eye*. It does not cease to be a lie because it is fed down a chain of informants, sources or gossips, to the point where Mr Ingrams himself may well be misled into believing it and publishing it.'

Mr Justice Brown reminded the jury that Mr Silvester and Mr Ingrams continued to assert the truth of the original articles.

'Members of the jury, what are you going to make of all that? There is not one single word of evidence before you which supports it. On the contrary, there is a great deal of evidence which indicates that it is wholly untrue.'

He turned to the curious episode of the mis-spelling by me of Mr Ingrams' name.

'One can very well understand a moment of pique, though one might feel perhaps rather unworthy to have felt it, but for it to colour, as Mr Ingrams said the mis-spelling of his name did colour, his whole approach to that letter might betray, you might conclude, the sort of vanity and self-importance that Mr Ingrams would have been all too alert to puncture in another.'

The judge drew to the end of his summing up and released the jury for the day until 10.30 the following morning when they would consider their verdict.

That verdict the reader already knows. Those principally concerned, were left to reflect upon the huge costs: me as plaintiff and, especially, Pressdram and Richard Ingrams as defendants, as they had to pay them.

It cannot be right that going to law to protect one's reputation should be so expensive and that the costs of such an action should amount to nearly five times the award of damages, even when they include exemplary damages. As I said earlier in this introduction, the redress of libel is available only to wealthy men and women or large corporations. A law which is not available to all cannot be a just law. I have long thought that the separation of the legal profession into solicitors and barristers adds greatly and unnecessarily to the expense of going to law and my experience in this case confirms me in my view.

Those in favour of fusion, as it is called, argued before the Royal Commission on Legal Services which reported in 1979 that the two-branch profession was inefficient, harmed the confidence of clients and was more expensive. I am emphatically on their side.

They also argued that the present system caused delay. Failures in communication flowed from the relationship between barrister and solicitor because it was too formal, because the written instructions to counsel were in some cases inadequate and late in arriving, and because barristers were reluctant to complain about inadequate

instructions for fear of offending a solicitor client. The Commission rejected these arguments. I would urge that all concerned, from the Lord Chancellor's Office down, should consider them again. I found that the triangular client-solicitor-barrister relationship was inefficient, difficult and frustrating. Counsel were hard to contact at week-ends, solicitors had not foreseen what the course of the action might be or the line which defendants' counsel might develop and much time and money was spent and wasted at the last minute organising defences against an attack on my reputation which was as predictable as it was inevitable. Negotiations went on for a settlement both before and during the hearing, but the discussions came to nothing.

Legal convention prevents me from detailing the course of the negotiations between lawyers, but I can say that Richard Ingrams phoned my chief of staff, Peter Jay, in October asking if I was out to destroy them or prepared to settle. My reply was that I was always prepared to settle but it must be on a fair basis.

As soon as the formal business of the court was over, I was surrounded by journalists asking me what I intended to do with the £55,000 damages awarded. My first thought was to give them to a children's charity or to research into finding a cure for AIDS. I reflected further on my way from Court Eleven to The Strand and decided that was right. I told assembled radio and TV journalists that assistance for AIDS research would be appropriate because the benefits of one infected organ would be going to find a cure for another. It was the kind of remark *Private Eye* might have made though it would not have been with a charitable intent.

CHAPTER ONE

Day 1

Murder, rape, mayhem? It was not to be quite so sensational for the jurors who filed into Court Number Eleven of the Law Courts that Monday morning in November.

They ranged in age from the early twenties to a granny figure around the eighty mark. There was a young man, who was later chosen as foreman. There was a middle-aged woman with each of her fingers smothered with a variety of rings. One woman, built like busty 'Carry On' actress Barbara Windsor, had a ticklish cough which interrupted the judge's summing up and prompted glasses of water and soothing pills to be passed up be a sympathetic female court usher.

One article in the *Daily Express*, published while they had four days away from court, prompted them to complain to Mr Justice Simon Brown. The piece said: 'The trial has unfolded with humour, horror and jokes, which the gum-chewing, yawning jury do not seem to appreciate. In fact, there was even a slight hiccup in this court-room drama when some of the jurors were reluctant to return to their seats after lunch. One of them complained that another smelled abominably'.

The judge told the jury: 'All I would say is that in so far as it refers to you, it seems to me to be gratuitously offensive ... the suggestion that you are a gum-chewing, yawning jury who are not appreciating the case seems to me to be thoroughly misplaced and misconceived criticism. I shall not even mention the other offensive remark. All I can urge you to do is to ignore it.'

These were the people who were to be at the centre of one of the most intriguing and controversial cases of libel ever heard in an English court of law.

The judge forecast as much in his first words to them. 'Members of the jury,' said Mr Justice Simon Brown, 'I gather you were all summoned for Old Bailey jury service ... and here you are, in the Strand.

'You are empanelled not to try - as you supposed you would - murder, rape, mayhem or something like that but, rather, a libel action. I suspect you will not find it any the less interesting ...' The jury would soon discover the truth of that prediction - and the fact that 'a rattling good book' would come in handy for the periods they were sent out of court while legal debates went on.

'From time to time', the judge told them, 'questions of law arise - and that gives you an opportunity to have a break and stretch your legs, which I dare say you will welcome. I know that this is not the most comfortable place to spend long hours.'

With that the jury were given their first short break while the judge debated with Mr Richard Hartley, QC, for Robert Maxwell and Mr Andrew Bateson, QC, for *Private Eye*.

Andrew Bateson had been described as the portly Rumpole of the High Court. He also reminded people of the famous barrister played by Charles Laughton in the film 'Witness For the Prosecution'.

True to form (his words) he knocked over all the bundles of documents as he walked into court on the first day. As a flurry of people picked them up and attempted to place them in order he announced: 'You ain't seen nothing yet. Wait till I knock the water over.'

IN THE HIGH COURT OF JUSTICE
QUEEN'S BENCH DIVISION

Royal Courts of Justice
Thursday, 6th November 1986

Before:

MR. JUSTICE SIMON BROWN
(and a Jury)

B E T W E E N:

MAXWELL   Plaintiff

- and -

PRESSDRAM LTD. & Anor.   Defendants

(Transcribed by Beverley F. Nunnery & Co., Official Shorthand
Writers and Tape Transcribers, 25 Dulverton Mansions, Gray's
Inn Road, London, WC1X 8EJ.
                              Telephone: 01 278-7047/0975)

MR. R. HARTLEY, Q.C. and MR. T. SHIELDS (instructed by Messrs.
Nicholson Graham & Jones) appeared on behalf of the Plaintiff.
MR. A. BATESON, Q.C. and MR. D. BROWNE (instructed by Messrs. Wright
Webb Syrett) appeared on behalf of the Defendants.

PROCEEDINGS

In fact he didn't, but the solicitor sitting in front of him managed to knock a full glass over Mr Bateson's notes. This brought the loud return from the 61-year-old QC: 'I am allowed to knock water over my instructing solicitor, but he is not allowed to knock it over me.'

Bateson and Hartley told the court they were very good friends, but there were to be times when the jury wondered. On one occasion, while Richard Ingrams was being cross-examined by Mr Bateson, his opponent

ABOVE LEFT: *Mr Justice Simon Brown.*
ABOVE RIGHT: *Frontispiece to the transcripts of the action.*

asked in an aside: 'What is defamatory? Bateson (with a deep sigh): 'Oh dear, poor Richard.' Hartley: 'Which Richard?' Bateson: 'You.' At this point Mr Justice Simon Brown looked down from the bench and asked: 'Would you like us to leave you two to it?' Mr Hartley got to his feet. 'At the risk of rousing my learned friend's wrath...' Bateson (sitting) muttered: 'Not wrath. Sympathy.'

Bateson would let slip his love of horse-racing when addressing the jury at the end of the case. He listed Mr Maxwell's Mirror Group Newspapers and was prompted by his junior for leaving out *The Sporting Life*. He made the aside: 'Well, I was leaving *The Sporting Life* on one side, interested though I may be in it for other reasons.'

Just before the jury were recalled, the judge pointed out that mention might be made of the Boundary Commission: 'I actually was counsel in that particular case,' he said. And although 'I cannot suppose that is going to be of any great excitement to any party ...I merely make that clear.'

The jury were brought back, and Mr Hartley outlined the case brought by Mr Maxwell, chairman of Pergamon Press, the British Printing and Communications Corporation, and Mirror Group Newspapers, publishers of the *Daily Mirror*, *Sunday Mirror*, *The People* and *The Sporting Life*.

'Mr Maxwell,' said Mr Hartley, 'is aged sixty-three. He had a distinguished war record including being awarded the Military Cross. He has been, and is proud of it, a member and active supporter of the Labour Party for many years. He was Member of Parliament for Buckingham from 1964 to 1970.

'His publishing interests started in a very modest way in the early 1950s and have grown over the years to the present position where the companies of which he is chairman publish newspapers, books and journals worldwide.

'Mr Maxwell's hobbies, when he has time for hobbies, are football and chess, and those of you who are football fans may know that he is Chairman of Oxford United Football Club which, after successful seasons in 1984 and

1985, is now in the first division.

'He is very happily married and has seven children.

'Mr Maxwell has been one of *Private Eye*'s favourite targets for very many years, with frequent references to him in the *Private Eye* column 'Street of Shame', which is a reference to Fleet Street. And he is also featured in a strip cartoon called "Captain Bob", a reference to Mr Maxwell.

'For the most part, Mr Maxwell has ignored *Private Eye*'s campaign against him. But there was one previous occasion when Mr Maxwell brought libel proceedings against *Private Eye* and other occasions when he threatened to bring proceedings.'

The first occasion was in 1975 and Mr Hartley asked the jury to read the piece complained of.

It said: 'The wretched hacks of the ailing *Sunday Observer*, having heard already that 'Dirty Digger' Rupert Murdoch wishes to take

over their newspaper, will not be encouraged to hear that a counter-bid is now being made by none other than Captain Robert Maxwell (nee Hoch) former MP and famed publisher.

'The awful Maxwell's lawyer spent much time last week negotiating with the Astor family, who nevertheless seem unwilling to sell to the Czechoslovak financial genius.

'Members of the staff of the *Scottish Daily News*, of which Maxwell is the much publicised supporter, are wondering how he could raise the money to take over the *Observer*.

'Although Maxwell has raised £120,000 for the *News*, he was pressed to raise the £25,000 cash deposit needed on Good Friday this year. Having himself managed to raise only £15,000, 'Hoch of the North' borrowed the other £10,000 from two senior *News* journalists (names and addresses supplied) out of their redundancy money from the defunct *Scottish Daily Express*.

'Moreover it took MacSwell three months to pay back the £10,000 to the two Caledonian hacks.

'Maxwell is taking his job at the *News* very seriously, having installed a £70 divan bed and a supply of personal food to be cooked by the canteen staff. Most of the *News* workers, especially the journalists, favour Maxwell, and some sub-editors have been seen to clap when he goes past.

'Less impressed by Maxwell are the three sources of possible large-scale loans:
1) The Government.
2) The print unions.
3) Sir Hugh Fraser, the Glasgow industrialist and proprietor of the *Evening Times* with which the now tabloid *News* might be combined.'

The following month, said Mr Hartley, *Private Eye* published a letter under the heading 'Hacks Fight Back'.

'It said:
  Dear Sir,
We the two "wretched hacks" of the *Scottish Daily News*, must point out that if your organ had been more awake and made the slightest effort to check the rash statements made in your lead piece of last week you would have discovered:

'1) That Mr Maxwell was not pressed to raise the £25,000 cash deposit needed on Good Friday, since he handed the co-operative a cheque for £125,000 that morning.

'2) Therefore he did not need to borrow the other £10,000 from two senior *News* journalists.

'3) Nor was he involved in any way in delaying the re-payment to us.

'The facts are these: The undersigned wanted to make a temporary investment of £11,000 in the *Scottish Daily News* at the last minute on Good Friday, but it was too late to deal with the matter formally. It was therefore decided by us and by Mr Allister Mackie, the Chairman, that our investment should be combined with that of Mr Maxwell on the understanding that our temporary investment would be returned to us after other permanent investors, who were in the pipeline, had taken our place. This has now happened.

Yours sincerely
RAY CHARD
Managing Editor
ALLAN SAXTON
Chief Sub, Foreign Desk
Scottish News Enterprises Ltd, 195 Albion Street, Glasgow G1 1RX'

'You might have thought,' said Mr Hartley, 'that in the light of having received that letter, *Private Eye* would have immediately apologised. But that is not their style. They in fact added insult to injury by the little footnote that you see under that letter.'

'The only inaccuracy in our story was the suggestion that Maxwell had paid back the £10,000 to the two authors of this letter. The money was in fact paid back by the company, a fact which has engaged the attention of *SDN's* accountants French & Cowan, and their solicitors Boyds of Glasgow, both of which firms had taken the *SDN* business from genuine idealism and have not been entirely happy at the financial involvement of MacSwell. *Ed.'*

Faced with that, Mr Hartley told the jury, Mr Maxwell issued a writ.

'But, undeterred, two issues later *Private Eye* returned to the attack.

'Under the heading "Street of Shame", it said:

"As was foretold by the *Eye*, that 'brave experiment in worker cooperation' the *Scottish Daily News*, is now in the hands of bouncing Czech Robert Maxwell. Already his inimitable managerial style is appearing in the pages. From an internal memo to senior editorial staff on September 18, we publish MacSwell's plan for the dying rag.

"The paper is too serious, both in content and presentation... The editor, senior editorial staff and all editorial staff should at all times in the next few months remember that they should go for stories which can help advertising and circulation (in that order) whenever they possibly can.'

"This sits ill with Hoch's claim that the circulation has risen by 90,000 copies a day since he took full charge. Moreover, the paper's print order has not been increased, and the weekly cash loss continues at £17,000.

"MacSwell's current strategy is not to ask for more Government money directly, but to persuade the government to drop its first option on the SDN building. This, it will be recalled, is the taxpayer's only security for the £1,200,000 loan made to the paper. If the government drops the option, as seems likely, MacSwell will be able to raise more commercial cash on a new mortgage on the building.

"MacSwell's accommodation problems have been exercising his mind of late. He lives in a penthouse suite at the Albany Hotel, and was much distressed when American folk-singer Johnny Cash arrived to perform in Glasgow and insisted on staying at the Albany's penthouse. An enterprising *SDN* sub-editor drafted the headline 'Czech bounced for Cash' before the story was brusquely killed.

"Hoch's new friend is middle-aged C.P. hack Nathan Goldberg. Rumour has it that Goldberg may soon be made editor of the *Scottish Daily News* in place of Fred Sillito, the present occupant."

'It was followed by a "Saying of the Week":

'After all these years, I have finally served a writ on *Private Eye*, and shut them up for good. I don't expect them to print any more about me Maxwell.'

'Libel actions brought by Mr Maxwell following those two articles were settled when the publishers of *Private Eye* and its editor, Richard Ingrams, paid damages and costs.

'And *Private Eye* apologised unreservedly.

'Over the following years, Mr Maxwell featured frequently in *Private Eye*. But he ignored its jibes at him.

'Then, in 1983, *Private Eye* published a fictitious letter drawing an extremely offensive comparison between Mr Maxwell and Ronnie Kray, one of the notorious Kray twins.'

What they did, said Mr Hartley, was to put above the name Kray a picture of Mr Maxwell, and above 'Maxwell' a picture of Ronnie Kray. A month later, *Private Eye* published an agreed apology for that. There was the plainest possible undertaking not to publish offensive material defamatory to Mr Maxwell in the future.

But that was a hollow undertaking - because *Private Eye* embarked on a new form of attack.

Said Mr Hartley: 'They regularly published a lookalike letter purporting to be written by Mr Maxwell's wife; lookalikes of the Duke of Edinburgh, and Adolph Eichmann; Edward Heath and Leon Uris; Brian Walden and Ian Brady, the Moors Murderer; and Bishop Tutu and Larry Adler.

'As I say, each time they purported to be signed by Ena B. Maxwell of Headington Hill Hall.

'The letters started within nine months of the earlier undertaking - so so much for an undertaking given by *Private Eye*.'

Coming to the present action Mr Hartley said: 'Can there be any doubt that what *Private Eye* is alleging is that Mr Maxwell, according to *Private Eye*, has acted as paymaster for Mr Kinnock, the Leader of the Labour Party, and is in effect bribing Mr Kinnock, or attempting to bribe him, in order to get a peerage?

'What I suggest to you is that not only is it extremely offensive, but a very serious allegation to make - bribery, or attempted bribery.'

Mr Maxwell heard about it in the *Mail on Sunday*, in a piece by Lady Falkender. He wrote to the editor of the *Mail on Sunday* and, naturally, he was extremely annoyed at the original publication in *Private Eye* and of course the repeating of the allegation in the *Mail on Sunday*.

'In the Mirror Diary on Monday, July 15 an article was published referring both to the article in Private Eye and to that in the Mail on Sunday.

Under the heading 'Another Whopper', it said: *Private Eye*, or Public Lie as it ought to be called, last week alleged that *Mirror* publisher Robert Maxwell was paying for Neil Kinnock's trip to Africa this week and that he had financed Kinnock's visit to Moscow last year.

'Not so.

'But that didn't stop Lady Marcia Falkender picking the story up and repeating it in the *Mail on Sunday* column yesterday.

'That is astonishing for two reasons

1. When Marcia was Harold Wilson's secretary at No. 10 there was no newspaper or magazine she hated more than *Private Eye*. She said it always told lies about her.

2. Harold Wilson's office was largely financed by a number of private individuals and no one knew more about this than Lady Falkender.

'Mr Maxwell last night wrote to the editor of the *Mail on Sunday*, Mr Stewart Steven, demanding a withdrawal of the allegation, an apology and a contribution of £25,000 to the *Mirror's* appeal for the victims of the Ethiopian famine.

'Failing that writs will be winging their way towards Mr Steven and Lady Falkender - as well as *Private Eye*.

'Mr Steven is, of course, well remembered for two 'whoppers'. First - while on the *Daily Express* - he discovered Martin Borman, Hitler's deputy, living in South America. Needless to say, it wasn't Borman. Then - while on the *Daily Mail* - he wrote a story about a Leyland slush fund. Another whopper - based on a forgery - which cost his proprietors several hundred thousand pounds in libel damages and legal costs.

'Incidentally, Lady Falkender claims credit in her colum for inventing the "walkabout" by politicians. When she did it for Harold Wilson she said it "contributed significantly to restoring his flagging fortunes."

'She omitted to point out that she invented the walkabout for the 1970 General Election.

'Wilson lost.'

The same day that this piece appeared, Mr Maxwell wrote to the editor of *Private Eye*, Mr Ingrams. So did Patricia Hewitt, Mr Kinnock's press secretary. Both letters were published in *Private Eye*.

Said Mr Hartley: 'You might have thought that, faced with those two letters, *Private Eye* would have done the decent thing and withdrawn their allegations against Mr Maxwell unreservedly. Unhappily, they did not.

'In, if you can believe it, the very same issue they published another very offensive article, with accompanying cartoon, about Mr Maxwell.'

Under the heading "Street of Shame", it said:

'The guest list for the glittering, champagne-all-the-way party marking Cap'n Bob's first glorious year at the helm of the *Daily Maxwell* is awesome indeed. On it was Prince Charles (who puzzlingly failed to turn up) and, of course, Neil Kinnock.

'On the day, Maxwell ordered political hack Julia Langdon to confirm with Kinnock that he would be coming. Kinnock told her he had no intention of gracing the affair as he was concerned with more important matters of state that evening. The fat man's response was typical. "Tell him," he boomed, "that if he doesn't come to my party the *Mirror* will not be reporting his African tour."

'Kinnock was furious. "You tell him," he stormed, "that I will not be bribed!" Thankfully good sense finally prevailed. Mindful of His Master's Voice, Kinnock duly turned up. Maximum publicity for the African junket, which Maxwell lamely denies financing, was promised. Kinnock and the rest left happily clutching their souvenir of the evening: a mock-up of the *Mirror* featuring the gigantic form of Maxwell on every page.'

And there was a picture of Mr Maxwell, and

Mr Kinnock as the little lap dog obeying everything that Mr Maxwell says. 'In that article you have ringing out loud and clear, do you not? the same allegation: that Mr Maxwell is trying to bribe Mr Kinnock, that Mr Kinnock is in Mr Maxwell's pocket, with the cartoon emphasising that Mr Kinnock is, in effect, Mr Maxwell's lap dog?

'And if that was not enough, the plain indication that Mr Maxwell is lying when he says that he had not financed and is not financing Mr Kinnock's overseas trips.

'Faced with this persistent allegation of bribery, Mr Maxwell issued a writ immediately and took out an application for an injunction to stop the sale of that particular issue of *Private Eye*.'

It was refused. But Mr Maxwell went to the Court of Appeal. The Court adjourned the case so that the defendants could swear an affidavit, stating on oath that the allegations were true. Faced with that affidavit - which was the clearest possible assertion that the very matters of which Mr Maxwell complained were true - the Court of Appeal, naturally, refused the application for an injunction.

But it granted Mr Maxwell's application for a speedy trial.

Said Mr Hartley: 'In the course of preparing for this trial, the publishers of *Private Eye*, and Mr Richard Ingrams their then editor, have not produced one shred of documentary evidence to substantiate these very specific allegations that Mr Maxwell had funded Mr Kinnock's trips to Moscow and Central America and was going to fund a trip to East Africa.

'So we are still totally in the dark as to what this mysterious evidence is, these 'sources', which of course they are not going to disclose - these 'reliable sources'.

'We are totally in the dark. But what they have said is they will call evidence by which they can identify the method whereby funds from Mr Maxwell were channelled to Mr Kinnock's private office.

'We are going to call evidence which is going to show that this assertion is absolutely untrue, and, we say, that the Court of Appeal was misled.'

The jury had two matters to decide. Firstly, whether those two articles do bear the meaning that Mr Maxwell was acting as paymaster for Mr Kinnock's trips abroad, with the intention of bribing Mr Kinnock, or attempting to bribe him, to give Mr Maxwell a peerage; secondly, if they did find, yes, this is an allegation of a bribery or something very near it - is that allegation true? 'This question obviously falls into two parts. First, did Mr Maxwell act as Mr Kinnock's paymaster? And, secondly, if he did, was it done with a view to curry favour and hoping to get a peerage?

'A sort of quid pro quo - 'I'll give you all this lovely loot and you can repay me by elevating me to the House of Lords'.'

One theme was that at the Labour Party Conference in October 1984, Mr Maxwell gave a donation of £43,000 to the Labour Party's funds.

'Mr Maxwell does not deny this; he freely admits that. You may wonder, 'Well, why shouldn't he?' He and the companies of which he is chairman–have made donations to the Labour Party and they are not ashamed of it.

'It is exactly the same way that many well-known individuals and, indeed, many famous household public companies give donations to the Conservative Party; and there is nothing wrong with that either.'

Mr Hartley added: 'In scraping the barrel of things that they could throw at Mr Maxwell, they alleged also that during 1985 Mr Maxwell provided a word processor, or the funds to buy the same, for use in the private office of Mr Kinnock.

'They were asked for further and better particulars of that. They have not been able to give them and that allegation has been struck out.

'I am suggesting to you that that is again indicative of the limits to which *Private Eye* will go. That is an allegation which is totally false.

'Another matter which they raised and, again, has had to be struck out from the defence is that during 1985 a legal dispute occurred between Mr John Silkin and the editorial staff of the *Tribune*.

'It was suggested that in an effort to resolve the dispute Mr Maxwell had offered Mr Silkin extended credit for the *Tribune*, amounting to over £100,000.

'Again wholly false. How does that ever come to be in the defence?'

Mr Hartley said: 'You may think that if you are in politics, you are bound to attract publicity - and you will remember that Mr Maxwell had been a Labour Member of Parliament.

'Equally, of course, as a newspaper publisher and chairman of a football club - and you may or may not have read of his support for the Commonwealth Games - I suggest to you there is nothing wrong in any of these activities and the publicity he has received from them.

'But what I suggest to you is offensive - which is what we will come to in a moment - is the suggestion that Mr Maxwell does all this cynically, with his eye on a peerage.

'I say to you, Mr Maxwell makes no secret of the fact that he supports the Labour Party and, indeed, that he would like to see a Labour Government in this country.

'But if a person who has supported a political party, as Mr Maxwell has done, if the gutter press, such as *Private Eye*, should see that as something cynical - that is, trying to buy a peerage - it really does speak volumes for *Private Eye*. And one hopes that the affairs of this country have not sunk that low.

'It is quite untrue to say that it is the plaintiff's personal ambition to be elevated to the House of Lords as a Labour peer and it is quite untrue to suggest that Mr Maxwell has given moneys with that in mind.'

Mr Hartley said: 'We say they had it in for Mr Maxwell.

'You have seen how they break undertakings, and what we say the defendants said to themselves, was: "Well, this is all good stuff. We can make more money out of defaming Mr Maxwell, and the fun our readers will get in reading that, than in any damages that we will have to pay out to Mr Maxwell".'

If the jury thought that *Private Eye* were saying a sort of 'hee, hee, hee' to Mr Maxwell, they might think they were quite clearly taking a risk - and enjoying taking the risk. 'Well, if we have to pay out any money to Mr Maxwell, our circulation figures will benefit anyway, so we'll get it back that way.'

Turning to the counterclaim by *Private Eye* about the Daily Mirror's 'Another Whopper' article, Mr Hartley said: 'They are complaining about very little.

'Mr Maxwell admits that, as the publisher of the *Mirror*, he is responsible for the publication of those words and he says that they are true in substance and in fact.'

Then he listed apologies made by *Private Eye* … to conductor André Previn, publisher Lord Weidenfeld, former MP Harold Soref …

'There are a good deal of these,' Mr Hartley told the jury, 'and we will have to go through them, seeing over the years the whoppers which we say the defendants have published.'

The list continued. Among others who received apologies from *Private Eye* were Sir James Goldsmith, over the Lord Lucan affair, former *Times* editor Harold Evans, film director Blake Edwards, industrialist Lord Weinstock, union leader Clive Jenkins, Princess Margaret's friend Roddy Llewellyn, Lord Goodman, actress Penelope Keith, broadcaster Desmond Wilcox, Lady Havers, wife of the Attorney — General, Ken Livingstone, Lady Rothermere, Sarah Keays, Sir Larry Lamb, former union leader Moss Evans, Jocelyn Stevens, former Prime Minister Edward Heath, Cecil Parkinson, and the London Symphony Orchestra.

Said Mr Hartley: 'It is a very sorry tale indeed. It is a litany of lies. We say they speak for themselves. We say Mr Maxwell was perfectly justified, as publisher of the Mirror, to publish that article describing it as "another whopper". Of course it goes without saying that we are asserting that the articles about Mr Maxwell are false - part of the litany of lies.'

The first witness called was Alex Kitson, former Deputy General Secretary to the Transport & General Workers' Union.

He told the court that in 1980-81 he was Chairman of the Labour Party and made an appeal for funds at the annual conference. During the conference, Robert Maxwell told him: 'Anything you can raise, Alex, I'll double.' The appeal raised £44,514 and subsequently the Labour Party received a cheque to the same amount, drawn on the Pergamon account. But Mr Maxwell never said anything about how the money should be spent.

LEFT: *Alex Kitson, Excutive Officer of the Transport and General Workers Union.*

He was asked: 'What do you say to the suggestion that funds were made available to Mr Kinnock's private office by being channelled through your union and, indeed, that those funds were provided to you?'

Mr Kitson replied: 'It's incorrect and a lie.'

Next to be called was Henry Timpson, Executive Financial Secretary of the Transport & General Workers' Union. He was asked by Mr Hartley: 'It is suggested that some money had been channelled through the Transport & General Workers' Union, by Mr Kitson, to the Leader of the Labour Party, Mr Kinnock. Is that possible?'

'No, that's not possible - not without involving myself or some others. It's just not possible,' he replied.

He was asked if he'd have known if there had been any payment by Mr Maxwell to the Union.

'Yes,' he said - and it was inconceivable that he would not have known about it 'unless the perpetrators fooled local regional officials and fooled the auditors at local level and national level'.

With Mr Timpson's evidence over, the jury withdrew while counsel debated legal points.

It was the end of a long Day One.

CHAPTER TWO

Day 2

Michael Foot was first into the witness box on the second day of the trial. The former leader of the Labour Party first enjoyed a light moment with Mr Hartley when he asked him: 'I think you share Mr Maxwell's recreation of football, but you support a different club?'

'Yes,' said Mr Foot, a keen supporter of Plymouth Argyle. 'We are moving up into the same division.'

Then Mr Hartley turned to allegations that, at a meeting in the Gay Hussar restaurant, Mr Maxwell handed over a cheque for £75,000 towards legal costs in a case brought against the Boundary Commission.

Mr Foot said the case was brought by himself, the Chief Whip of the Labour Party, Mr Michael Cocks, the party's General Secretary, Mr James Mortimer, and its national agent, Mr David Hughes. The case - in which the Labour Party itself was not involved, and towards which it paid 'not a penny' - was unsuccessful. They were then faced with a bill for their own costs and those of the Boundary Commission, and set out to raise the money by talking to people who were friendly to the Labour Party.

'But,' said Mr Foot, 'we never had any discussions with Mr Maxwell on this subject, either at the Gay Hussar or anywhere else. So that is absolute rubbish.'

He did, though, have a lunch at the restaurant in early 1983 'on an entirely different matter'. 'It was concerned solely with the question whether we would be able to start a new Labour paper in time for the General Election.'

There that day were Mr Geoffrey Goodman, then *Mirror* industrial editor, Mr Robert Edwards, then Editor of the *Sunday Mirror*, and Mr Maxwell - who then had no link with the *Mirror*.

Their discussion 'didn't come to anything', said Mr Foot. No cheque was handed over. 'And I paid for the lunch.'

A fund was launched for the Boundary Commission case. But there was a shortfall of around £8,000 and Mr Foot and Michael Cocks met Mr Maxwell in his office to discuss it. A sum of £8,534.08 was paid - with a Pergamon Press cheque - to the Boundary Commission Fighting Fund 'and that wiped the slate clean'.

The judge then asked the jury to withdraw 'and stretch your legs' while counsel debated a legal point. When they returned, Mr Hartley announced: 'The defendants accept the essential propriety of the plaintiff's payments and payments made by companies associated with him to the Labour Party and the Boundary Commission Fighting Fund so long as they were made with no improper motive.

'The defendants further accept that by mid-August, 1986, they knew that Mr Foot's evidence-in-chief would be as it was given in this court.'

With that over, Mr Foot was recalled and asked by Mr Hartley: 'How does the Honours system work?'

He replied: 'The Leader of the Opposition has the right to nominate people who may become members of the House of Lords. Of course their submissions go to the Prime Minister and she or he, or whoever, submits the names to the Queen.'

RIGHT: *Rt. Hon. Michael Foot, former Leader of the Opposition.*
BELOW: *Rt. Hon. Michael Cocks, Labour Chief Whip.*

And when those submissions are made, said Mr Foot, the Leader of the Opposition has to state that there are no improper motives and no payments have been made. 'An undertaking has to be made by the person who nominated the peer ... and this has to go to the committee that was established to investigate the appointments of members of the House of Lords.'

Cross-examined by Mr Bateson, Mr Foot agreed that, of English writers, he had a particular interest in satirists, and he knew Richard Ingrams, a satirist, rather well. Mr Bateson asked: 'I think your nephew, Paul Foot, contributes to *Private Eye?*'

'I think he did at one stage', said Mr Foot. 'I am not quite sure whether he still continues. They say that the paper has deteriorated a little in recent months, but I do not know whether that is the case.'

'Well, Mr Ingrams has retired, you see, Mr Foot,' said Mr Bateson.

Michael Foot agreed that he followed, and subscribed to, *Private Eye* for a number of years 'with sometimes approval and sometimes strong disapproval'. He was in favour of 'the strongest possible satire'. But, as a journalist, he believed it was very important for journalists to check the facts on which they based satire. 'There are some facts which can be easily checked, and I would have thought this might be the case in this one.'

Talking of the Honours List, Mr Bateson read a sentence saying, 'Every tycoon knows that the short cut to a title is to cough up cash to the party in power.' Did that come as a surprise to Mr Foot - that this is the public attitude so often in the case of honours?

'I think the definition of the words 'the public attitude' is a very broad use of the term … it is impossible to give an answer,' said Mr Foot.

But was it the sort of attitude he would expect tycoons to have? 'No,' said Mr Foot. 'I think it varies.'

Then Mr Bateson asked about a book on the honours system by political researcher John Walker. In it, he said, Walker points out that former Labour leader Harold Wilson received financial backing from people like Sir Rudi Sternberg, George Weidenfeld and Joseph Kagan.

Said Mr Foot: 'I am not responsible for what Harold Wilson may have written or said, or even the appointments that may have been made when he was there.'

Mr Bateson asked: 'Would you agree with me that people who gave considerable financial assistance to Harold Wilson got peerages?'

'I am not prepared to comment on that,' said Mr Foot. 'What I had to do when I was asked to nominate people was to vouch by my signature that the person concerned had not been engaged in any improper payments and had not been involved in anything that was improper.'

He was asked again: 'Is it within your knowledge that individuals who gave financial assistance to Mr Wilson obtained peerages?'

Said Mr Foot: 'It is not in my knowledge that they did. I don't know what they gave, and I think that is a question to be addressed to Mr Wilson and not me.'

Re-examined by Mr Hartley, Mr Foot agreed that he'd expect even satirists to get their facts right.

What, he was asked, should happen when they get their facts wrong? 'I think,' said Mr Foot, 'that the first thing they can do is to apologise and to print in their newspapers or journals the retractions, or attempt to put right the wrong that they have done. I think that is the simplest way for journalists to put it right.

'Journalists sometimes make mistakes - that becomes inevitable in all newspapers. But the best way is for them to correct their mistakes as soon as possible and not to try and persist in basing their attacks on the foundations of inaccurate facts.'

Mr Foot's evidence was completed, and the court called Mr Michael Cocks, the MP for Bristol South.

Like Mr Foot, he denied that there had been a meeting with Mr Maxwell at the Gay Hussar restaurant at which a cheque for £75,000 was handed over. The cost of the Boundary Commission case came to around £60,000, he said, and Mr Maxwell was approached to contribute to the fighting fund. In addition to payments totalling £30,000 there was the £8,534 for the shortfall.

The next witness was Mr Richard Clements, executive officer in charge of the Office of the Leader of the Opposition. He told the court that the office was basically financed by public funds, and money for Mr Neil Kinnock's overseas trips was raised by approaches to trade unions.

Mr Hartley read to him a claim that some of the financial support Mr Maxwell provided to the Labour Party had gone to fund visits abroad by Mr Kinnock, including visits to

Moscow and Central America. 'Such funds,' it was said, 'were made available to Mr Kinnock's private office by being chanelled through the Transport and General Workers' Union or its officers.'

But, said Mr Clements, no funds at all were paid by Mr Maxwell to him or through the TGWU.

The defendants, Mr Hartley told him, said that not only did Mr Maxwell pay for trips to Moscow and Central America but also a trip to East Africa. 'They say that there was an unspent surplus of funds provided by Mr Maxwell for the Moscow trip which Mr Kinnock's private office intended to towards the cost of the East African visit. Is there any truth in that at all?' he asked. 'Is there any unspent surplus of funds?'

'There is no truth in that whatsoever,' said Mr Clements. And there had been no agreement - express or implied - that Mr Maxwell would in any way put money into Mr Kinnock's bank account and no question of putting a gift through the TGWU.

ABOVE: *Richard Clements, executive officer in charge of the Office of the Leader of the Opposition.*

After the lunch adjournment, the court heard from Mr Ian Nicholas Grant, who is employed by Pergamon Press as an adviser to Mr Maxwell. Previously, he said, he'd been employed by the Labour Party as Director of Publicity.

Mr Hartley read to him an allegation put in the defence: 'In 1985 the Labour Party wished to end the employment of Mr Nick Grant, the Party's headquarters' press officer. 'Mr Grant had served the party a long time, but was unpopular with Mr Kinnock. Had Mr Grant been dismissed, substantial compensation would have been payable by the Labour Party and considerable embarrassment would have been caused. The plaintiff, on learning of the position, offered Mr Grant immediate alternative employment as his public affairs adviser, and thereby saved the Labour Party from having to pay compensation.'

Mr Grant denied that he was unpopular with Mr Kinnock and said the question of dismissal did not arise. He told Mr Bateson: 'I don't agree for a moment that the tension in the Labour Party headquarters was created by my presence.'

After Mr Grant's evidence, the judge dismissed the jury early. 'The jury may be told that I think it is unnecessary that they should be brought back to court. They may be told that they are sent away with regret and legal argument will occupy the rest of the afternoon. Please be prompt for 10.30 tomorrow morning.'

So ended Day Two.

CHAPTER THREE

Day 3

Day Three of the trial was one keenly anticipated by the jury, the assembled Press and the public - the day Robert Maxwell would give evidence against *Private Eye*.

The 63-year-old Chairman of Mirror Group newspapers began by agreeing with Mr Hartley some details of his life: Labour MP for Buckingham from 1964 until 1970 - during which he helped through the Clean Air Act - and a former chairman of the Labour National Fundraising Foundation and of the Labour Working Party on Science, Government and Industry.

Mr Maxwell told the court he was born in Czechoslovakia and came to Britain from France as a soldier in September 1940. He served in the British Army and was awarded the Military Cross.

He was very happily married, with seven children.

Talking of the first time he took action against *Private Eye*, he said he did so 'because it was a tissue of lies and implied that I borrowed money from my employees, which was wholly untrue, or that I had difficulty in meeting my obligations and commitments'.

A further article, under the heading 'Street of Shame', was 'continued fabrication and lies'.

Turning to the *Private Eye* piece headed 'Kray Twins', Mr Hartley asked: 'Did you see anything funny in that?'

Mr Maxwell replied: 'I did not, my lord. 'Not only did I not see anything funny, but for years after this libel action in 1976 and the apology they gave, unreservedly withdrawing it, they kept on, time again, publishing stories about me. Being a public figure, I ignored them. But when this appeared not only was I not amused, but far worse, Mrs Maxwell and all of our children were utterly shocked to have me, their father, compared to a convicted major gangster. We were so upset about this that we had to again go back to issue proceedings for libel. That was how we got into this situation.'

Later, he agreed, *Private Eye* published look-alike pictures with letters seemingly written by his wife - 'yours sincerely, Ena T Maxwell', with his address at the bottom.

Mrs Maxwell was very upset with me that I settled this action of the Kray Twins,' he said. 'She said to me that if I had taken the libel action and gone to the court instead of taking their word, she would not be dragged regularly into *Private Eye*. I was really very upset about it, as was she, as were the children.'

Mr Hartley mentioned an issue of *Private Eye* in December, 1981 with a letter purporting to be written by Mrs Maxwell with 'look-alike' pictures of the Duke of Edinburgh and Adolf Eichmann.

Mention of the Nazi exterminator was too much for him and he broke down in tears. 'My family were destroyed by Eichmann,' he sobbed, reaching for a white linen handkerchief. He blew his nose, looked across at Mr Justice Simon Brown and declared: 'I'm sorry, my lord.' It was several minutes, and a number of questions from his counsel later, before Mr Maxwell felt it safe to push the handkerchief back into his pocket.

RIGHT: *Mr Robert Maxwell*

Mr Hartley mentioned a *Private Eye* article and, alongside, a cartoon with Mr Maxwell's face on a gramophone - 'His Master's Voice'- with Mr Kinnock, 'as if a little dog' at the side. 'What effect did that article and cartoon have?' he asked.

Said Mr Maxwell: 'It was not only accusing me of bribery of the Leader of the Opposition. But this is an allegation - if it is not instantly withdrawn - not only gravely damaging to me and to the Leader of Her Majesty's Opposition, but an allegation of bribery for purposes of buying a peerage. That,' he added, 'is destructive of the body politic of the government and the country, and it could not be left on record. If they did not withdraw it unreservedly, there was no alternative but to go back to court to clear my name of this gross allegation and lie.'

Mr Maxwell instructed his solicitors to issue a writ and to try to obtain an injunction to halt further copies of that issue of *Private Eye* being distributed. As a publisher, he felt it would be wrong to go for an injunction against a periodical unless the allegation was so grave and serious and they were unwilling to withdraw it. But, said Mr Maxwell, 'I had no alternative.'

When the case went to the Court of Appeal, counsel for the defendants said they intended to justify what they had said.

Said Mr Maxwell: 'I remember being utterly shocked that counsel could give such an undertaking.'

He was asked how he felt when the defendants said they had evidence about funds from him being channelled to Mr Kinnock's private office.

'Past experience,' said Mr Maxwell, 'has shown that *Private Eye* will do anything - publish anything - in order to get an increased circulation and increase its profits. I was utterly shocked that a journalist should be willing to tell his counsel to tell a lie to the Court of Appeal. I am still amazed, still shocked, that this is what this so-called periodical is capable of doing.'

Mr Maxwell - a member of the Labour Party for between twenty-five and thirty years - said he had never made any payments to the private office of the Leader of the Opposition. He denied ever attending a lunch at the Gay Hussar at which a cheque for £75,000 was handed over. He did, though, help the Boundary Commission Fighting Fund with cheques of £10,000, £20,000 and £8,534 ... £20,000 from himself and £18,534 from Pergamon Press Ltd.

Mr Maxwell agreed that when he acquired control of Mirror Group Newspapers in 1984 he fulfilled a long-standing ambition to become a national newspaper proprietor. But he denied a claim that he had 'exploited his position as a newspaper publisher to seek to advance his own personal standing with, and influence over, the leadership of the Labour Party'.

'It is not true,' said Mr Maxwell.

He dealt with a further claim which said he has 'exploited his control over Mirror Group Newspapers Limited to attract for himself as much personal publicity as possible in order to seek to create for himself a public image as an influential and respected figure in public life'.

Mr Hartley asked: 'Being in public life, do you inevitably attract a certain amount of publicity?'

'Regrettably that is so, because I am not only a publisher. I am also engaged in many take-over bids and football. All of these activities regrettably attract publicity.'

Another claim was that it was Mr Maxwell's 'personal ambition to be elevated to the House of Lords as a Labour peer'.

'Not true,' said Mr Maxwell.

And the claim that he 'seeks to achieve this as others have done before him by patronage of a political party and by the self-publicity he can create through his control of Mirror Group Newspapers Limited?'

'I have no ambition to be a member of the House of Lords,' he said.

Mr Hartley then turned to a story which said that in July, 1985, Mr Maxwell held a party to celebrate the first anniversary of his acquisition of the Mirror group. Mr Neil

Kinnock was among those invited. When, it was said, Mr Maxwell heard that Mr Kinnock had other commitments that evening, he threatened to withhold publicity in his newspapers for Mr Kinnock's tour of East Africa later that month. Eventually, it was added, Mr Kinnock did attend the party and, with other guests, was given a mock-up picture of the *Mirror* containing pictures of Mr Maxwell.

Asked about the story, Mr Maxwell told the court he believed the reason Mr Kinnock had for not attending was that on the same night he had an invitation from Mr Rupert Murdoch's *Times* newspaper. 'And since he had rejected attending the event at *The Times*, he thought he ought to be even-handed and not attend the *Mirror's* either. I said words to the effect 'Well, if he won't come to the Mirror party, we won't go to his African party.' It was, I hope, a funny joke. Certainly everybody else laughed about it.' And it was certainly not a threat, as the defence suggested.

In fact, said Mr Maxwell, Mr Kinnock was outraged that he had not been told by his staff about the invitation. 'Once Mr Kinnock heard about it, he and Mrs Kinnock were delighted to attend the reception.'

Dealing with his recruitment of Nick Grant, former Labour Party publicity director, Mr Maxwell said there was no question of employing him 'to save any embarrassment or expense to the Labour Party'. He had not entered into any agreement with Mr Kinnock or Mr Roy Hattersley or anyone to take Mr Grant, as it were, off their hands.

When he was cross-examined by Mr Bateson, Mr Maxwell was asked: 'If you were offered a peerage, would you accept?'

He replied: 'The answer to that I can only say is this: I have been offered it twice before and I have said No.'

'When', asked Mr Bateson, 'were you offered it before?' 'Some few years ago by Mr Goronwy-Roberts, who asked me whether I would allow my name to go forward for a peerage, and I said No because I couldn't support the defence policies of Michael Foot.'

The second occasion, he added, was last year, when the deputy leader of the Labour Party, Mr Hattersley, 'asked me a similar question - whether I would like to be considered - and I said, 'No.' I don't recollect giving a reason. I just said 'No.' Thank you very much.'

Mr Bateson asked if Mr Maxwell liked a position of influence and power.

'Sometimes I like it and sometimes I don't,' he said.

He was asked: 'If a peerage was offered to you that gave you additional power or influence, you would accept it, would you not?'

'I have already told you,' said Mr Maxwell. 'I have rejected it twice.'

Asked the question again, he replied: 'I see no reason why my answer a third time should be any different from what it was twice.'

The judge agreed. 'I think that is a fair response,' he said.

Mr Bateson asked: 'It is a fact, is it not, that giving aid and assistance to a political party - particularly financial - is a very good route to a title?'

'Certainly not,' said Mr Maxwell.

Then Mr Bateson turned to an article written by John Smith in *The People* newspaper, which Mr Maxwell publishes. It said: 'Every tycoon knows that the short cut to a title is to cough up cash to the party in power.'

Mr Maxwell said he would not agree with that. But it was 'the publication by *The People* of a star reporter exercising his right of freedom of expression in our free society. He has a total right and freedom to express himself, subject only to the laws of libel.'

Of the *Daily Mirror* article headed 'Another Whopper', Mr Maxwell said he wrote it 'jointly with another'. It mentioned the financing of Harold Wilson's office, and Mr Bateson asked: 'Did anybody ever suggest that either Lord Kagan or Lord Sternberg - which I think were the two you knew - bribed Mr Wilson for their peerage?'

Mr Maxwell replied: 'I didn't really know

Polytechnic Institute of New York

ROBERT MAXWELL
Doctor of Science

Yours is a story-book success that demonstrates in an exemplary fashion the combination of private entrepreneurship with a commitment to the world of ideas and knowledge.

You have endured the upheavals of World War II and dislocation to foreign lands where you joined the citizens of the United Kingdom, your adopted country, and, commissioned as a captain in the field, fought to preserve democracy. After the war, you shared in rebuilding, and later served the public as a Labor Member of Parliament.

Starting with little more than dreams and ambition, you have built a major corporation. Along with success, you have continued to maintain an insatiable curiosity about the world around you, a desire to provide mankind with useful information with which to build a better life, and a commitment to open doors to knowledge.

As chairman of the Mirror Group of newspapers, which includes London's Daily Mirror, one of Britain's most popular newspapers, you do not hesitate to raise your voice in political opposition, take firm stands on a variety of issues, and compete vigorously with rivals in a robust exercise of the finest traditions of the Fourth Estate.

You showed an early willingness to risk your investments to publish scientific journals and books—not merely for monetary return, but because of your unswerving conviction that this would be beneficial to society. The years have proven you a man of vision. You are founder and chairman of Pergamon Press—a vital and effective intellectual conduit for scientific ideas and developments. By means of its journals and books, scientists share their knowledge around the world, not only to push back the edges of darkness but to send a signal to the corners of the globe that scientific cooperation can help, pave the way to peace.

From such acts of personal conviction, many lights can be lit; many answers can be found to scientific queries; and men and women move closer to the light. This is a heritage of which you can be truly proud and satisfied, for you have given the world another means to reach across boundaries to share truth.

In recognition of your contributions to increasing the sharing of scientific knowledge, we confer on you the highest academic distinction Polytechnic Institute of New York affords, the degree of Doctor of Science, honoris causa.

June 5, 1985

Chairman of the Corporation

President

Polytechnic Institute of New York

Upon the recommendation of the Faculty

and by authority of the Regents of the University of the State of New York

the Corporation of the Polytechnic Institute of New York

hereby confers upon

Robert Maxwell

the degree of

Doctor of Science
honoris causa

with all pertinent rights, honors, privileges, and responsibilities.

In witness, the authorized officers have affixed their names and the

corporate seal in the Borough of Brooklyn, City of New York

June 5, 1985

Joseph J. Jacobs
Chairman of the Corporation

George Bugliarello
President

Sternberg at all. I only met Kagan once or twice. Nobody suggested to me, nor do I believe, they bribed Mr Wilson. I think it is a monstrous allegation and ought not to be made.

'Lord Wilson is not here. He is being defamed under the privilege of the court, and I think it is disgraceful that this should be possible. Lord Wilson is not here to defend himself.'

The judge interrupted to say: 'Mr Bateson is not for a moment suggesting, as I understand it, that either of those gentlemen bribed Mr Wilson or that Mr Wilson succumbed to financial blandishments of that character.'

Mr Maxwell agreed that the fact that Mr Wilson's private office was funded by private individuals was very well known. 'Could I say,' he added, 'that I refused to participate when invited to finance Mr Wilson's office some years ago. I was invited to - before the funding of the office of the Leader of the Opposition become possible through public funds.'

The judge asked: 'You say that nobody thinks the worse of anybody - be they Labour or Conservative - who make these private contributions to the Opposition private office?'

'That is so, be they peers or individuals or companies, my lord,' said Mr Maxwell. 'In our society - since, I regret to say, we are not funding the political parties through the public purse - the political parties, if we are to retain our freedom and to avoid becoming dictatorships, have to be funded by people and institutions and organisations who can afford to contribute money for their efficient running. That is quite a different thing to implying bribery and corruption, which is a monstrous allegation against all political parties in this country and ought not to be made.'

LEFT: *Award presented to Mr Robert Maxwell, an unusual American recognition of a British success story.*

In the light of that observation, Mr Bateson drew Mr Maxwell's attention to his letter of complaint to Richard Ingrams, in which he mentioned 'the disgraceful allegation that I provide Mr Kinnock with 'freebies' (which presumably is intended to mean "bribes")'.

'What you are saying there,' said Mr Bateson, 'is that you detect this bribery allegation out of the use of the word 'freebies'.'

'And all the rest,' said Mr Maxwell.

Mr Bateson asked: 'I understood you to say that you did not see anything wrong in, or there was no general disapproval of, funding the Leader of the Opposition through private subscription?'

'That is so,' Mr Maxwell replied. 'But where it gets wrong - when you link this to a peerage - that is the appalling thing. This is where your clients have caused a monstrous lie and libel.'

He was asked: 'If you had been told that Mr Kinnock required money in order to make these trips abroad, would you have given it?'

'No,' said Mr Maxwell. 'I would have taken exactly the same line as I did in Mr Wilson's Prime Ministership. I would not have given it.'

'There was nothing wrong about it, was there?' asked Mr Bateson.

'There is nothing wrong about it except this,' replied Mr Maxwell. 'When I was in the House of Commons' the jury will recollect, I was Chairman of the Labour National Fund-Raising Foundation, whose business it was to raise money for the Labour Party. Without money, parties in a democracy cannot survive - and our freedoms depend on it. I took the view then, and hold it now, and made strong representations, that it is in the national interest that our parties should be funded from public funds to prevent the kind of allegations that are being made in this monstrous libel. Having taken that view and having got partial acceptance through the Short money, I have taken the view then and hold it now that if the Leader of the Opposition needs money to carry out his official duties, he should get it from central funds. And if he can't, then he ought to at least do in this modern time what

Mr. Kinnock has done - go for funds to public bodies such as the trade unions.

'Nothing has done more damage to our public life than this kind of allegation that you can buy peerages. This died in our country under Lloyd George. It was as a result of that that the whole honours system was changed, and you had to sign a statement by the person nominating you that there was no inducement and no money went in.

'So the answer is that because I said "No" to Mr. Wilson's office, because I strongly believed that parties and Leaders of the Opposition should be funded from central funds, then I would have said "No" to Mr. Kinnock.

'But I am very happy to say that Mr. Kinnock has dropped the practice as far as I know, and certainly nobody has come to me to ask me to help fund his office.'

Asked about "freebies", Mr Maxwell said: 'A "freebie" is really counted in tens of pounds - maybe a hundred pounds. Anything above that is a straightforward bribe. It cannot be taken as a generality that freebies are all right in our society. They are not. I certainly don't treat them as all right, and I am very suspicious about freebies. I never accept them for myself, and we look with suspicion on them in our newspapers.'

Mr Maxwell glanced at the clock, and Mr Bateson told him: 'I am afraid you are going to be there a little time. If you have another appointment or something, do say so.'

Mr Maxwell told him: 'I have nothing more important than to finish my duties to his lordship and the jury.'

When the case resumed after lunch, the jury had a question for the judge. He'd told them, right at the start of the trial, that if they wanted anything - even to answer a call of nature - they should send him a note. Now they'd sent him one. 'I have a note from the jury,' he said, 'which reads "Please could we be informed exactly what a peer is and what his compulsory - if any - duties would be?".'

Said the judge: 'Perhaps I may venture a simple, no doubt simplistic, answer to that. A peer is no more, no less, than a member of the House of Lords, be it a male or female - we have both peers and peeresses. Nowadays, as you probably know, practically all new peerages are life peerages and they are not hereditary, so that you cannot pass them down the generations of your children and grandchildren to come.

'As a member of the House of Lords, nobody is compelled to attend the debates or do any work as such at all. However, if you are created a life peer, as sometimes happens, on the recommendation of a political leader of one of the political parties, you would probably expect, and be expected, to play some part in the debates and deliberations and votes of the House of Lords.'

During the afternoon session, Mr Maxwell was asked about the Daily Mirror and agreed that when he took it over he said he would maintain its existing political stance and editorial independence, policies and practices. And that included editorial freedom.

He was asked about a front-page guarantee that one of his readers would win £1 million. It was accompanied by his photograph, and Mr Bateson asked: 'Does any other newspaper proprietor feature on the front page of his newspaper like that?'

'I do not know,' said Mr Maxwell.

'Was this,' asked Mr Bateson, 'the most important item on that day to go on the front page?'

'If it is on the front page,' he was told, 'that is the most important item on that day.'

Didn't he think that the miners' strike which was going on at that time might be more important for the front page?

'I just do not recollect what I thought, going back more than two years, Mr Bateson,' he replied. 'If you remember what you thought two years ago, of course, you are very good at it. I am not.'

Mr Bateson mentioned several *Mirror* pages carrying pictures of Mr Maxwell in connection with the newspaper's bingo campaign.

TONY HEALEY

TYCOONS CROSS SWORDS — LORD GNOME CRUSADED AGAINST?

Mr Maxwell told him: 'The *Daily Mirror* is not like that now. These are selected pages and a specific campaign for the £1 million bingo - and it is grossly unfair of counsel to say that is how the Mirror is now. And he knows it.'

Then Mr Bateson mentioned a page with the headline: 'The *Mirror* mercy flight is on its way', and a picture of Mr Maxwell standing in the plane.

Said Mr Maxwell: 'I am very proud to have initiated that mercy flight. Hundreds of people's lives were saved and millions of our readers throughout the whole country were delighted about it and were very proud of it. The *Mirror* responded quickly, immediately, to what we saw as an appalling tragedy on our television screens, and we would do it again my lord, if that was required.'

The *Mirror* was also proud, he added, of its 'Win a Million' campaign. 'It gave fun to our readers - millions and millions of people who enjoyed playing the game.'

Mr Bateson told him: 'It has been said that you turned the *Mirror* into your family album. Would you agree with that?'

'I would not agree with that, no,' Mr Maxwell replied.

'The gentleman who said it,' Mr Bateson told him, 'was a Mr Pilger. Do you know him?'

'The gentleman,' said Mr Maxwell, 'was an employee of ours, very highly paid, who did no work for us, and we were happy to be shot of him - a disgruntled employee.'

Asked about an article on a visit he made to Bulgaria, Mr Maxwell said: 'Part of my business a a publisher of the *Mirror* is to interview a head of state as important as Mr. Zhivkov to have his opinions and views about relations with our country and about his peace in the Balkans.'

A Mirror reporter, Anton Antonovicz, had covered the visit.

Said Mr Maxwell: 'What he reports is part of the freedom of his press. It is his opinion. The article he wrote and that the editor published - they considered this was the part that would interest the *Mirror* readers. There are other parts which he decided not to publish

- business which we did with the President of Bulgaria which are not in this article. Is that clear?'

Mr Justice Simon Brown said: 'No, not entirely, and it is probably my fault. You went because you thought it was relevant to the *Mirror's* business for you to interview this head of state?'

'Correct,' said Mr Maxwell.

'I can quite understand why that is *Mirror* business if it produces copy - in other words, if an article is written indicating what the President said to you. But apart from that, what other *Mirror* purpose is served by the discussion?'

'The briefing of what line he is likely to take in the matter of war and peace, in the matter of Comecon, in the matter of relations between Bulgaria and Great Britain,' said Mr Maxwell. 'We have to have this background information in order to take the right editorial line. I was accompanied by a political editor as well as Mr. Antonovicz. He wrote a light-hearted piece which he considered would interest millions of our readers.

'Many others would not be interested in the higher level politics, but we as a national newspaper need to have the benefit of advice of Heads of State in as many parts of the world as we can get. That is the business of the Mirror.'

'Yes,' said the judge. 'I entirely understand that.'

Another foreign trip - this time to China - was raised by Mr Bateson, who referred to a picture of Mr Maxwell with the Chinese leader, Deng Xiao Ping.

Said Mr Maxwell: 'The Mirror is particularly proud to have secured that interview. This is the first time a British businessman and publisher was given the opportunity to meet the Chairman of the Chinese People's Republic, and we have done very well for our readers of Mirror Group Newspapers and the British Printing and Communications Corporation - a most important visit. From it resulted a new newspaper, the China Daily.'

Was the trip, Mr Bateson asked, also made to further other business interests?

Mr Maxwell said: 'That sounds, my lord, as though there is something sinister about it. I wish Mr Bateson would relate to BPCC and the Pergamon Press. We employ thousands of people in these businesses, and their business with China is very important to us, to the people who work for us, and for this country.'

He explained: 'We are making the whole of this newspaper, transmitting it by satellite from Peking to London and producing it and distributing it on the same day in London and Paris. It is a great British achievement. We are very proud of it, and it shows what modern technology now does and can do.'

Mr Bateson also asked about Mr Maxwell's chairmanship of the Commonwealth Games, and the medals he presented to Tessa Sanderson, Daley Thompson and Steve Cram.

He explained: 'One of the suggestions was that as part of my responsibilities for taking over the Games would be the presentation of medals. I refused that. But on the day in question, I was chosen - and pleased to be chosen - by the Commonwealth Athletic Federation to present the medals.'

Of a Mirror article saying that 'the wild and wasteful party in Fleet Street is over', Mr Maxwell told the court: 'This is the famous article where I told the Fleet Street unions that enough is enough - that their gravy train had finally hit the buffers.'

Mr Bateson asked: 'You then proceeded, did you not, to fight the unions? To lay off men, generally...'

Mr Hartley protested. 'My lord, may I ask what this has got to do with this libel action?'

Mr Bateson told him: that 'Mr Maxwell's motives are not motives dictated by altruistic socialism. There is nothing in his conduct and his treatment of his employees that comes even remotely close to socialism. What he will do, it is my submission, is to use socialism as a vehicle for the power that he wants...'

The Jury withdrew, while a legal debate on these points went on, and the debate continued until the court adjourned for the day.

CHAPTER FOUR
Day 4

When the case entered its fourth day, Mr Justice Simon Brown ruled against the defendants' line of questioning the previous day. There were ample authorities, he declared, to the effect that cross-examination cannot 'properly admit wide-ranging, scatter-gun allegations of misconduct'.

Then the jury filed in, and Mr Maxwell was recalled to continue his evidence.

He was asked first about an interview he gave on Anglia Television in May 1984, but said he could not recall it. A transcript was provided, but before long Mr Hartley was asking the judge if the jury could retire again. 'In my submission,' he said, 'this is yet another attempt to get things in the back door.'

The judge agreed, and the jury left the court again, while the legal debate went on. When they returned, the judge told them: 'There is only one piece of advice that ought invariably to be given to juries - and that is to bring to court a rattling good book!'

Then Mr Maxwell was asked again about the television programme. Mr Bateson told him that he was asked in the interview: 'You've got an excellent sense of humour. Why bother to sue them?' To which, he said, Mr Maxwell had replied: 'I am sorry, *Private Eye* is a satirical magazine whose proprietor, a gentleman I believe called Mr Wigwam - a Mr Ingrams, I beg your pardon - is in the habit of going after innocent people. I am one of those that he knows if he steps out of line, he'll be swatted like a fly.'

Later, said Mr Bateson, Mr Maxwell added that he'd brought the 'Kray twins' action 'not for myself, but for many hundreds of other people who have been hurt and haven't the ability to hit back'. Mr Bateson asked: 'Have you brought these proceedings to swat Mr Wigwam, for the benefit of hundreds of other people, or for your wife and family?'

Mr Maxwell replied: 'I have brought these proceedings for the protection of my reputation, for the protection of the political system and its integrity. If I am accused of bribing the Leader of the Opposition, that is an appalling accusation. My wife and family were utterly dismayed by being deliberately brought in by *Private Eye* to help their circulation and to increase their profits. I certainly do not dissent from the fact that I am also hoping as a result of this action that a lot of other innocent people, who keep being attacked and who cannot afford to defend themselves in an expensive libel action, will equally be helped.'

Re-examined by Mr Hartley, Mr Maxwell was told, 'As I understand the defendants' case, they have not withdrawn any allegations … How do you feel about that and the time you have spent in the witness box and the questions you have been asked?'

He replied: 'Appalled and shocked that, notwithstanding the cruel and wicked allegations made against me, they have produced no evidence whatsoever to justify them. And they did not have the guts or the decency to withdraw the allegations. I am very, very sorry about that.'

That ended the case for the Plaintiffs, and Mr Bateson began to outline his case to the jury. He told them: 'I expect you know what a bribe is, the same as anybody else does. You

bribe a policeman by giving him a fiver not to report you and get a prosecution on a parking offence. You can bribe somebody, as they do in video piracy these days - you bribe a projectionist to get the film for the night so that you can take copies of it. That is a bribe.

'Now there is nothing in this article that says anything about bribes like that. It says, "How many more Kinnock freebies will Maxwell have to provide before he is recommended for a peerage?" So that if it was a bribe to get a peerage it has not worked. It is not saying "Oh, he paid the money and got the peerage". It was not a bribe in that sense of the word.

'There is nothing wrong in our society today about giving assistance, financial assistance, to political parties, political leaders, or anything of a similar nature. There is nothing even wrong, I suggest to you, in our modern society about people paying money to a political party in the hope that they will get a peerage, if that is what they want. If and when society changes, perhaps even the law changes, it may be that it will be a serious matter for complaint. At the moment it is not. And you will hear that it is a frequent feature of political life - the way in which people support political parties and how their elevation to the peerage coincides with the cash having been provided. And there is nothing wrong with it. Mr Bateson ended by saying:

'Finally, of course, there is the reputation of Mr Maxwell. And it is in fact an important part of my client's case that the plaintiff has a general bad reputation as an ambitious self-publicist and a bully. Members of the jury, I will be calling evidence about that.'

Then the court adjourned for lunch.

After the lunch break, Mr Bateson called Mr Christopher Silvester, political correspondent of *Private Eye*, who agreed he had written the article on Mr Maxwell published on July 12, 1985.

LEFT: *Neil Kinnock, Leader of the Opposition, and his wife Glenys, setting off on their African trip.*

Asked where he obtained his information, he said: 'My information came from a source who is highly respected within the Labour Party. He is a prospective Parliamentary candidate. He was also privy to what went on in Mr Kinnock's private office.'

Did he intend to suggest in the article any question of bribery? 'I did not intend to suggest anything of the sort,' he replied.

Questioned about the honours system, Mr Silvester told the court: 'I think it is a fact of modern political life that people who make donations to political parties - all political parties - receive honours.'

Cross-examined by Mr Hartley, he said his article was 'true in substance'. Asked what was true, he replied: 'We have not been able to prove the allegation that Mr Maxwell paid for the overseas trips of Mr Kinnock, but I believe the article to be true in substance - that he made payments to the Labour Party. Indeed, when I wrote the article I believed the information on which I relied to be 100 per cent accurate.'

His source, he said, had been consistently reliable. But when Mr Hartley asked: 'Are you prepared to name him?' Mr Silvester replied: 'I would be no more prepared to disclose a source than I would expect Mr Maxwell's journalists to disclose their sources to a court of law, unless the source wished to be disclosed.'

He agreed it would be easy to make up a story and, when challenged, said: 'Well, I have got it on the highest authority and source, but I won't disclose it.' But his source, he added, 'had indicated to me that he would not be particularly keen to actually appear in the witness box for reasons of possibly jeopardising his own political career.'

He was prepared to accept that the article may have been inaccurate, but did not accept that what he wrote was a lie. *Private Eye* did not publish an apology 'because from the very beginning of these proceedings Mr Maxwell's demands both for damages and costs in this matter have been outrageous.' He added: 'I think it is outrageous that Mr Maxwell presumes the word 'freebies' to mean bribes, and I think it is outrageous of Mr Maxwell to demand the sum of £10,000 in relation to this matter. I also think it is outrageous that he attempted to emotionally blackmail us by citing the *Mirror's* Ethiopian Appeal Fund, which has been the subject of a couple of articles in the magazine and about which other proceedings are - as I understand it - still in existence between us and Mr Maxwell.'

Asked who wrote the 'Street of Shame' article, Mr Silvester replied: 'An employee of Mr Maxwell.' But: 'I am not prepared to disclose the source of that story, either, for very obvious reasons.' Mr Silvester added: 'We receive contributions to all the columns in the magazine from journalists working on all newspapers on a freelance basis. I was aware that the author of the article was shortly going to leave Mr Maxwell's employment on a voluntary basis, but in fact that did not subsequently take place. The person is still there, still working for Mr Maxwell, still privy to what goes on in his offices.'

There was laughter in court when Mr Hartley asked: 'So *Private Eye* has got a mole inside Mr Maxwell's office?' and Mr Silvester told him: 'Not just one, Mr Hartley.'

Questioned further about his source, he said: 'The source for the first story - who was a frequent visitor to Mr Kinnock's private office on official business - was told by two individuals that this was the nature of the relationship between Mr Maxwell and Mr Kinnock's private office. And furthermore that the method by which the monies had been channelled to Mr Kinnock's private office was through Mr Kitson. My source in fact was told by Mr Kitson that "I organised and got Mr Maxwell to subsidise the Moscow trip". My source had spoken to Mr Kitson and Mr Kitson had said: "I got Mr Maxwell to organise and subsidise the Moscow trip.'

'So if your source is correct,' asked Mr Hartley, 'Mr Kitson is not only a liar, but he is a perjurer?' Mr Silvester replied: 'If my source is correct.'

Mr Silvester was still in the witness box when the case was adjourned for the day.

CHAPTER FIVE

Day 5

When Christopher Silvester returned to the witness box on the fifth day of the trial, he was asked by Mr Hartley: 'Are you saying the reason you did not approach Mr Maxwell before this article went into *Private Eye* was because you did not think it was defamatory of him?'

He replied: 'We write articles, as I explained, from week to week about Mr Maxwell. We would not dream of approaching him about those articles. We know that he has a hostile attitude towards our magazine, so what would be the point?'

'How does one stop *Private Eye* publishing

BELOW: *Christopher Silvester, Political Editor from* Private Eye.

lies?', asked Mr Hartley. 'Perhaps you could give everybody a little hint on what they should do.'

Mr Silvester told him: 'I don't believe *Private Eye* published lies, because I believe that a lie is a deliberate untruth, and we are not in the business of publishing deliberate untruths.'

Asked about a *Private Eye* apology to Lady Havers, Mr Silvester said: 'The apology is a lie'. And he added: 'The apologies are drafted by counsel. They are not necessarily what we believe. The fact that they are published in our magazine does not mean that is what we believe.'

Said Mr Hartley: 'I think you have made one thing plain to everybody in this court: that apologies in *Private Eye* are worthless.' But Mr Silvester said: 'That is not true'.

Later, Mr Silvester said there was a third source in Mr Maxwell's employ. But he was not prepared to give his name, and the source was not prepared to give evidence.

'When did you know that?' asked Mr Hartley. He replied: 'I knew that at precisely the same time as I knew that the other potential witnesses were not prepared to give evidence. We didn't expect the proceedings to be carried through. When we realised Mr Maxwell was in earnest ... we realised that it would be a good idea to seek further assurances from these people that they would give evidence for us. They all declined.'

When Hartley asked: 'What is the improper motive, if any, of those payments on Mr Maxwell's behalf?' Mr Silvester told him: 'The improper motive is as stated... "seeking to advance his own personal standing with, and influence over, the leadership of the Labour Party". Mr Maxwell is a man who wants power. He enjoys quite a good deal of it already, but he wants more. My personal belief is that Mr Maxwell would like to be a peer of the realm.'

Mr Hartley asked: 'Would you agree with me that over many years Mr Maxwell has become a special target for *Private Eye*?'

'One of many,' said Mr Silvester. Among others were 'just about every politician you care to mention (and) other members of the Establishment'. He added: 'I would say that *Private Eye* and Mr Maxwell have locked antlers on many occasions and there is no prospect of those antlers becoming disentangled. There is not a campaign in the sense of deliberately seeking to offend or defame Mr Maxwell. There is a consistent desire to criticise and comment upon his conduct.'

Mr Silvester was asked about an article about Miss Sara Keays with which, he agreed, he had been concerned. He said: 'That was based on the circumstances surrounding the Cecil Parkinson-Sara Keays affair which, of course, was first published, brought to public notice in *Private Eye*. It concerned the original article. If you will recall, there was a great deal of rumour and speculation about the relationship between Miss Keays and Mr Parkinson at the time. However, one of my sources intimated to me ... that Miss Keays had been involved in a relationship with Mr Marcus Fox, MP. We subsequently discovered it was untrue.'

But he told the court he was not prepared to disclose his source on that story.

Other cases in which *Private Eye* apologised were mentioned, and again Mr Silvester refused to disclose his sources.

Re-examined by Mr Bateson, Mr Silvester was reminded of a 'look-alike' feature in *Private Eye* about Lord Weinstock and Mr Andropov. 'Has that,' he was asked, 'resulted in any complaint or proceedings?'

Mr Bateson intervened. 'My lord, Mr Andropov cannot. He is dead'.

Soon afterwards, Mr Silvester left the witness box and made way for the man whose evidence had been eagerly awaited - Richard Reid Ingrams, who until October, 1986, was the editor of *Private Eye*.

Ingrams said that during his editorship, which began in 1962, *Private Eye* consisted of 'really two halves - one is composed of what is supposed to be jokes, political satire, humour of one kind or another, and the other half of stories. It exposes gossip, reporting.'

Asked by Mr Bateson what sort of line *Private Eye* has taken over the years, he said: 'Our aim is to be satirical, which involves making fun of public figures, and those set in authority over us. I suppose, also, in a very broad sense it has been to expose humbug of one kind or another.

'The exposure side of *Private Eye* ... does divide itself up into different sections. In the middle part you find satire, humour and parodies of newspapers and that sort of thing, cartoons ... and at the front and back you find stories and exposures about politicians and also, of course, a great deal about Fleet Street, which *Private Eye* has specialised in since it started. Exposing what goes on in Fleet Street.

'Certainly in the old days - I think it has changed somewhat now - nobody else ever wrote about what Press lords did and what went on in various newspapers. It used to be a policy that dog does not eat dog. In other words, one newspaper should not attack another.

'Now that has all rather changed. But when *Private Eye* started, that was the case - *Private Eye* did a lot of reporting, about Fleet Street particularly.'

Private Eye, he said, had no political affiliations, and over the years had been responsible for a number of exposures involving political figures, political scandals. Among them the Thorpe case and the Poulson affair - 'a corrupt architect who employed a number of politicians' - were the two most notable. Mr Ingrams added: "There are a great many others one could mention, but I don't want to blow my own trumpet.'

Asked about what policy was adopted about the truth of falsity of an article, he said: 'Our policy would be basically the same as any other paper, except of course that the kind of material that *Private Eye* is dealing with is somewhat different. If you like, more risky.

'So *Private Eye* certainly has a reputation - whether it is deserved or not I do not know - for being rather more daring and outspoken about what it says about various things than,

for example, the *Daily Telegraph*.

Asked about checking stories he said: 'As the magazine has become more and more successful and has a larger circulation, these checks have become more and more necessary, because *Private Eye* has become more and more a target for litigants.'

He had never deliberately published an untruth, and he said it was quite wrong of Mr Maxwell to say that 'Past experience shows that *Private Eye* will do anything to tell lies to increase circulation.'

He added: 'In my opinion, any paper that was based on that principle would quickly collapse, not only because it would be sued a lot, but because people wouldn't believe it. I think any paper depends for its survival on the confidence of its readers, and if it printed lies week after week, and if the word got around, no-one would buy it.'

Private Eye satirised humbug of one kind or another and looked at politics, the Press, television and finance - 'which I myself find difficult to understand, but it has a very high reputation in the City'.

Mr Bateson asked about the article on Mr Maxwell in *Private Eye* of July 12 and asked what he thought of its accuracy.

He replied: 'Well, I considered it at first sight a very likely type of story. It seemed to me a convincing story.

'I didn't regard it as of great importance in relation to the other items. I was aware that Mr Maxwell was a long-time benefactor of the Labour Party and it didn't strike me as being particularly remarkable that he had made these payments. So in terms of a sort of scoop, I didn't rate this very highly.'

Of the second article, he said: 'I thought that was a much more interesting story than the previous one. It showed the relationship between Mr Maxwell and Mr Kinnock. Again it seemed to me a convincing story, and I think as a matter of fact that it was my idea to have the cartoon showing the HMV dog.'

Asked about the truth of the two stories, Mr Ingrams said: 'I knew from Mr Silvester that he had a good informant in regard to the first article. I know who his informant was. I had met him on a number of occasions. He contributed to *Private Eye* a number of stories. I liked him very much. I thought he was a reliable source. On the second article, the one about the party, this came from one of our regular informers on the *Daily Mirror*. Again, I knew that person to be a reliable informant.'

What was his view about the substantial truth of the first article?

'I still believe it was in substance correct. My main reason for believing that is that our source has always stuck to his guns and not, as sometimes happens, back-tracked.'

Asked about payments to the Labour Party, he told the court: 'I know Mr Maxwell had made payments to the Labour Party. I always thought of him as a sort of sugar-daddy to whom the Labour Party could turn if they were in need of a bit of cash, which he was happy to provide. So when I saw the story saying he has paid for this or that trip, I thought: "Well, so he has."

'Both stories, it seemed to me, were really attacks on Mr Kinnock, not Mr Maxwell. It was Mr Kinnock who was most badly presented by being associated with Mr Maxwell. Mr Maxwell was just doing what he had always done, which was to be a sugar-daddy.'

Cross-examined by Mr Hartley, Mr Ingrams said he attached importance to the counter-claim in the case (involving the article headed 'Another Whopper').

Mr Hartley asked: 'Are you saying you would have brought proceedings in respect of it, had it not been for the fact that Mr Maxwell sued you and the publishers of *Private Eye*?'

'I would not have brought proceedings, because I have never myself believed in bring proceedings for libel,' said Mr Ingrams. And he agreed it was 'tit for tat'.

Did he accept that the allegations, stating that Mr Maxwell has contributed to certain overseas trips of Mr Kinnock and is intending to contribute to his latest trip, were untrue? 'No,' said Mr Ingrams.

He agreed with Mr Hartley that the people most likely to know the true state of affairs of the money article were Mr Kitson - because it was suggested funds were chanelled through him - Mr Maxwell, who is supposed to have paid the money, and Mr Kinnock, who was supposed to have received it.

All three - two on oath in court and Mr Kinnock through a Telex from Tanzania and a letter from his Press secretary - had said no such payments were made, said Mr Hartley. 'Does that not in your mind suggest to you that your source might well be wrong?'

Said Mr Ingrams: 'He might be wrong, yes, but I still believe him.' And he couldn't see what would shake him from that belief.

Replying to a question from the judge, Mr Ingrams said: 'As an editor I am constantly having to assess the reliability of sources and journalists. Unfortunately, some of them get discarded because they turn out to be unreliable.'

Mr Hartley asked: 'Would you not accept that one of the best tests of reliability is a preparedness to come out from the cloak of anonymity and come into the witness box to be cross-examined?'

Mr Ingrams replied: 'No, not at all, because I think many informants by doing so would be sacrificing their jobs.'

Mr Hartley asked: 'Do you give Mr Maxwell credit for anything he has done recently?'

Said Mr Ingrams: 'Yes, I think he has done a lot for Oxford Football Club.'

'And that,' asked Mr Hartley, 'is a serious answer and is the limit to which you are prepared to go?'

Mr Ingrams: 'I think he has. I live in the Oxford area myself.'

Asked how Mr Maxwell could be said to be advancing his career in relation to Mr Kinnock, Mr Ingrams said: 'If Mr Kinnock, for example, were to go to Moscow and he was to say "I am a friend of Mr Maxwell and he helps me", then the next time Mr Maxwell went to Moscow he might get a better reception. So it would be a great help to him in all his business activities to be seen and known to be a close friend and associate of Mr

Kinnock.'

Answering further questions, he said he was not against ambitious people. 'I am suspicious of them.' But he was not suspicious of successful people, and they were not all targets in *Private Eye*.

'There are a great many successful people. For some reason the figure of Yehudi Menuhin springs to mind as an extremely successful man who would not be a target in *Private Eye*.'

Then Mr Ingrams referred to 'another

ABOVE: *Richard Ingrams, gas mask at the ready, prepares to read copy for* Private Eye.

element in the story which has not been mentioned at all'. He said: 'Newspaper proprietors are invariably offered peerages, so Mr Maxwell - on two counts, as it were - would be a very likely candidate. Almost every newspaper proprietor in my experience eventually becomes a peer.'

On that note, Day five came to an end.

CHAPTER SIX

Day 6

Richard Ingrams was back in the witness box when the case entered its sixth day and second week, and was asked by Mr Hartley if his unidentified sources would be paid for stories.

'No,' he said, 'They wouldn't be selling their story. If someone came in, as sometimes did happen, asking for more money for a particular story, I was inclined not to do a deal with them ... I have always been suspicious of people offering stories for money.'

Asked again about *Private Eye's* sources, he said he would prefer to say nothing about them.

Soon afterwards the judge told the jury that they must withdraw again. 'We have one or two things to discuss - things which are matters of law and do not really concern you,' he said. When the jury retired, there was a long legal debate about the *Private Eye* sources. The judge, ruling on the arguments, said that Mr Hartley had argued that the sources be disclosed.

The arguments for an order for disclosure were powerful, he said. But the public interest in the non-disclosure of sources should still be regarded as outweighing the requirement, in the interests of justice, for them to be named.

When the jury returned, the judge apologised for the fact that they'd been away for a long time. But, he added, 'I fear it is not going to be the last time that we have to ask you to be out of court for a substantial time.'

Then Mr Ingrams was cross-examined by Mr Hartley, partly on the question of *Private Eye* apologies. He was asked: 'What do the words in *Private Eye* mean when you say you withdrew an allegation against somebody?'

He replied: 'It is not *Private Eye* language. This is lawyers' language. I never use language like that, nor do journalists. It is lawyers' language.'

The judge asked: 'But it does indicate in lawyers' language that the publishers are recognising the untruth of the original publication?'

Mr Ingrams told him: 'I don't think it necessarily does, my lord. There could be circumstances where one was forced - through lack of evidence or some such - to print such a statement. But it would not necessarily follow from that that I believed that article to be untrue ... it is quite conceivable that *Private Eye* would say "We unreservedly withdraw this story" and for me, personally, as editor, to believe - or even to know - that the story was true.'

Later the judge told the jury: 'When you were outside court this morning I was asked to give certain rulings. One of those, counsel desires to have tested in the Court of Appeal.' And as the Court could deal with it that afternoon, it meant that they - and he himself - could have the rest of the afternoon off.

The Court of Appeal case was heard by Lord Justice Kerr and Lord Justice Parker. They were told that during the *Private Eye* case, the judge had ruled that Mr Silvester and Mr Ingrams were not obliged to disclose their source of information. They ruled that for a journalist to be required to disclose his source, the court had to be satisfied that the disclosure was necessary in the technical sense of the administration of justice. The judge had been right in concluding that the only issue left was

ABOVE: *Richard Ingrams, retired editor of* Private Eye, *broods over his libel actions with Mr Robert Maxwell.*

damages, and in thinking that the issue could be dealt with by summing-up to the jury.

The Court of Appeal dismissed an interlocutory appeal by Mr Maxwell from the judge's ruling.

Day six ended, then, on a note of anticlimax.

CHAPTER SEVEN

Day 7

Back in court next day, Mr Hartley told the judge that the Court of Appeal had agonised over the question of sources for quite a long time. And the judge observed: 'It was obviously a borderline case.' Then he asked for the jury to return and he told them of the Appeal Court's ruling.

Mr Ingrams, recalled and cross-examined by Mr Hartley, was questioned again about *Private Eye* apologies. The judge asked him: 'Are not at least the bulk of your apologies - whether printed or in open court - sincere and genuine?'

He replied: 'It's rather like the curate's egg - parts of them may be.'

Asked how many of the magazine's 53 apologies would be genuine, he said: 'I would say, very roughly, that 75 per cent are genuine and the others slightly more questionable.'

Mr Hartley asked if Mr Ingrams would despise people who bring libel actions.

He replied: 'Not at all. I think in many cases they're justified. All I said was that I personally wouldn't ... It's a regrettable fact that in this day and age bringing a libel action is, on the whole, restricted to people who have a great deal of money.' But he agreed that he, too, was bringing a libel action in the case, and that was 'tit for tat'.

Mr Hartley asked: 'Can the jury treat your counter-claim with not only a pinch of salt, but regard it as the grossest piece of humbug on your part?'

Said Mr Ingrams: 'No, it isn't humbug. It's a genuine counter-claim. If he sues me, I'm going to sue him. If he calls me a liar, then I will sue him.'

Turning to the Kray twins 'look-alike' feature, Mr Hartley asked how Mr Ingrams felt after hearing Mr Maxwell's evidence.

He replied: 'Well, I was not aware until Mr Maxwell told us this last week that his family had been destroyed, as he said, by Adolf Eichmann.'

Mr Hartley asked: 'Knowing what you now know, would you not agree that it is about as offensive a thing as could be said about Mr Maxwell and Mrs Maxwell that you could possibly think of?'

Mr Ingrams told him: 'I can see that in the circumstances it would have caused him distress, but I did not intend that.' But, looked at in retrospect, it could seem to be a very sick joke.

Towards the end of his cross-examination, Mr Hartley asked Mr Ingrams about *Private Eye's* finances. He said that although he was chairman of the company and signed the accounts, he had always tried to distance himself from the financial running of the magazine.

Asked if they put aside something like a third of the turnover for payment of libel damages and costs, he said: 'You'll have to ask our managing director about that.'

His name? 'Mr Cash,' said Mr Ingrams.

Mr Who? 'Mr Cash,' said Mr Ingrams. 'It always gets a laugh.'

It was a rare happy moment on which to end Day Seven.

RIGHT: *David Cash, Managing Director of* Private Eye.

CHAPTER EIGHT

Day 8

When Richard Ingrams returned to the witness box next day, Mr Hartley asked about 'constant attacks' in *Private Eye* on Mr Harold Evans (former editor of *The Times*).

They were written, Mr Ingrams told the court, by Auberon Waugh in his fictional diary. 'And I think *Private Eye* readers, knowing Mr Waugh's column as they did, would not have taken references to Mr Evans literally. I remember one that described him as being in the habit of biting people when he was angry. I would assume that *Private Eye* readers would have assumed this was a joke.'

He agreed that on one occasion an action brought by Mr Evans was settled when he and the publishers gave an undertaking not to pursue any campaign of malice and denigration against him.

That undertaking, given in 1975, was ignored, he agreed, and added: 'Mr Evans was a very persistent litigant - the most persistent, in my experience of *Private Eye*. He was constantly taking offence at the slightest references to him.

'In fact, in the end, after he had complained, I made a unilateral, full-page declaration that I would never again refer to him in *Private Eye* because I couldn't face the thought of any more litigation coming from him.'

That was sincere - Mr Evans had never been mentioned again - but Mr Ingrams said he was not prepared to do the same for Mr Maxwell. Why? 'Because it's not the same. Mr Evans I considered to be, by that stage, an insignificant figure. Mr Maxwell is a very powerful and significant figure.'

Turning to an apology to GEC chief Sir Arnold Weinstock, (later Lord Weinstock) Mr Hartley asked what the source of the article had been. 'That was written by Mr Paul Foot,' he was told.

Asked if he knew what checks Mr Foot had made, Mr Ingrams replied: 'Mr Foot is a very thorough, experienced and, in my opinion, brilliant journalist ... I would assume that if Mr Foot submits to me an article, that he had made a thorough investigation of it. Mr Foot is - perhaps you know - employed by Mr Maxwell on the *Daily Mirror*.' That article, he agreed, was 100 per cent untrue. But it would not have been written by Mr Foot deliberately as a lie.

'I would prefer to put it that his source got it wrong, that he had misled him. If the source had made up a story which he gave to Mr Foot, he would, I presume, have done so with the express intention of getting *Private Eye* into trouble, because he would know that we would publish it or might publish it, that litigation would ensue and that we would get into trouble.'

Mr Hartley asked: '*Private Eye* would not survive if you did not say nasty things about people?'

Mr Ingrams disagreed: 'They're not all nasty things. There are quite a lot of, I would hope, funny things about people. I don't want to be nasty about, for example, Mr Denis Thatcher, who is regularly written about in *Private Eye*, every week. I would hope that we are amusing. We don't intend to be nasty.'

Mr Ingrams answered questions about several apologies given to people who'd been

ABOVE: *Harold Evans, former editor of the* Sunday Times, *'a very persistent litigant' (Richard Ingrams).*

mentioned in *Private Eye*. Among them was one to actress Penelope Keith and her husband Rodney Timson, which he said was a genuine apology.

Mr Hartley asked: 'An allegation against a Detective Constable, Mr Timson, that he and his wife "had obtained a large, expensive bracelet by some dishonest means", is a particularly serious allegation to make, is it not?'

Mr Ingrams agreed: 'Yes, it is.'

Hartley: 'You must have known that it was likely to affect his career.'

Ingrams: 'I would not think that. The story, as I recall it, as it appeared in *Private Eye*, was to say that Penelope Keith had appeared on the television, wearing this bracelet, and that somebody had rung up the television studio, claiming that this bracelet was stolen goods. That was the story.'

Hartley: 'It was not meant as a joke, was it?'

Ingrams: 'No, it was not.'

Hartley: 'And you knew perfectly well that people would think that Penelope Keith and her husband were party to the stealing of that bracelet?'

Ingrams: 'Well, that wouldn't necessarily follow from what was said. That could be read into it, I agree.'

Hartley: 'Mr Ingrams, did you intend the article to mean that Mr and Mrs Timson had obtained a large and expensive bracelet by some dishonest means?'

Ingrams: 'I was not intending to suggest anything at all about Mrs Timson, I don't think.'

Hartley: 'Did you intend it to mean that Mr

Timson was involved in obtaining the bracelet by some dishonest means?'

Ingrams: 'Yes ... that ... story stated that somebody had contacted Granada Television and claimed that this piece of jewellery had been stolen. That was what the story said, and it would be possible to read into that an allegation that Superintendent (sic) Timson was in some way involved.'

The judge: 'The only other possible imputation is that there are some pretty zany viewers of television.'

Imgrams: 'Yes, my lord.'

Hartley: 'Do you accept that it had caused both Mr and Mrs Timson "shock, anger and distress"?'

Ingrams: 'I accept that.'

Hartley: 'What were your feelings when you put that particular issue to bed and there is this very nasty allegation against Mr Timson, a serving police officer? What did you think that it was likely to do in the Penelope Keith household when they got to hear of it?'

Ingrams: 'I don't think in those terms, Mr Hartley. One has no means of knowing how people will react to articles about them in *Private Eye*.'

Hartley: 'You are a very uncaring person, are you not?'

Ingrams: 'No, I'm not saying that at all.'

Hartley: 'You do not mind how any of your targets react? You do not mind what distress it causes them or their family?'

Ingrams: 'I'm saying one has no means of knowing. Some people take articles in *Private Eye* humorously. Often one thinks one's written something very offensive to somebody, and they ring up and say how amused they are by what has been written.'

Hartley: 'Did you expect Mr Timson to ring up and say how amused he was?'

Ingrams: 'No, I did not, but I was thinking about my general attitude towards printing *Private Eye* - that, on the whole, I do not think beforehand "What effect is this likely to have if it is put in?" because one has no means of knowing.'

Hartley: 'You drop a bomb and you do not mind what damage is caused?'

Ingrams: 'No, I wouldn't put it like that ... sometimes what you think will cause offence doesn't. And sometimes what you think is a joke, causes great offence. For example, the look-alike which we talked about yesterday. I thought that that was a joke, but it caused great offence to Mr Maxwell. I accept that.'

Hartley: 'Mr Ingrams, it is precisely because you have this reckless frame of mind, you do not think it through, that I am suggesting to you that you do publish these wild statements in *Private Eye*, not caring whether they are true or false, and not caring what effect they have.'

Ingrams: 'I do care whether they are true or false, and, as I reiterate, I have never put anything into *Private Eye* which I knew to be false.'

Mr Hartley then turned to a story in *The Sun* newspaper which said: '*Private Eye* lied about a Minister,' and asked Mr Ingrams: 'Are you saying that that is defamatory of you?'

He replied: 'Yes, it is.' But asked if he'd written to the newspaper to ask them to correct it, he said: 'I believe, along with Buckingham Palace, Mr Hartley, that one does not comment on stories in *The Sun*.'

Just before the court adjourned for lunch, Mr Bateson asked the judge: 'My lord, all I ask is for permission, during the adjournment, to see my client Mr Ingrams and take instructions from him.' The judge agreed, and when the case resumed after lunch, there was a shock announcement from Mr Bateson. He asked the judge for leave to withdraw the counter-claim concerning the *Daily Mirror's* 'Another Whopper' article.

The judge agreed and, after legal debate, the jury returned and he told them: 'The defendants have not thought it right to continue with their counter-claim. That, accordingly, has been dismissed with costs.'

Then he explained why Mr Alex Kitson, former Deputy General Secretary of the Transport and General Workers' Union, was again in the witness box. Mr Kitson - the first witness in the case 'all those days ago' - had been mentioned by both Mr Silvester and Mr Ingrams as being at least someone who spoke to the source in the first publication. 'That matter,' said the judge, 'was never put to Mr Kitson, and he is now going to be asked questions about it.'

Mr Hartley said Mr Silvester told the court that his source was told by Mr Kitson that he had arranged for Mr Maxwell to subsidise Mr Kinnock's trip to Moscow. He asked Mr Kitson: 'Is there any truth at all that you have told anyone at all that you have arranged for Mr Maxwell to subsidise the Moscow trip?'

Mr Kitson replied: 'No truth whatsoever. I never spoke to either Mr Maxwell or anyone else in connection with these trips, and in fact Mr Kinnock was in Moscow before I knew that he was going to Moscow.'

After that, Richard Ingrams was recalled, and cross-examined by Mr Hartley.

He was asked if Mr Hugh Stephenson, former editor of *The New Statesman*, had been approached to give evidence to support the contention of Mr Maxwell's alleged general bad reputation.

He replied: 'He may well have been.'

Mr Hartley said: 'I am frankly amazed that Mr Ingrams does not know.'

But the judge told him: 'For all he knows, half-a-dozen witnesses have been approached by *Private Eye* to give evidence and have all flatly refused. Is that right?'

'For all I know,' said Mr Ingrams.

Later, Mr Hartley asked if Mr Ingrams did not think it was a very serious matter to call someone a bully.

He replied: 'Well, I would qualify my answer by saying it would depend on who it was. If you said the Archbishop of Canterbury was a bully, it might be different from the Labour Chief Whip.'

Mr Hartley asked: 'Are you saying that Mr Maxwell made the payments to the Boundary Commission Fighting Fund through any ulterior motive?'

Mr Ingrams: 'No, I'm not.'

Mr Hartley: 'Are you saying that he made the £44,000-odd payment to the Labour Party conference with an improper motive?'

Mr Ingrams: 'No.'

Mr Hartley: 'Do you challenge Mr Maxwell's assertion that he does not want to be a peer, a member of the House of Lords?'

Mr Ingrams: 'Well, I do find that hard to accept ... I could concede that when he was offered a peerage last year, he refused. But he could change his mind next week.'

Mr Hartley asked: 'You have said more than once that it is your belief that Mr Maxwell has, in effect, got it in for you, and would like to close *Private Eye* down?'

Mr Ingrams replied: 'Well, I think he said that he wanted to "swat me like a fly".'

'Is that an unreasonable view,' Mr Hartley asked, 'to hold about somebody who you feel is always stinging you and hurting you?'

Said Mr Ingrams: 'I would regard it as unreasonable for a man who owns newspapers and who, indeed, has called himself on occasion a journalist, to harry another paper - and also to move heaven and earth, as Mr Maxwell has done, to get a journalist to reveal his sources.'

It was coming to the end of another day in court.

The judge gave all concerned their starting times for tomorrow: 'Ten forty-five, members of the jury. Ten thirty the rest.'

CHAPTER NINE

Day 9

The reason for that slightly later starting time for the jury on day nine of the trial was because there was a legal debate about exemplary damages before they returned. When they did, Mr Hartley cross-examined Richard Ingrams about further *Private Eye* apologies and a statement in open court about Mr Gordon Kirby, who featured in the Helen Smith case.

Mr Ingrams explained: 'Mr Kirby was involved in a long-running campaign by *Private Eye* to vindicate Mr Ron Smith, whose daughter died in Jeddah in mysterious circumstances.

'The campaign was not directed against Mr Kirby - the campaign was on behalf of Mr Ron Smith, who was trying to investigate the circumstances in which his daughter had died and was being continually obstructed.'

Mr Hartley asked: 'You know that that campaign waged against Mr Kirby pretty well destroyed him, did it not, and his family?'

Mr Ingrams: 'Well, Mr Kirby wasn't dismissed from his job or anything like that - he was supported by the Foreign Office. The Foreign Office paid for him to sue *Private Eye*. Why should I accept that he has been destroyed? He is still in the employment of the Government.'

Then Mr Hartley returned to an earlier apology and asked if it was genuine.

'Well,' said Mr Ingrams, 'parts of it. This is what I think I referred to as a curate's egg apology. Parts of it are true and parts of it are not.'

The judge observed: 'Of course, the point about a curate's egg is that it is a nonsensical answer and it means the whole thing is infected and bad, does it not?'

'No,' said Mr Ingrams. 'It doesn't mean that. The answer of the curate was that parts of it are excellent, my lord.'

The judge was not happy. He said: 'But he is asked by the bishop, or whoever it is, "How's your boiled egg - it stinks to high Heaven." And, being loath to say, as was the case, that the egg was rotten, he said "Part of it is all right." But I mean it is only a way of saying "the whole is rotten".'

Mr Ingrams told him: 'Well, I didn't mean it in that sense. All I meant to say was that parts of it were fine and other parts were not so fine.'

Later, Mr Ingrams was asked if, since Mr Maxwell had become Publisher of the *Daily Mirror*, there had been a number of very good causes for which he has asked for money from the public.

'I am aware of the Ethiopian appeal,' said Mr Ingrams. And he accepted that after the Bradford Football Club fire, there was a Mirror Group Soccer Disaster and Safety Fund. But it was part of his case that Mr Maxwell had exploited his position as Publisher of the *Mirror* to advance his personal standing.

'And,' asked Mr Hartley, 'is it your contention that he does that "to advance his own personal standing with an influence over the leadership of the Labour Party?"'

Mr Ingram replied: 'Partly the Labour Party, partly with foreign governments, like the government of Poland or Bulgaria, where he seeks to secure business advantages by writing propaganda for the leaders of those countries in his newspapers.'

'Is it nor a good thing for Britain that business is done ...?'

Mr Ingrams said: 'I don't think it is a good thing for anyone that the President of Bulgaria, who is a Communist tyrant, I think of the most odious kind - responsible, for example, for the murder of Mr Markov who used to work at the BBC - should be treated to a kind of propaganda full-page puff in the *Daily Mirror*.

'I don't think that is of benefit to anyone, and it is not of benefit to the *Daily Mirror*, because I believe the *Daily Mirror* readers, particularly Labour Party supporters, would be appalled by that type of article, and, indeed, they showed it by abandoning their paper.'

Mr Hartley suggested: 'As we have seen your moral standards when it comes to publishing *Private Eye* and what you put in there, it really is a humbug for you to take that sort of line against the *Mirror*.'

He was told: 'I would not write an article praising someone who I knew to be a murderer.'

Mr Hartley reminded him that after the Brussels football disaster, there was a *Mirror* fund set up. Was that cynically done? he asked.

'No,' said Mr Ingrams. 'I would not say cynically done.'

The *Mirror* also has funds for the National Society for the Prevention of Cruelty to Children. Was that done cynically? Mr Hartley asked.

'No,' said Mr Ingrams. 'This is, I would say, standard newspaper practice. Newspapers launch appeals on behalf of various charities or good causes of this kind. The *Mirror* is no different here than any other newspaper.' He agreed that the only appeals ever included in *Private Eye* are those for funds to pay out libel damages.

He was asked: 'Do you agree that to save the Commonwealth Games was a good thing to do, or a bad thing to do?'

'I think in the circumstances it was a good thing to do, but Mr Maxwell didn't do it in a way which I would necessarily approve. He made it abundantly clear that he was getting the maximum amount of personal publicity from it. It would have been perfectly possible for Mr Maxwell to provide funds and not indulge in personal publicity stunts.'

In the afternoon the court heard from Mr Christopher Hird, a financial journalist who had worked on *The Economist, Daily Mail, New Statesman* and the Insight pages of *The Sunday Times*, and for the independent TV production company Diverse Productions.

Questioned by Mr Desmond Browne, junior counsel for the defendants, he was asked about Mr Maxwell's reputation in relation to his motives as a newspaper proprietor and Labour Party benefactor.

He said: 'The *Daily Mirror* is an unusual paper in the sense that it contains editorial matter that relates to the proprietor and to his business interests. That is not the case with most newspapers in this country.'

Of Mr Maxwell as a Labour Party benefactor, he said: 'His general reputation in that matter is that by being a supporter of the Labour Party he hopes to advance his own interests.'

It was thought that Mr Maxwell tried to influence the policy of his newspapers excessively and that he dealt with his employees in 'a rough-handed way'.

Cross-examined by Mr Hartley, Mr Hird said he taught in the Journalism Department of the City University one morning a week, and agreed that his students were told to check their sources.

He was asked: 'If one is publishing a defamatory story about someone and there is a likelihood of being sued, you would tell journalists that they must get a statement from that source?'

He replied: 'Yes. It is my policy that if one is going to publish something that is defamatory, to confront the person about whom you are making the statement.' If a source was involved, he would check that it was reliable.

Questioned about Mr Maxwell and the *Daily Mirror*, Mr Hird agreed that when he took over, there was overstaffing in certain departments in Fleet Street. But 'there were other ways of solving the difficulties of overmanning at papers such as the *Mirror* than the course Mr Maxwell chose to take.'

Said Mr Hartley: 'Well, he does not have barbed wire around his...' 'No,' said Mr Hird. 'He doesn't, no.'

He agreed that Mr Maxwell took a different view from the newspaper barons of the 1920s, 1930s, 1940s, 1950s and 1960s 'where anything went as long as the paper came out. It did not matter how much money was lost'. And modern Fleet Street proprietors were, to some extent, following Mr Maxwell's lead.

When he was re-examined by Mr Browne, Mr Hird said that, in his experience as a journalist, sometimes sources of important stories would be reluctant to go to court. He taught his student journalists that they should not reveal their sources. That was an accepted journalistic ethic.

'Journalists have no right,' he added, 'to cost people their jobs because they tell them the truth about something that they know.'

Asked about a newspaper proprietor who sought to compel journalists to disclose their sources, he said: 'I think it's disgraceful. It is such an attack on all the fundamental rules by which we operate. It's incredible that a newspaper proprietor could do that.'

Then Mr Browne returned to the question of barbed wire, raised earlier. He asked: 'Mr Hartley put to you a rather oblique question, the significance of which the jury may have missed, about there being no barbed wire at the *Mirror* building. Could you read between the lines for us and tell us precisely what he was getting at?'

Mr Hird told him: 'Yes. There is barbed wire around the new offices of *The Times* and *The Sunday Times* down at Wapping as a result of the industrial dispute that arose out of Mr Murdoch's moving of the printing of those papers from Gray's Inn Road down to Wapping. That's where the barbed wire is. But there's no barbed wire around the *Mirror*.'

The jury retired again while a legal debate went on, and when they returned they heard from Mr John Walker, a local government officer and author who worked between 1980 and 1985 for the Labour Research Department - an organisation funded by trade unions. Part of his duties there, he told Mr Bateson, was to examine company accounts and the details of political donations declared by companies.

He noticed a striking link between companies which made significant donations to the Conservative Party and leading directors of them receiving major honours from the present government. After more research, he ended up writing a book on the history of the honours system, called 'The Queen Has Been Pleased', which included a chapter on 'The Press Barons'.

Mr Bateson asked him about an article in *The People* newspaper which included the words: 'Every tycoon knows that the short-cut to a title is to cough up cash to the party in power.'

Asked what he thought of that, Mr Walker

Lord Elwyn-Jones.

replied: 'It's a very crude way of putting a slightly more exact statement. But I think the evidence would suggest that at certain times in recent history businessmen whose companies have contributed generously to political parties have received major honours, knighthoods and peerages, in circumstances where they wouldn't otherwise have done so.'

In cross-examination, Mr Hartley asked: 'Would you accept that a lot of people can give quite considerable sums of money - whether it be to the Labour Party, the Conservative Party, the Liberal Party, the SDP or indeed Uncle Tom Cobbley's party - without, in fact, desiring or seeking a peerage, or any honour at all?'

'Yes,' said Mr Walker. And he agreed there was one entry in his book about Mr Maxwell. It said: 'The message from the Press list is that if you want fame and honour, get on to the *Mirror* and wait for another Labour Government. No doubt Robert Maxwell's intentions as proprietor of the Mirror Group of newspapers are different.'

The next witness was Lord Elwyn-Jones, and the court heard of his impressive career: Labour MP for West Ham from 1945 to 1974, Attorney-General in the Government from 1964 to 1970, and a Lord of Appeal since 1979. He is editor-in-chief of the Criminal Law Library, published by Waterlow, a subsidiary of Mr Maxwell's BPCC, and has known Robert Maxwell and his family for about thirty years.

Lord Elwyn-Jones said he'd spoken for Mr Maxwell when he was Labour Parliamentary candidate for Buckingham in the 1959 General Election: 'I hope that is not why he lost,' he commented. He spoke for him again in the 1964 election, when he was elected a Labour Member of Parliament.

Mr Maxwell, he said, had been a lifelong supporter of the Labour Party and, he believed, shared his view that a Labour Government would be beneficial to the people of this country.

Mr Hartley asked: 'How would you describe him, apart from being a personal friend?'

Lord Elwyn-Jones replied: 'What has struck me outstandingly about him is his moral and physical courage. That was manifested on the battlefield when he came from his own country, having suffered the murder of seven members of his family by the Nazis. This made a considerable emotional impact on me, as I was one of the prosecuting counsel in the Nuremberg Trial, and I know what the sufferings of the survivors meant. To say nothing of the victims.

'Therefore the willingness of the man, in the face of that, to go into action … and to the best of my knowledge and belief I think he was one of the few private soldiers to be commissioned in the field, and I think I am right in saying that Field Marshal Montgomery himself pinned the Military Cross on his chest. Those things are not forgotten in my mind, especially in the context of his own devotion to his family.'

Mr Maxwell, sitting at the front of the court, showed considerable emotion has he listened to his old friend give that glowing testimonial. For the second time during the case, his eyes filled with tears, and he dabbed his eyes with a handkerchief.

What about his alleged reputation as a bully? 'I've never met it,' said Lord Elwyn-Jones. 'I wouldn't expect to meet it I must say … he's a pretty tough character. That I knew. That's manifested in what I've said already.'

What about Mr Maxwell as a self-publicist? 'I don't think he's averse to self-publicity. It may well be that being connected with the newspaper is part of the explanation of that.'

And did Lord Elwyn-Jones think any the worse of him for what he had done in that regard? 'I don't,' he replied. 'I have admired what he has done as far as the newspaper is concerned, which he has pretty well rescued from a very poor position to obviously a very strong and successful position. Whether the propagation of himself is part of the process of his idea of improving the prospects of the newspaper is a matter for his judgment, not for mine.'

Cross-examined by Mr Bateson, Lord

Elwyn-Jones agreed that Mr Maxwell's picture appearing in the *Daily Mirror* was a fairly frequent occurrence. But he didn't think hiding one's light under a bushel was the habit of newspaper proprietors.

Had he seen Lord Hartwell's picture in the *Daily Telegraph*?

'I don't think I have, no,' said Lord Elwyn-Jones. And there was laughter as he added: 'I've seen him in the House of Lords, however. Whether that is an adequate substitute, I do not know!'

Said Mr Bateson: 'I am sure you see all sorts of people in the House of Lords, but that is not what this case is about.'

'You see the best people,' said Lord Elwyn-Jones.

When he was re-examined by Mr Hartley, Lord Elwyn-Jones was asked if he had been

Mark Young, General Secretary of BALPA.

able to see Mr Maxwell's attitude towards his staff. He replied: 'Towards the domestic staff? I've been a guest in his home, and I have not observed any extraordinary feature of rudeness. But I've had nothing to do with his business, except for this matter which you mentioned earlier - that I am the editor-in-chief of this interesting series of books on criminal law.'

The last witness in the case was Mr Mark Young, general secretary of the British Airline Pilots' Association since 1974, and secretary of the National Joint Council for Civil Air Transport. Mr Young, who is also an international co-ordinator who occasionally acts on behalf of the International Airline

Pilots' Association, told the court he'd known Mr Maxwell for about twelve years.

He had been chief union negotiator when the now-named British International Helicopters was transferred from British Airways to Mr Maxwell and his *Scottish Daily Record* and *Sunday Mail* company. He'd found Mr Maxwell very pro-union - and 'a very, very tough negotiator'. He added: 'He is a man who focusses very clearly on what his objectives and interests are and makes it clear to everyone with him where they lie. But I also believe he's a good negotiator because he takes into account the interests of the other side. I think in seeking an agreement he not only wants to reach his own interests. He also wants to make sure that the other side he negotiates with also reaches their goal.

'I think also that once the priciples of the negotiation have been settled, he's an extremely generous man on what I call the small print of an agreement - but matters which are very important to trade unions.'

Mr Young was asked why BALPA recommended the deal with British International Helicopters.

He replied: 'I said I'd known Mr Maxwell for some time, and I believed I knew his character. But I went out of my way to talk to senior trade union figures - people who I knew who had closer contact and relationships with him - and asked them their views. They all advised me that he was a tough man to deal with, but on the whole all the companies he ever took over prospered and that in turn provides security of employment for people and generally they grew and created new employment. Since that was one of the major prerequisites of the unions in the industry in the transfer of ownership, I recommended that we should negotiate a deal with Mr Maxwell.'

They did so, and Mr Maxwell kept to his side of the bargain 'absolutely'.

Asked about Mr Maxwell being a self-publicist, he replied: 'I do not believe that.'

And that was almost that.

Mr Justice Simon Brown told the jury: 'This finally concludes the evidence in the action.' All that was left were speeches from counsel and his summing-up.

But there were questions of law still to be raised. So the judge told the jury their timetable: 'Tomorrow off. A long weekend. Back Monday.'

CHAPTER TEN

Day 10

While the jury had a day off, it was work as usual for the judge, counsel and the court.

The judge announced: 'Mr Bateson submits that the plaintiff's claim for exemplary damages in respect of the second article should not go before the jury.' After a short address, he said: 'My ruling is that the exemplary damage claim can go to the jury, but only in regard to the further distribution or publication of the relevant issue once the matter is before the Court of Appeal. This ruling, too, can - and I understand will - be the subject of the proposed further interlocutor appeal to the Court of Appeal. Accordingly again I am comforted to think that it is not necessarily my ruling that is going to be decisive as to how this issue is left to the jury.' He gave leave to appeal.

CHAPTER ELEVEN

The Court of Appeal

After hearing legal argument from both counsel in the Court of Appeal throughout Monday, Lord Justice Nourse and Lord Justice Ralph Gibson gave their judgment on Tuesday morning, the twelfth day of the case:

Lord Justice Nourse: 'I will ask Lord Justice Ralph Gibson to give the first judgment on this appeal.'

Lord Justice Ralph Gibson: 'This is an interlocutory appeal in a libel action. The trial is pending before a jury and Mr Justice Simon Brown. The evidence has been completed: submissions to the jury have not yet been made. The defendants, with leave of the learned judge, appeal to this court asking that two rulings of the judge be reversed. The first ruling is that the plea of justification as it now stands in truncated form upon the pleadings is not open to the defendants and is not supported by any evidence fit to go to the jury, and the second is that within the limited terms only, as stated by the learned judge, there is sufficient evidence in support of the plaintiff's claim to exemplary damages to justify the leaving of that part of the claim to the jury.

'As to the matter of justification, it is necessary to state how that pleading now appears on the pleadings. The plaintiff's claim by writ of 24th July 1985 is for damages for two libels published in *Private Eye*. The first is an article in the issue dated 12th July 1985 and the second is an article and cartoon in the next following issue on 26th July. It is in respect of the second publication only that exemplary damages are claimed. A statement of claim served on 26th July sets out the words complained of as to the first libel. I shall omit some parts which do not appear to me to be relevant for these purposes. It was as follows: '"Mirror Group publisher Robert Maxwell may not be popular with some sections of the Labour movement, but he is definitely de rigueur with Party Leader, Neil Kinnock.

'"Patricia Hewitt, Kinnock's once fun-loving press secretary is shortly to announce a visit by the Welsh windbag to the East African capitals of Dar-es-Salaam and Nairobi, though she won't be revealing that Maxwell is acting as paymaster for the trip.

'"Members of Kinnock's kitchen cabinet are fond of boasting how they 'made money out of the Moscow trip' (another Maxwell subsidy) and recall how the Captain picked up the tab for Kinnock's Central American tour after the international charity War on Want backed-off for publicity reasons.

'"How many more Kinnock freebies will Maxwell have to provide before he is recommended for a peerage?"

'With reference to that libel the statement of claim asserts in paragraph 4: "The said words in their natural and ordinary meaning meant and were understood to mean that the plaintiff had acted or was acting as paymaster for trips made by Mr Neil Kinnock, the Leader of the Labour Party, to East Africa, Central America and Moscow and was thereby guilty of bribery or attempted bribery."

'As to the second libel alleged, the words were set out in paragraph 5 of the statement of claim, and they were as follows: "The guest list for the glittering, champagne-all-the-way party marking Cap'n Bob's first glorious year at the helm of the *Daily Maxwell* was awesome indeed. On it was Prince Charles (who puzzlingly failed to turn up) and, of course, Neil Kinnock.

'"On the day, Maxwell ordered political hack Julia Langdon to confirm with Kinnock that he would be coming. Kinnock told her he had no intention of gracing the affair as he was concerned with more important matters of state that evening. The fat man's response was typical. 'Tell him,' he boomed, 'that if he doesn't come to my party the *Mirror* will not be reporting his African tour.'

'"Kinnock was furious. 'You tell him', he stormed, 'that I will not be bribed!' Thankfully good sense finally prevailed. Mindful of His Master's Voice, Kinnock duly turned up. Maximum publicity for the African junket, which Maxwell lamely denies financing, was promised. Kinnock and the rest left happily clutching their souvenir of the evening: a mock-up of the *Mirror* featuring the gigantic form of Maxwell on every page."

'The cartoon referred to shows what were intended to be understood as the likeness of the plaintiff's face in the horn of a gramophone and Mr Kinnock's face on the attentive dog.

'With reference to the second libel, the statement of claim asserts: "The said words and cartoon in their natural and ordinary meaning and/or by way of legal innuendo bore or were understood to bear the meaning attributed to the first, namely, to put it shortly, that the plaintiff was guilty of bribery or attempted bribery. The reference to the innuendo was made by reference to the "special facts" of the first article having been printed and, it was suggested, read by many readers of the second.

'The defence of the defendants was served in August 1985. By paragraphs 4, 5 and 6 it denied that the words published or the cartoon "bore or were understood to bear or were capable of bearing the meaning alleged" by the plaintiff or any meaning defamatory of him. Further or alternatively, the defence asserts on behalf of both defendants that "the words complained of … are true in substance and in fact". The particulars relied upon in support of the plea of justification were set out in seven sub-paragraphs.

'Some of the most important matters have gone from the case because the defendants have called no evidence in support of them. They include sub-paragraph 3 of the particulars, in which it was alleged: "Some of the financial support that the plaintiff has provided to the Labour Party has gone to fund visits abroad by the Leader of the Labour Party, Mr Neil Kinnock, including visits to Moscow and Central America", such funds being made available through the Transport and General Workers' Union.

'Sub-paragraph 4 also disappeared from the case. That alleged that Mr Kinnock made a visit to East Africa in July 1985, the month of the publications complained of, and that until publication the visit "was to be funded by or on behalf of the plaintiff" through the Transport and General Workers' Union. Mr Bateson told us that those allegations had been withdrawn.

'The failure to call evidence to support those allegations which were the basis of the main case of justification was examined closely in cross-examination of the defendants' witnesses who, putting the matter very shortly, said that they had received information through apparently credible and reliable sources that it had proved impossible, by any means which the defendants were willing to use, to get the providers of information to give evidence. The witnesses, Mr Silvester and Mr Ingrams, declined to identify their sources and relied upon Section 10 of the Contempt of Court Act 1981. Mr Justice Simon Brown declined to order disclosure on the grounds that he was not satisfied that it was necessary in the interests of justice so to do.

'On appeal by the plaintiff to this court Lord Justice Kerr and Lord Justice Parker on 11th November 1986 upheld the judge's ruling. Our attention has been drawn by Mr Hartley to the reasons there given in the judgments delivered. It is clear that on behalf of the plaintiff Mr Hartley will have many formidable points to make. The judge will also no doubt comment severely in his charge to the jury upon some aspects of the defendants' conduct.

'Returning to the pleaded defence, it is necessary to note what remains of the particulars of justification. Paragraph 7(1) said: "The plaintiff, who is a millionaire, is a member of the Labour Party, a former Labour MP and an active Labour Party supporter." That is formally admitted. Paragraph 7(2) says: "Over a period of years the plaintiff has made available and offered to make available to the Labour Party funds under his control both by way of cash donations and by way of financial support for particular projects or purposes."

'The evidence with reference to that, as I understand it, came from Mr Maxwell as to payments by him or by Pergamon Limited, a company controlled by him, being some £38,000 to the Boundary Commisssion Fighting Fund paid by three or four separate payments, and £44,000 odd to the Labour Party conference of 1984.

'Paragraph 7(5) is also formally admitted and is in these terms: "The plaintiff has at all times sought considerable publicity for himself and his activities, including his political activities in supporting the Labour Party."

'As to Paragraph 7(6), the first sentence only is admitted and was to the following effect: "When the plaintiff acquired control of Mirror Group Newspapers Limited in 1984 he fulfilled a long-standing ambition of his to become a national newspaper proprietor."

'That is followed by various allegations relevant to the so-called "wider meaning" of the libels to which I shall come, that the plaintiff has exploited his position as a newspaper proprietor "to seek to advance his own personal standing with and influence over the leadership of the Labour Party. The plaintiff has also exploited his control over Mirror Group Newspapers Limited to attract for himself as much personal publicity as possible in order to seek to create for himself a public image as an influential and respected figure in public life. It is the plaintiff's personal ambition to be elevated to the House of Lords as a Labour peer. The plaintiff seeks to achieve this as others have done before him by patronage of a political party and by the self-publicity he can create through his control of Mirror Group Newspapers Limited."

'Lastly in Paragraph 7(7) there is the reference to the party in July 1985 which is the subject-matter of the second article. It includes the assertion that Mr Neil Kinnock was among those invited and that "on or about the day of the party the plaintiff sought confirmation that Mr Kinnock would be attending. When the plaintiff was informed that Mr Kinnock had other commitments on the evening in question, the plaintiff threatened to withhold publicity in the *Mirror* newspapers for Mr Kinnock's tour of East Africa later that month. Mr Kinnock duly attended the plaintiff's celebration party and in common with the other guests was provided with a mock-up of the *Mirror* containing pictures of the plaintiff." The sentence about the threat to withhold publicity is not admitted, and we are told that no evidence was produced to support it. Also the word "duly" before the word "attended" is obviously in issue.

'As a result of the failure by the defendants to produce evidence in support of the more important allegations in their particulars of justification, the learned judge struck out the defence of fair comment. There was no appeal about that, nor could there have been. As was pointed out to us, Lord Justice Kerr, on the appeal to this court, said at page 14F of the judgment: "He" (the learned judge) "was clearly right in doing so, because since the defendants accepted that they could not prove the truth of the matters published, it became impossible for them to seek to maintain that their comment on those matters was fair. There is now no appeal against that ruling by the learned judge."

'Lord Justice Kerr also referred to the defendants' counter-claim against the plaintiff based on the publication in the *Daily Mirror* which was said to suggest that the defendants had lied deliberately in publishing the libels complained of by the plaintiff. Lord Justice Kerr expressed surprise (at page 19E) to hear that the defendants proposed to maintain the counter-claim after they had been forced to abandon the whole of the gist, or the important part, of their claim for justification. That expression of surprise was very soon entirely justified by events - we are told that the counter-claim was abandoned during the cross-examination of Mr Ingrams.

'We can therefore ask, as Lord Justice Kerr asked, "What really remains by way of defence in this action?" What remains has been described to us substantially as it was to the court on 11th November, and it appears in the brief reasons given by Mr Justice Simon Brown for his ruling on justification. It is as follows. The primary defence to the plaintiff's claim is that the two publications were not defamatory. Alternatively the defendants seek to justify. The judge continued as follows (at page 2B): "The plaintiff asserts of the first article that its natural and ordinary meaning is that he had acted or was acting as paymaster of

the trips made by Mr Kinnock, the Leader of the Labour Party, to East Africa, Central America and Moscow, and was thereby guilty of bribery or attempted bribery. The defendants assert that the article, if defamatory at all, should be understood to bear both a lesser and wider defamatory meaning. The 'lesser' meaning is that the discreditable conduct of which the plaintiff is guilty is not bribery or anything as serious or extreme as that, but rather that he should be regarded as having made the relevant payments with the lesser improper motive of seeking to influence Mr Kinnock to recommend him for a peerage. The 'wider' defamatory meaning for which the defendants contend that the words are capable of bearing is that the plaintiff has an ambition to be a peer and improperly is seeking to achieve this by patronage of the Labour Party and by the self-publicity which he creates through his control of the Mirror Group. In support of his entitlement to assert and rely upon such wider meaning he relies upon the unreported decision of the Court of Appeal in Williams v. Reason. The defendants would then seek to justify such wider meaning by reference to and reliance upon, first, not the payments for Mr Kinnock's foreign travels but rather other payments, namely the payments I have already referred to, the £44,000 and the £38,000.

'Continuing at page 3, the learned judge said: "Secondly, of the matters on which the defendants would seek to rely, that the plaintiff is a self-publicist, an allegation made in para 7(5) of the defence which is indeed admitted. Third, that the plaintiff, as is alleged in paragraph 7(6), seeks to exploit his position in the Mirror Group to create not only self-publicity but a public image as an influential and respected public figure.

'"The defendants accordingly would be seeking to justify the lesser and wider defamatory meaning to which I have referred by reliance upon the remaining pleaded particulars."

'The plaintiff's contentions in reply before

the judge were as follows. First, not enough is still alleged to justify a plea of justification, even if evidence could be regarded as having been given in support of the surviving allegation. Secondly, the evidence given does not in fact support those surviving allegations.

'It was common ground before the judge, as it has been before us, that what the judge called "the lesser defamatory meaning", namely that if the words were defamatory at all they meant no more than an allegation of misconduct short of bribery, was a meaning which the jury could properly be invited to consider. The dispute arose on the wider meaning and upon whether there was any evidence fit to go before the jury of justification of the lesser or wider meaning. The contentions advanced by Mr Hartley on behalf of the plaintiff on the wider meaning were recorded by the judge as follows at page 4: "He does however dispute that the words are capable of bearing the 'wider' meaning which the defendants seek to put upon them. In particular he makes these points: first, there is within the article no suggestion of patronage by the plaintiff of the Labour Party. Indeed, no reference to any payments other than directly from the plaintiff to Mr Kinnock for foreign travels. Now, however, the defendants seek to rely not on those payments at all but rather on payments from the plaintiff to the Boundary Commission Fighting Fund and from Pergamon to the Labour Party and the Boundary Commission Fighting Fund.

'"Secondly, even less is there any reference in the published article to self-publicity or to exploitation of the plaintiff's position as controller of the Mirror Group.

'"Thirdly, the sting of the article, which of course is all that the defendants are required to justify, is not only in the last three lines but is also to be found in the earlier phrase in respect of one of the alleged payments, that Patricia Hewitt, Mr Kinnock's press secretary, 'won't be revealing that Maxwell is acting as paymaster for the trip', an allegation tantamount to an assertion that the payments were all intentionally secret."

'The learned judge accepted the second point on the ground that he was bound so to hold on the authority of Williams v Reason, an unreported decision of this court consisting of Lord Justice Stephenson, Lord Justice O'Connor and Lord Justice Purchas. That is to say it was not open to Mr Bateson to allege as part of the contended for wider meaning of the article anything about self-publicity or the plaintiff's control of the Mirror Group.

'It is necessary to note what the words were to which the judge was referring when he spoke of the "contended for wider meaning of the article". There were two articles. They have been set out above. They were separate publications, and if found to be defamatory consitute separate causes of action. The reason why the judge referred to "the article" in the singular is explained at page one of the transcript of his reasons where he said: "Although there are two articles complained of, I shall henceforth refer only to the first since the second is in my judgment essentially but a reiteration of the first, albeit arguably with aggravating features, in particular the use of the word 'bribed', the cartoon and the context of both which is in the same issue that the plaintiff's strong denial of the truth of the first is published."

'During the argument I had thought that the judge's approach to the two articles was not in issue and that this court was not being asked to approach the ruling which he gave on the basis that the two articles are to be separately analysed for the points in issue in this appeal in order to see whether the wider meaning might be a reasonably possible meaning of the second article in the light of the first but would not be possible on the first alone. Mr Hartley, however, after Mr Bateson's reply, pointed out that the articles were separate causes of action and submitted that the question before the court is to be answered by reference to the first article on the ground that the second article does not add much. It may be that he had made this point perfectly clearly earlier in his submissions and I have failed to follow it.

'It seems to me, therefore, that if Mr

Bateson is to succeed entirely in this appeal against this ruling he must make good his contention by reference to the first article as well as the two articles read together that the wider meaning is one which a reasonable jury could give the words after being properly directed that it was a meaning they could reasonably bear.

'I have found this part of this case to be difficult, as did the learned judge. It is I think largely a matter of impression on reading the article. The specific allegations of making the payments for the trips mentioned are not true. The defendants, while saying that the article as a whole is not defamatory, wish to argue that, if defamatory at all, the proper meaning which the jury should attach to it is, as stated, that the plaintiff is ambitious to be a peer and is improperly seeking to achieve that by patronage of the Labour Party and by his self-publicity created through his control of the Mirror Group. The defendants want to argue the possible defamatory meaning in order to give themselves the chance of persuading the jury, if there is evidence to support it, that they have justified the sting in the libel. The plaintiff seeks to have the possible defamatory meaning removed from consideration of the jury in case the jury should be unfairly misled into settling for a less serious meaning than the words plainly bear and even into thinking that the defendants have justified a grave libel by proving something different which they had not alleged.

'I agree with the judge that in the first article alone there is scant reference to self-publicity or to exploitation of his position as controller of the Mirror Group. There is no more than the reference to the plaintiff as publisher of the Group. I take the view, however, that the wider meaning contended for is one which the words of the first article could reasonably bear. The allegation of payment for foreign travel of Mr Kinnock in his capacity as Leader of the Labour Party is not, I think, so distinct from patronage of the Labour Party as Mr Hartley contends, although of course Mr Hartley may well persuade the jury that they should regard the article in the way Mr Hartley has invited us to read it. Nor do I think, although again I see the force of the point, as no doubt would the jury, that the reference to Patricia Hewitt not revealing that Maxwell is acting as paymaster is of such force that the court is required to, or should properly, rule that the wider meaning is not one which the words can properly bear. It is not necessary in my judgment to deal further with this issue by reference to the two articles read together, because on that basis it would be entirely clear to me that the wider meaning is one that the words can reasonably bear.

'The judge, having referred to what I have pointed out with reference to the second point argued, considered the way of putting the defendants' case on this issue which he regarded as the strongest. At page 4 of the transcript he said: "May not the words indeed bear the wider meaning that the plaintiff was ambitious to be a peer and improperly seeking to achieve that by patronage of Labour interests? And would it not then be open to the defendants to invite the jury to conclude that the plaintiff had made, either personally or through Pergamon (his creature) payments to the Boundary Commission, unpublicised payments, which is all that Mr Bateson contends that the article was in any event asserting about the Kinnock payments, with that improper motive? Would not that constitute justification of the sting of the libel?

'"Certainly in my judgment that puts the defendants' case at its strongest. But I have concluded, not without doubt or difficulty, that it still falls outside the permitted scope for a plea of justification in this type of case, even though I recognise that that scope has clearly been enlarged by Williams."

'The judge gave two further reasons in support of that conclusion or made comments as follows: "It seems to me of some significance that when the whole question of justification arose, as here it did, before the Court of Appeal in July 1985 when the plaintiff was seeking to enjoin against further publication, the defendants never even envisaged that they could possibly seek to justify this libel on the now suggested basis, or indeed on any basis other than by the proof of at least some of the specific payments which the article alleged had been made for Mr Kinnock's travels. It is pertinent in that regard to note that Mr Ingrams' evidence before this court is that he was already at that time aware of the unpublished Boundary Commission payments, quite apart no doubt from the well publicised payment at the Labour Party Conference."

'For my part I have difficulty with both these added reasons or comments. I am very much aware that the learned judge has been trying this case for many days and knows it well, whereas we have had submissions for one full day upon the pleadings and documents. With great respect, however, I am unable to find anything of significant relevance to the present issue in how the defendants by their counsel dealt with the issue of justification before the Court of Appeal in July 1985. The case then put forward was an intention to justify the allegations of specific payments by witnesses who would speak to them.

'Important issues have been raised as to the good faith of the defendants' witnesses with reference to the then asserted intention to justify by the means stated. Those issues are for the jury, and it may well be that the jury will find it easy to answer them favourably to the plaintiff for the reasons suggested. I am unable, however, to see why a failure to mention or to rely upon an alternative basis of justification for a possible wider and less defamatory meaning throws any light upon the question whether that contended for wider and less defamatory meaning is one which, as a matter of law, the jury should be directed the words could reasonably bear. I take the same view in this context of the evidence of Mr Ingrams to the effect that he was aware in July 1985 of the unpublished Boundary Commission payments coupled with the fact that when the matter was before this court on the plaintiff's application for an injunction

nothing was said about those payments.

'For my part accordingly I would not uphold the judge's ruling that this wider defamatory meaning is not open to the defendants and that in effect the remaining particulars of justification are to be struck out. I differ from the learned judge on this matter only after much hesitation. It seems to me that the wider meaning contended for is a defamatory meaning which the words of these articles could reasonably bear. I do not know whether the jury will reach the conclusion that they will give such a meaning to the words or whether they will regard the contention as wholly unacceptable. It will be for them to decide, and it will be better if I say no more upon the subject.

'There remains the second contention put forward by Mr Hartley that there is not before the jury evidence fit to go before the jury, that is to say, in the judge's words, "evidence which a reasonable careful jury could find discharge the burden resting upon the defendants". He said (at page 5H): "To prove the plea of justification sought to be advanced, the defendants would have to prove, first, that the plaintiff is indeed ambitious for a peerage; and secondly, that the payments to the Labour Party - or perhaps more particularly to the BCFF - were made for the improper purpose of seeking to realise that ambition. As to the first, the plaintiff denies it. That no doubt is a good deal less than conclusive, but there is in my judgment no evidence to the contrary, and perhaps it is not a matter clearly to be inferred, let alone in the face of the plaintiff's unchallenged evidence that he has in fact twice refused to allow his name to go forward with a view to being recommended to Her Majesty for ennoblement. All that the defendants could rely upon, besides what Mr Bateson asserts is the unconvincing barrenness of the plaintiff's explanation for his refusals, are, first, the plaintiff's general tendency to self-publicity, and secondly, the past practice of peerages being conferred on those who have patronised political parties.

'"As to the second of the matters which the

defendants would need to prove, namely, the payments in fact made by the plaintiff were made for the improper purpose of realising his ambition, this is to my mind the consideration of overriding importance on the question of the evidence. The fact is that Mr Ingrams, the editor of the first defendants and himself the second defendant, expressly accepted that there was no improper or ulterior motive behind either the payment to the Labour Party or the several payments to the Boundary Commission Fighting Fund. It thus seems to me quite impossible for the jury to conclude by reference to that conduct, which is all that on any view of the first issue as to the justification of a wide meaning of the published words, for the jury to uphold such a plea."

'It seems to me that an interlocutory appeal upon such an issue at the present stage of this case presents very great difficulties to this court. It is of course right that the parties to a jury action of this nature should have access to the Court of Appeal to test, before verdict and judgment, the correctness in law of rulings made as to the case to be left to the jury. If possible it is right to avoid the fearsome burden upon the parties of a re-trial if, after verdict, a ruling or direction is shown to have been wrong.

'Where, however, the question raised is the judge's ruling on whether there is evidence fit to go to the jury upon an issue, it will frequently, if not in most cases, be impossible for this court to assess the sufficiency or fitness of the evidence which is before the jury. We have no transcripts. It is essential that the trial be interrupted for the shortest time possible. The intention is that the hearing of the trial should continue today after the giving of the judgment in this court as and when the learned judge directs. Mr Bateson has fairly and frankly acknowledged the difficulty.

'It is, as I understand it, common ground between the parties that if this court should uphold the judge's ruling that there is no evidence fit to go before the jury on the remaining issue of justification and uphold it

on the ground that we cannot say it is wrong because we do not know what the evidence is, it would be open to the defendants after verdict and judgment to complain in this court that the issue was wrongly excluded by the judge by reference to the transcripts of evidence.

'Mr Bateson, however, argues that the reasons given by the judge for holding that there is no evidence fit to go to the jury are not sustainable and if his contention is made out this court should say so and leave the matter to the judge to direct the jury in the light of our judgments and of any further submissions made to him. The first point made by Mr Bateson is that the question of whether the plaintiff is ambitious for a peerage should not be withdrawn from the jury merely because the plaintiff has denied it and there is no positive evidence, such as admission to a witness. The answer to the question, he says, may properly, and should in this case, be left to the jury to decide by inference from the material before them and in the light of their assessment of the plaintiff's evidence, including his denial.

'Mr Bateson has listed the material before the jury and the matters admitted in the defendants' particulars of justification to which I have already referred. He referred us to an article published in one of the newspapers of which the plaintiff is the publisher referring to "what every tycoon knows about the ways of getting a title". Mr Hartley objected that that is not something relied upon in the particulars of justification, and I therefore pay no further attention to it.

'Finally, Mr Bateson referred to the evidence given by the author of a book, without objection as to admissibility, showing the practice (I think Mr Bateson referred to it as the "facts of life") in the past with reference to the recommendations for the grant of peerages to those who have rendered distinguished services to political parties, including the giving of financial support, a practice which has included on occasions the recommendation for the grant of peerages to those whom Mr Bateson referred to as "press barons".

'Mr Hartley has objected to us that it was not suggested to Mr Maxwell in cross-examination that he had given or caused money to be given to the Labour Party or to the Boundary Commission Fighting Fund with the suggested motive of thereby obtaining for himself a recommendation that he be made a peer. Mr Bateson asserted that he had, as he said, put something like it to the plaintiff. I think the words said to have been used were "the giving of money is a good route to getting a title". It is of course common ground that Mr Maxwell repudiated any such suggestion made to him, but to that extent the suggestion was made and the jury heard the question and saw the plaintiff answer it.

'It is not clear to me that the learned judge did decide the second point, namely as to no evidence fit to go to the jury, on the absence of direct evidence about it. He said: "Perhaps it" (that is the existence of the motive of ambition) "is not a matter clearly to be inferred let alone in the face of the plaintiff's unchallenged evidence." It seems to me that in that passage he was commenting upon the weakness of the grounds upon which the jury might be invited to infer the existence of the suggested motive rather than stating his view that no such ground existed in the evidence. It was on the second of the matters which the defendant would need to prove, namely that the payments in fact made or caused to be made by the plaintiff for the improper purpose of realising his ambition, that the judge found the consideration which he described as of "overriding importance on the question of evidence". The way the judge put it I have already read out, and I refer briefly again to one part of that, namely the fact that Mr Ingrams accepted that there was no improper motive.

'Mr Bateson has contended that the answers in evidence of Mr Ingrams referred to by the judge cannot properly be given the effect attributed to them. He points out that the primary case of the defendant is that the words used were not defamatory at all. They do not, according to the defendant, mean that they had accused the plaintiff of attempted bribery or of any other discreditable conduct. Consistently with that defence Mr Ingrams said that he did not infer from the payment made to the Labour Party or to the Boundary Commission Fighting Fund any improper or ulterior motive. It is or should be open to the defendant, says Mr Bateson, to answer such a question candidly in accordance with his own view as to what it is right to infer from the making of those payments and at the same time have his counsel submit to the jury that if the jury find the article to be defamatory in the lesser or wider sense described earlier in this judgment the jury should infer upon all the material before them that the plaintiff, in making the payments, was acting from the improper or ulterior motive of seeking a title.

'Mr Hartley submitted to us that the judge was right to find in the reported answers to Mr Ingrams the conclusive force attributed to them. Mr Ingrams had been asked what "his case was", and his answer should be treated as conclusive. If Mr Ingrams had said that he, Mr Ingrams, had personally drawn the inference from the fact of payment to the Labour Party and to the Boundary Commission Fighting Fund that the plaintiff had made the payments with the improper motive suggested, then, said Mr Hartley, the position would be different.

'For my part I am unable to accept that the fact that Mr Ingrams accepted that there was no improper or ulterior motive behind either the payment to the Labour Party or the several payments to the Fighting Fund could, as I understand this case, have the conclusive and overriding effect contended for by Mr Hartley. I do not doubt that Mr Ingrams' evidence may be regarded by the jury as more than sufficient answer to the suggested ground of justification if the jury, finding the articles to be defamatory, are persuaded to regard them as defamatory only in the limited sense now suggested on behalf of the defendants. The jury may well be very impressed indeed by the fact that Mr Ingrams, who has had occasion enough to consider the matter, felt unable to infer from the payments made any improper motive in making them. If he did not, why should the jury?

'I see force in these points. I am, however, not persuaded that, for the reasons put forward by Mr Hartley, the remaining issue on justification should be withdrawn from consideration of the jury. I would therefore allow the defendants' appeal on the issue of justification. I would set aside the judge's ruling to the following extent. The wider defamatory meaning, namely that the plaintiff has an ambition to be a peer and is improperly seeking to achieve that ambition by patronage of the Labour Party and by the self-publicity which he creates through his control of the Mirror Group, is a meaning of the words used which the words of the articles could reasonably bear. Further, as to the sufficiency of the evidence in support of the plea of justification of the meaning of such words, if the jury should find the words defamatory but to no greater extent than to such a meaning, I would, for the reasons already explained, make no ruling that there is sufficient evidence but rule only that the acceptance in evidence by Mr Ingrams that there was no improper or ulterior motive behind the payment is not as a matter of law a consideration of overriding importance which renders it impossible for the jury to conclude that the plea of justification should be upheld.

'I turn now to the second matter of appeal, the judge's ruling that there is evidence fit to go to the jury in support of the plaintiff's claim to exemplary damages. The claim is advanced only with reference to the publication of the second article. The learned judge directed himself by reference to the law as stated in Cassell & Co v Broome (1972) A.C. 1027 and the case of Riches. It is not suggested that he misdirected himself in any way, save as to the precise date and time relevant to the issues of exemplary damage. We were invited by Mr Bateson to accept as an accurate statement of the law the principles listed in paragraph 18.27

in the Second Edition of Duncan and Neill on Defamation. It is sufficient to read only sub-paragraph (a) of the stated principles: "Exemplary damages can only be awarded if the plaintiff proves that the defendant when he made the publication knew that he was committing a tort or was reckless whether his action was tortious or not, and decided to publish because the prospects of material advantage outweighed the prospects of material loss. What is necessary is that the tortious act must be done with guilty knowledge for the motive that the chances of economic advantage outweigh the chances of economic, or perhaps physical, penalty."

'Mr Hartley did not suggest that anything needed to be added to, or taken from, that statement of principle. Mr Bateson has disclaimed any attack upon the judge's view that there was in general sufficient evidence with reference to knowledge or recklessness as to the defamatory and untrue nature of the publications or as to the calculations by the defendants as to the chances of economic advantage out-weighing the chances of economic penalty. He takes only the point of law that the judge misdirected himself as to the date and time at which proof of the required knowledge or recklessness and calculation of economic advantage is required.

'The judge's ruling is as follows: "So far as the second article here is concerned, I take the view that although there is sufficient evidence of recklessness to be left to the jury in regard to the initial stage of the publication, by which I mean the distribution up to the point at which it stood when the matter was before the Court of Appeal, I have concluded that there is here no sufficient evidence that the defendants were taking the view that it would pay them to publish and risk the consequences. In my judgment, as at that stage the profit to be made from including in the second article the only clause which in my judgment attracts the allegation that it is defamatory that is now advanced in this action, is the phrase "which Maxwell lamely denies financing". That may or may not be regarded by the jury as not only a reckless but a lamentable dig against the plaintiff. The fact is, in my judgment, it cannot be said to have been included in any way so as to boost sales. Indeed, I find it difficult to suppose that the article gains much in the way of essential interest or saleability from it. The article essentially tells a different story, itself possibly anti-Maxwell, albeit not the subject of any complaint as a separate libel in this action.

'"I take a different view, however, of the position that arose when the matter came before the Court of Appeal at two o'clock on Wednesday, 24th July, the date of publication, at a time when a large number of issues were no doubt sold and others unrecoverable, but when a substantial part of the issues clearly could have been - had the court granted injunctive relief - prevented from further distribution. As at that stage it seems to me that the plaintiff's case on recklessness is one properly to be put before the jury. After all, at that stage not only was there the original strong denial of the plaintiff and Miss Hewitt but also the telex from Mr Kinnock and the plaintiff's preparedness to go on oath, and indeed to bring the injunction proceedings. The only step taken at that stage by the defendants to ensure the truth of the article was apparently to ask the source, whom they have declined to name in these proceedings, whether he was maintaining his story and prepared to give evidence in support of it. It will be for the jury to decide whether that amounts to a sufficient taking of the obvious steps which were then necessary."

'Mr Bateson had contended that at 2 o'clock on 24th July when the matter came before the Court of Appeal publication was already complete. He fastened on the words in the passage from the textbook which I have read: "Exemplary damages can only be awarded if the plaintiff proves that the defendant when he made the publication knew" etc. The evidence showed, said Mr Bateson, that the issue of *Private Eye* went to the printer on Monday 22nd July and the copies of subscribers were sent out by post. On Tuesday 23rd July the

remainder of the printing went to the distributors for distribution to retail outlets. They were on sale from retail outlets on the morning of Wednesday 24th July, but distribution was not complete, according to some evidence, until the following day.

'Mr Bateson referred us to the affidavit of Mr Silvester which was put in when the matter was before the Court of Appeal. I do not find it necessary to set out the evidence. The contention made is that because publication, or the important or essential parts of it, was or were complete before 2 p.m. on 24th July, it was not open to the judge to leave the matter to the jury in the terms indicated by the judge's ruling. I am unable to accept this submission, and I can see nothing to support the contention that the judge was wrong. The jury will pay careful attention to the arguments propounded before us by Mr Bateson. If there is not guilty knowledge and recklessness before 2 o'clock on Wednesday 24th July and not guilty calculation of loss and gain, how can any jury be confident that there was any such guilt with reference to such publication as there was after 2 o'clock on that date and which the defendants could have stopped?

'I can see some force in that argument. I am, however, unable to see that as a matter of law a defendant who has published part of an issue of a magazine and is not proved to have made that publication with the guilty mind required for proof of a right to exemplary damages is thereby protected against a finding of liability to pay exemplary damages with reference to further publications of the same issue with reference to which there is evidence of that guilty action.

'I would accordingly dismiss the defendants' appeal on this issue.'

Lord Justice Nourse: 'I agree, and although we are allowing the appeal in regard to the justification issue I find that there is nothing which I can usefully add to the reasoning of my lord on either point, with which reasoning I am in complete agreement.'

Mr Bateson: 'In those circumstances I think

we both rise to our feet, but might I suggest that the appeal on the question of justification be allowed with costs and the appeal on the question of exemplary damages be dismissed with costs?'

Lord Justice Nourse: 'What do you say, Mr Hartley?'

Mr Hartley: 'That is certainly one way of doing it, or just say costs in cause for the whole lot or each side pay their own costs.'

Lord Justice Nourse: 'We think the correct order is to make no order as to costs.'

Mr Hartley: 'I wonder if your lordship would say that the transcript - I know a full note is being taken - could be available just as soon as possible, because I know that Mr Justice Simon Brown would very much value it before he sums up.'

Lord Justice Nourse: 'Clearly we will do anything which it is open to us to do, which does not include the impossible, but we can make a direction that the transcript be expedited.'

Mr Hartley: 'I am grateful. Without being approved by your lordships? For judge and counsel only.'

Lord Justice Nourse: 'We have to live dangerously sometimes. Yes.'

CHAPTER TWELVE

Mr Bateson for the Defense

Mr Bateson, as counsel for the defendants, had the task of leading off the final speeches to the jury. It was his job to present at length and in full detail the case on behalf of *Private Eye* and Richard Ingrams.

'You know by now, for your sins I am sure, that this is a case of libel. There are three libels - two that the plaintiff says were committed on him, one that the defendants say was committed on them; that last one you do not have to concern yourselves with anymore.

'I propose to deal, if I may, with the plaintiff's case first and the fundamental function of a jury at the outset of their deliberations when you sit in the jury room working out what your answer is going to be, is that you and you alone decide what the words mean. His lordship, in the course of his summing up, will direct you on what the words are capable of meaning. He will also direct you on all questions of law. You must take it from him. If anything I say on that point disagrees with what my lord directs as a matter of law, you will take it from him and you will disregard anything I have said. The first question, then, of meaning.

'A plaintiff in a libel action has to put in the worst meaning that he alleges - he does not necessarily put in the only meaning - and if there is another meaning that you decide the words have, which is less than saying 'bribery', you can, of course, give the words that meaning. But let us look at what is said here on the basis that what is meant here is bribery.

'I suggest to you, the words do not mean bribery. If you are bribing somebody, you are paying them in exchange for getting something back. There is no suggestion here that this payment is to get something back - there is nothing here about bribery. He [Mr Maxwell] is not paying money to get something back; he is not slipping a fiver to a policeman and getting back the fact that the policeman does not prosecute him - nothing like that. And we come to the whole crux of this article - the last two lines: "How many more Kinnock freebies will Maxwell have to provide before he is recommended for a peerage?" Now, it is out of those words that bribery is spelt. That is where it comes from.

'You will see that is what Mr Maxwell himself says: "The disgraceful allegation that I provide Mr Kinnock with 'freebies' (which presumably is intended to mean 'bribes') for the purpose of securing for myself a peerage recommendation is as insulting as it is mendacious." So there we have it - freebies means bribes.

'Members of the jury, meaning is for you. I suggest to you that putting that sort of interpretation on these words is stretching our language to a breaking point. We have, of course, had transatlantic invasion from language - "freebies" is one of them - and it is very difficult to find out precisely what it means, although you, of course, can draw your own conclusions. I did find it in one dictionary - an up-to-date one - and that defined it as "something provided without charge". Now, something provided without charge is not a bribe. So, let us have a little closer look at this, because there are one or two things that are rather important, you may think. First of all, political parties cannot exist, whether they are

Labour, Conservative, or SDP, without subscription, without payment, without donations, and the bigger the political party, the greater, probably, the need for donations. People who pay that money are not doing anything wrong at all. To say that somebody is paying money to a political party is not, and I suggest cannot be, a libel.

'The second thing that I would ask you to bear in mind is, if somebody has an ambition to be a lord, there is nothing wrong in that either. Nobody could say that because you have an ambition to be a lord it lowers you in the opinion of right-thinking men. What has happened here is that there is a combination of getting a peerage and payment of political donations. Members of the jury, I suggest to you there is nothing wrong in that. Let us try and test, if I may, Mr Maxwell's basic considerations - his claims to libel - by seeing where he draws the line. It is very difficult, I suggest to you. If it is said in a publication that Mr Maxwell pays money to a political party in the hope of a peerage, that is not a libel. If it is said you pay money to a political party for the use of the leader of that party, in the hope of getting a peerage, I understand that nobody suggests that this is a libel. If it is said you pay money direct to the leader of a party because he asks for it, and you pay it in the hope and expectation that you get made a lord - just the motive, just the hope, nothing said, you just hope it - that is not a libel. Supposing it is said, "The leader of the party is going abroad - he hasn't got enough money, can you provide some for his trip abroad?" and you do, and when you provide that money you provide it

because you are hoping to get a peerage and somebody says so in writing - that, members of the jury, is not a libel. And that, I suggest to you, is all these words mean.

'I suggest to you that unless you can get something like bribery out of these words - and you cannot - it is not a bribe. You cannot make or cook-up a libel out of it at all. It does not say in the article "bribery", does it? That is not a word that the article uses. But in coming to these conclusions, as you must, about the meaning of words, do not think to yourself about the evidence - the meaning is for you. Look at the words. What sort of sense do they make to you, twelve ordinary decent people, giving up their time to sit and hear this case.

'There is one inference that you have got to draw, if the plaintiff is to succeed, and that, I suggest to you, is bribery. I suggest that this means no more nor less than that he will go on making payments with the result that in the end he will get a peerage - he will be made a lord. When you are deciding about what words mean, do not think in terms of whether they are false or not - that does not matter. The meaning is just the word. So you have got to spell out of these last two sentences: 'How many more Kinnock freebies will Maxwell have to provide before he is recommended for a peerage?' not saying, as it appears to, "How much more money has Mr Maxwell to provide before the result is he is recommended for a peerage?" There is nothing about bribery in that. But it is for you - and if you decide that these words do not reflect on Mr Maxwell at all, you will find for the defendants. You see, what you really would have to have is a statement in the article saying, "Kinnock will have to have several more payments from Mr Maxwell, whereupon the latter has been promised a peerage". That might yield bribe into it. But it does not say that. It does not even begin to say that. And what you have to think of, if you are thinking in terms of what is defamatory, is that the test is the test of what right-thinking people generally think the words mean. It is not any good to take the fact that some people in the community may disapprove of paying money with a motive of getting a peerage - it has got to be the general opinion of society.

'You may remember that I asked Mr Maxwell about a number of lords who were made lords by Lord Wilson in 1976, and they had received peerages after considerable financial support to Mr Wilson. I asked whether he suggested, or whether he knew anybody else who had suggested, that either Lord Kagan or Lord Plurenden bribed Mr Wilson for a peerage, just because they had paid moneys over to the Prime Minister's pocket, and he said, "Nobody suggested to me, nor do I believe, that they bribed Mr Wilson. I think it is a monstrous allegation and ought not to be made." Nobody has made it, except, possibly, Mr Maxwell has made it up, and you will have to consider that in the course of your deliberations.

'Turning to another matter, I asked him about freebies and we then got a rather odd definition of that, because what he said was: "A freeby is only counted in tens of pounds, maybe a hundred pounds but anything above that is a straightforward bribe." So what he is suggesting is that you have got some sort of new meaning, or some sort of meaning, to the word "freeby" so that when it gets into thousands of pounds it becomes a bribe. If it is only hundreds of pounds it is not a bribe. Members of the jury, the meaning is for you, but is that not stretching language again to breaking point?

'We know that Mr Maxwell lives and breathes and exists in an area where being made lords is a frequent occurrence. He makes payments to the Labour Party. He is a newspaper publisher. He is very influential in one of the senior political parties in the country. It can hardly be suggested, can it, that to state of him in those circumstances that he is a man who, if he goes on paying political parties and their leaders, will qualify for a peerage? You have heard the evidence. This is what happens with these individuals all the time. And that may be very important on other aspects of this case.

'We have, of course, an additional defamatory meaning which implies that Patricia Hewitt was deliberately keeping the matter secret and that is defamatory to Mr Maxwell. I am not even sure why. If Miss Patricia Hewitt is keeping payment of this kind a secret, it may reflect on Mr Kinnock for keeping such a payment secret. It is his secretary who is keeping the secret. But apparently that is now said to reflect upon Mr Maxwell. Members of the jury, the meaning is for you. It is not for you to consider the evidence, and say: "I think Mr Maxwell is nice or nasty, *Private Eye* are fun or nasty, look at all the evidence I have heard, isn't it dreadful?" None of that matters. You look at the words. And it does not matter if you think one or the other of them is particularly nasty - that has got nothing to do with the first decision you have to make on the meaning of words.

'The next matter you have to decide, having decided the meaning of the words, is whether they are true. Now, the burden (as we lawyers call it) of proving that the words are true, always rests in a libel action, on the defendant, and the burden on the defendant is that he has got to show that the words, as we put it, on the balance of probabilities, or probably, are true. That depends on the meaning you put on the words. We do not contend, on behalf of the defendants, that if the words mean Mr Maxwell bribed Mr Kinnock, that that is true. We say that the words do not mean that and it is nonsense to suggest that they do. But if you decide that they do mean that, we do not say that the words are true. We do, of course, accept that Mr Kinnock's trips were not paid for by Mr Maxwell - we have to, we have called no evidence to support the suggestion. However, you may take the view that it does not mean bribes but it does mean, in your view, that for somebody to be said to be paying money to a political party with the motive of getting a peerage out of it, brings him into hatred, ridicule and contempt, or lowers him in the estimation of right-thinking people - two tests for whether something is a libel.

'Of course, one of the other things you must not mix up when coming to that conclusion is that you may think that this business of paying money over to the Labour Party resulting in somebody getting a peerage is a sole reflection on the leader of that party. Let us not bother with whether they are Labour, Conservative, SDP or anything else. Mr Kinnock, Mrs Thatcher, Dr Owen, Mr Steel are not parties to this action. This is an action for Mr Maxwell. So it has got to be that paying money to a political party in the hope and with the motive of getting a peerage, is in some way a reflection on Mr Maxwell. It is the defendants' case that if you take that view then the words are true. In order to arrive at that conclusion and faced with the fact that my clients accept that the trips abroad by Mr Kinnock were not paid for by Mr Maxwell, you have to look at other matters. The first thing you might remember is, he did pay - he paid, all told, a total of £82,800, either himself or his company.

'Now, those payments had one or two oddities about them. First of all, you may remember the enormous difficulty my clients had in getting details of those payments from Mr Maxwell. They were said to be by cheque - Mr Maxwell said on oath they were cheques. We know one of them was not - it was an order on a bank to pay, it was not a cheque. Those payments were made for the Boundary Commission Fighting Fund.

'So we get to the next area of dispute, which gives rise, I suggest, to a little bit of irony. It is said that because these four gentlemen, Mr Foot being the principal, had brought the proceedings against the Boundary Commission, it was not the Labour Party, and that these were not payments to the Labour Party. To say that those payments to the fighting fund were not paid to the Labour Party is, you may think, splitting hairs. Of course they were payments to the Labour Party. And, do not forget that Mr Maxwell, according to Mr Foot, had given a guarantee beforehand - not a formal one, but an oral guarantee for a given sum.

'Now, members of the jury, what is said here is that there was a meeting at the Gay Hussar which resulted in money passing, and that money was the £75,000. Another nice fine point is taken here. It is said: "Oh, well, there was not a payment of £75,000 at the Gay Hussar."

'But, members of the jury, there was still the payment of £38,000, as a result of which, as you will have seen from your other bundle, Mr Cocks wrote a letter of thanks to Mr Maxwell. Apart from anything else, it is pretty clear, is it not? that Mr Maxwell can be made a lord with these grateful politicians any time he wants to, and bear that in mind, if you would.

'Is it not pretty obvious that he is increasing his personal influence with the Labour Party by these payments - and successfully? 'Difficult to thank you enough for your help in this matter': is that not what it is all about? And these are the payments, you may remember, that featured in the Pergamon accounts, which said "No political donations". And it said that this went in "Charitable and educational" in the accounts. "Payments to Mr Foot and other leading figures of the Labour Party for the fight that they took in the Boundary Commission Fighting Fund which they called for to meet their costs which they had incurred on behalf of the Labour Party." It is a funny sort of charitable and a funny sort of educational donation, is it not?

'Let us turn to look at another matter of this man's influence and use of his position to dominate the Labour Party. Mr Maxwell was holding a party to celebrate the first anniversary of his acquisition of Mirror Group Newspapers. Mr Maxwell said this: he had a large meeting of editors and he was told that Mr Kinnock's reason for not attending 'was that on the same night there was an invitation from Mr Murdoch's *Times*, and since he had rejected attending the event at *The Times* he thought he ought to be even-handed and not attend the *Mirror* invitation either'. It is pretty clear, is it not? that he considered that he has the degree of influence over the Labour Party where he could make a joke. The joke does not even fit on any other explanation. Is that not holding the big stick? Mr Maxwell said it was not intended as a threat. You may think jokes like that cannot be anything else. I mean, did it get back to Mr Kinnock? "Why did it occur to you," I asked him, "to make this joke, as you put it?"

'Do you not find it fairly easy to draw the conclusion as to why that should have been his reaction? His answer was: "I don't know."

'Is it not perfectly clear that Mr Maxwell is using his power, his position and his payments to exercise influence over the Labour Party? And why? Because Mr Maxwell is an ambitious man - he is a man who drives to be in the public eye. He likes it. He likes playing parts in public life and parliamentary life. He was an MP for Buckingham from 1964 to 1970. He says he had been offered a peerage but had refused it twice. But why, is worth remembering.

'You will remember one of you asked his lordship for the definition of a peer, and what he said was "that a peer is somebody who becomes a member of the House of Lords and, of course, if they become peers through a political party they would follow that party line", and, of course, one can understand Mr Maxwell saying: "I don't agree with unilateral nuclear disarmament, therefore I won't be a peer and take, what is commonly called, the label 'wet'." Why should he? There is nothing, as I have said before, discreditable in wanting a peerage. It is nice to enjoy the position Mr Maxwell obviously does of being able to take a peerage whenever he wants one - that is the

evidence. Mr Maxwell, when I asked him: "If you were offered a peerage would you accept?" said this: "The answer to that I can only say is this. I have been offered it twice before and I have said 'No'." "That is not an answer to the question." He then went into the two offers.

'With "Forward with Britain", Mr Maxwell starts his position with the Mirror Group by saying, as we can see, in the second paragraph: "I am proud to be the proprietor of this group of publications." Of course, that changed: he called himself a publisher. The "Proprietor" is a Lichtenstein company. If you go to the next page, do you see Robert Maxwell's pledge? Look at the middle paragraph. "Mr Maxwell confirms his undertaking to safeguard jobs and honour all union agreements." This is the sort of thing you have to bear in mind when assessing the weight you give to Mr Maxwell's evidence, including about his ambition to be a peer or not. And you are entitled to consider them on that basis. People do not broadcast their ambitions; very often they keep them very close to themselves. Would you look to see what he has done? He has placed himself, has he not? in a position where he can have a peerage whenever he wants one, and it is his ambition to have one, I suggest to you, at a moment in time that he wishes it.

'It is for you to decide whether, with the meaning that I have suggested to you of these words, the defendants have satisfied you that the words are substantially true in most cases - it is my submission that they have. Mr Browne reminds me of the statement in *The People* newspaper - Mr Maxwell's newspaper: "Every tycoon knows the short cut to a title is to cough up the cash to the Party in power." Mr Maxwell knows that, does he not? If you decide that the words have a defamatory meaning and libel the plaintiff and that that libel is not true, your next question is a question of the damages you would award Mr Maxwell. Damages in this sense is compensation - I will deal with the different aspect of damages later. At the present moment I am dealing with compensation.

There must be compensation for damages to his reputation and injury to his feelings. How serious is the libel in the light of the meaning you give the words? We know it is not a libel to say he wants a peerage. We know it is not a libel to say he makes payments to a political party. How serious a libel do you think it is to put the two together? Other aspects: "Injury to the plaintiff's feelings, including aggravating factors."

'Members of the jury, you have seen Mr Maxwell. What impression did you have that this had done by way of injury to his feelings? None.

'Injury to his reputation? We got a rather mixed bag to look at on this point. There is an excerpt from an hour-long television programme in Mr Maxwell's own home. You do not do a one-hour programme in one hour - it takes four hours, perhaps even longer. In your own home you have to have electric wires, cables, you have got a camera crew, you have got lights - just imagine what it is like. Mr Maxwell says he does not remember it. I asked you to consider Mr Maxwell's evidence in the light of various pointers you get as to the extent to which you can believe him. That, I suggest to you, is one of the most marked.

'Is not this a case in which Mr Maxwell has taken the view that Mr Ingrams has stepped out of line again and therefore decided to swat Mr "Wigwam" like a fly? If you take the view that that is the true purpose of this action, or indeed, any part of it, by Mr Maxwell, you will make sure that he knows that is not the purpose of an English libel action nor is it the function of the English courts.

'What in relation to the look-alike was said was, 'That photograph of you next to one of the Kray brothers; you have got an excellent sense of humour, why bother to sue them?' And, again, after his answer about swatting Mr Ingrams like a fly, "You are a big enough man to walk away from that." So he said: "I didn't do it for myself, but for many hundreds of other people who have been hurt and haven't the ability to hit back." I have told you damages for libel are compensation for injury

to your reputation and injury to your feelings. They are not either to swat Mr Ingrams or for the benefit of other innocents.

'It is not for you to award damages to Mr Maxwell because of his white knight errantry in bringing this action for the protection of the political system and its integrity. Do you believe he needs compensation for damages to reputation, or that there is a genuine loss that needs to be compensated? Is it not clear what this action is really about? This is a man, ruthless, vindictive, with a vast ego, who did not like the pricks of a satirical magazine. You have seen all these papers in the defendants' bundle - page after page of Mr Maxwell doing this, Mr Maxwell doing that, Mr Maxwell's picture. You have seen the man, you have heard his answers. Do you remember that I put to him that a Mr Pilger had said that he had turned the *Daily Mirror* into a family album? And how he said that Mr Pilger was an overpaid lay-about they had sacked, and he had to be reprimanded by my lord? Does this not give you a picture of this man as he really is? Are you not getting the flavour of the man? Compensation should always be reasonable - how much do you give a man like that?

'Each of us lives by standards and ethics. I hope that in my profession our standards and ethics are probably higher than anybody else's: There is one fundamental ethic of the Pressman; regardless of the cost to himself, he does not disclose his sources unless the source agrees to be disclosed. We will have to look at that in a different context in a moment. Here is a man who has taken over the Mirror Group newspapers - *Daily Mirror*, *Sunday People*, *Scottish Daily Record*, *Scottish Sunday Mail*. Now, those four big national newspapers - and he knows the fundamental ethic about disclosure of sources - yet he tried to get two journalists to be forced by the courts to disclose their sources in this case. He said there was a special reason. Did you hear what it was? I did not. The only special reason I suggest to you is this: that it is some indication of the vindictiveness of this man and his hatred for *Private Eye*, some indication that it is his intention to get a verdict from you that will swat Mr Ingrams like a fly, as he said. That is not your function. Again, if it is your view that this forms all or any part of Mr Maxwell's motive, you will be at pains to ensure that your award shows him it has not worked.

'I pass now to another matter of damages. Damages always depend on the extent of the publication. The circulation here is a quarter of a million every fortnight. If you multiply that by four, as was done by the plaintiff, that comes to a million. They also saw, that million, the two letters, one from Neil Kinnock and one from Mr Maxwell. Those are matters which you are entitled to consider in the amount of damages that you award. And do not forget Mr Maxwell's own contribution to journalism, helped by "Another Whopper". Let us do the same mathematics as we did with *Private Eye*. A quarter of a million circulation, four readers to each buyer, a million people read it. *Daily Mirror*, three million people buy it, multiply it by four, twelve million people read it. More people read this than ever read *Private Eye* and that is something you should bear in mind.

'You have had to wait about a great deal. There have been all sorts of gaps in the trial of this case, and it must make it a great deal more difficult for you than, if I may put it this way, a straight run. I have a little bit more to do and may I turn to what I call the mitigating factor - the reputation of the plaintiff? What you have to do is to award damages as compensation to the actual damage to the actual reputation. Now, having said that, let me explain to you a little bit about what that means. Let me suppose that you have a person with a general reputation of being an absolute villain - a murderer. In fact he has never murdered anybody, he has never done anybody any harm, he would not hurt a fly, but his reputation is the reputation of a murderer. And it is reputation that you have to look at, and by reputation I mean general reputation - not what your friends think of you, not what people think of you who have dealt with you across the table, but your general reputation.

Now, you heard the evidence of Mr Hird. Mr Hird had no connection with *Private Eye* of any kind. He was a man who quite clearly was fully acquainted with the industry, including Mr Maxwell's part in it, and his reputation. Did you not get the impression from his evidence quite clearly that the reputation of Mr Maxwell was that of a self-publicist and a bully-boy? Lots of people have been kicked too hard by Mr Maxwell. That, members of the jury, is not a reputation that merits large damages - very, very much the reverse.

'There is also of course the behaviour of the plaintiff himself to the defendant, and in the action. Of course you will bear in mind the behaviour of the plaintiff when he said he would swat Mr Ingrams like a fly, when he tried to compel them to disclose the sources, and throughout this case, while you have been disappearing, members of the jury, taking every technical point he could. Those are matters that you can take into account in assessing compensation that you will give to Mr Maxwell, assuming you get that far - assuming that you accept that this is some way defamatory of Mr Maxwell; if you accept, as you will be suggesting, that it is untrue. Of course, I suggest that you should say it is not defamatory and it is true, but we are now dealing with the situation on the basis that it is a libel and it is not true.

'In dealing with general reputation, the plaintiff called two people, one the wholly delightful and much admired Lord Elwyn-Jones, who is known to all of us in this row with considerable regard. He in fact worked for one of Mr Maxwell's companies, but I do not know that that would have affected him in any way - he was an old friend and he was talking about his relationship with Mr Maxwell. The relationship of an old friend. He was not giving evidence at all, delightful though he was, of general reputation, other than, of course, to say that Mr Maxwell did love publicity. The other was a Mr Young. Mr Young had negotiated union agreements with Mr Maxwell twice. He was able to tell you that he found Mr Maxwell tough to negotiate with, but fair. That is not a man's reputation and it has got nothing to do with his general reputation. So that, in effect, you have the evidence of Mr Hird with no-one really to contradict it.

'I have dealt with the publication of the two letters on 26th July. Mr Maxwell also had published the fact that this was not true in the *Daily Mirror*. He then went to the Court of Appeal in public to say it was all untrue. So you have those four occasions and really there could not have been much doubt, could there? that people at the very least were not sitting in judgment on these articles and saying that must be true, therefore they are defamatory of him. That you must take into account. Is there - and this is one particular item that I would like to just dwell upon for a little while, although I will be developing it much more later - is there any evidence of malice by the defendants? You heard Mr Silvester, in particular, and he said he believed his source - he still does - and it does not matter what Mr Maxwell or Mr Kitson said about it. Members of the jury, that is the very opposite of malice. But he was, of course, asked if he disliked Mr Maxwell, and he said "No", and the matter was not further pursued.

'So the only thing that one has to consider, and which is left of the matters that I have been dealing with, is in relation to compensation. Has there been anything here to aggravate the damages? That is, to increase them by causing additional injury.

'The main ground for this is that there was no withdrawal of the plea of justification after my clients knew that their source was not coming forward. It was said, as I understand it, this was made worse by the source having two other sources, which, of course, is typical of any newspaper, as I am sure you appreciate. Now, when you come to consider the question of damages for not withdrawing the plea of justification, it is not your function to punish the defendants for failing to withdraw. We are talking about compensation.

'I suggest that there is not a shred of evidence that Mr Maxwell felt any greater insult, greater injury or greater damage because the plea of justification was not withdrawn, than he would have done if it had been. It is perfectly obvious that was not what affected Mr Maxwell's mind at all, and when my clients were asked why they had not withdrawn the plea of justification earlier, they said because Mr Maxwell's demands were so exorbitant. You have seen those demands in the letter which asks for an apology in terms of the draft, and the payment of £10,000 to the Ethiopia Appeal Fund.

'Fancy asking a newspaper to agree to say: "We acknowledge that the snide comment on freebies was and was intended to be insulting and wounding, and it was totally unfounded." It was not an apology, it was a piece of abject self-abasement in swatting Mr Wigwam. That was the idea. And the fact that my clients were not prepared to do that is, in my submission, no grounds for inflating the damages that you should award the plaintiff.'

At this point the court adjourned for the evening.

Mr Bateson rose to his feet to continue at 10.30 the following morning.

'Members of the jury, when we adjourned last night I had only one matter to deal with, and to invite you to consider, in relation to what the lawyers call compensatory damage, that is the damage that the plaintiff can recover for the injury to his reputation. That arises out of a section of the Defamation Act, 1952 (it sounds horrifying, but I will try to reduce it a little bit for you). The defendants may give evidence in mitigation of damages - that is in reduction of damages.

'Can we start to see in this case whether there were any such payments that you can have regard to? Clearly the article of Lady Falkender was taken from the *Private Eye* article. Clearly, it repeated it. In those circumstances, you are entitled to take into account, in assessing the damages paid by *Private Eye*, the £5,000 already paid by the *Mail on Sunday*. So that is the last of the factors that I am going to invite you to have in mind when you come to put your figure of damages in compensation to Mr Maxwell.

'There are a number of factors that you have, I am sure you have appreciated, to take into account when arriving at what that figure should be. I do ask you in your deliberations to keep them clearly in mind. They are important, and it is important particularly that your verdict should not be construed in any way as being a verdict designed to swat *Private Eye*.

'There is however one other matter that arises in this case and on which I must address you. There is a claim here for exemplary damages. I have told you all about the damages that are payable as compensation to the plaintiff, what he is entitled to receive. "Exemplary damages" is a particular type of damage in English law which is payable as a punishment to a defendant in certain circumstances. It is a very Draconian power that is used very rarely. It is my submission it does not arise in this case. It has of course this peculiar anomaly about it: that a punishment to the defendant, something in the way of a fine, is normally payable in criminal proceeding to some form of government authority who receive the money. With punitive damages there is no-one else to give it to but the plaintiff - in itself, I suggest to you, a reason for viewing this proposition with a great deal of reserve.

'Let me therefore try and give you such assistance as I can on what constitutes exemplary damages and how it arises in these cases. Exemplary damages can only be awarded (and it is important to remember this) in relation to the publication that is before you. It can only be awarded if that publication was published knowing it to be false, or recklessly not caring whether it was true or false. It also has to have as a necessary part of it the fact that a swift mental calculation is being done that they will get more money out of it if they let the publication go on, but they will have to pay for damages and costs in a libel action. Let me take these two ingredients first of all, because they both have to exist; they both have to exist in

relation to the second article, not in relation to the first, and finally they have to exist on 24th July after lunch at two o'clock in the afternoon, when the application was made to the Court of Appeal for an injunction.

'I shall invite you to look at that article in a moment, but you may remember this rather odd situation: *Private Eye* is printed on a Monday, and the volumes are sent out to subscribers by *Private Eye*; then it goes to the distributors on Tuesday and it is on sale Wednesday morning. So if we are taking two o'clock in the afternoon on Wednesday, it has already been on sale for half a day, so you are considering exemplary damages, not in relation to the total publication, which is a quarter of a million, but in relation to whatever is left after a morning's sale. It cannot be exemplary damages relating to the whole of that issue.

'Having said that, let us look at this second article. You cannot, I suggest, get out of it a meaning that "the plaintiff had acted or was acting as paymaster for trips made by Mr Neil Kinnock, the Leader of the Labour Party, to East Africa, Central America and Moscow, was thereby guilty of bribery or attempted bribery", because that is the meaning that this article is said to bear. This of course was a bribe. "If you don't come to my party, I won't cover your African tour."

'It is precisely the sort of thing such as saying to a policeman: "If you will take £5, you won't prosecute me, will you?" Of course, you can look at it in a different way. You might use different words. For instance, you can paraphase it, bearing in mind Mr Maxwell: "Kinnock was furious. 'You tell him', he stormed, 'that I will not be bullied'." What has got to be said here, though, in relation to exemplary damages, is that the defendants recklessly published part of *Private Eye* because of those few words and indeed because of the profit that they calculated they could make from it. Of course, that, in my submission - and I suggest to you - is wholly and utterly untenable. It does not even begin to make sense.

'Let us look at it slightly differently. You have to consider whether it can be said that the defendants were reckless, either knew that the article was false, or were reckless. I do not think there is much doubt that you cannot allege knowledge, but what does "reckless" mean? "Reckless" means that you do not take any care at all. The very difference between recklessness and carelessness is that carelessness may require you to take more care than you did; recklessness is when you do not take any care at all. What I believe the suggestion is that is going to be made, is not that he was reckless, but that he should have checked his source by some other way. Perhaps it could be said, if the only test for exemplary damages was carelessness, he should have taken more care. To say somebody should have checked more is not to say they are reckless. It may be saying that they are callous - and lawyers have a very good habit of spelling callousness out of practically every human endeavour if somebody is injured. But that is not recklessness.

'What is the evidence before you as to what happened' in the Court of Appeal that Wednesday? Mr Ingrams was not there; he was at home. He was spoken to by Mr Silvester and he gave Mr Silvester authority to deal with the matter in the Court of Appeal. The position was, in the Court of Appeal at that time, that Mr Silvester believed his source. I am going to deal with "source" in a moment. He believed his source was coming forward to give evidence. He had a short talk with the barrister then acting for him and went into court and said: "We are going to justify." He believed that source. That is not recklessness.

'Also you have to consider the second part - calculated that they would make more out of the sale of the rest of *Private Eye* than the damages that they would have to pay Mr Maxwell. This does not mean a mathematical calculation, of course. What it means is that there must be at least some evidence before you that Mr Silvester did that.

'It is probably an appropriate moment in which to deal with something which has occupied a lot of time in this case, namely sources. It may be suggested to you that because the source has not come forward, he is not very reliable. Let me just put this to you. We all live and do our jobs by some form of ethics and integrity. I suppose the best known is the ethic of a journalist that he does not disclose his sources. The reason is simple: if he disclosed his sources, then of course people would not talk to him; his sources would dry up, as the lawyers put it. Journalists face the risk - and it is not just *Private Eye*, members of the jury, every journalist of every newspaper in the land relies on sources - he may have a good, sound defence to an action if he could call his sources, and he takes the risk of not disclosing them. Those sources may come from high and low. To assume that they come from low, or are unreliable, is to divorce oneself from very basic human nature, is it not? We know that there is a source and of course it is accepted that there is a source for two reasons: (1) it was never suggested to Mr Silvester that there was not one; (2) when the point was raised with me in open court, I gave my learned friend assurance, which he accepted, that there was a source.

'So what we have to do is to look at this sort of comment that may be made and consider what we do know about the source. We know that he is a prospective Labour candidate. First of all, if he was revealed as the source... You are twelve ordinary decent people - what do you think would happen to his political career? He is not prepared to risk that career by coming to give evidence. That does not make him unreliable. That does not make him someone who Mr Silvester, on the afternoon of Wednesday, 24 July, should ignore.

'It is in those circumstances that I invite you to say that they have failed to satisfy you that the two basic ingredients here even remotely exist, certainly do not exist sufficiently to justify a Draconian order of punishment of this kind. I am afraid to say that the problem for you does not end there. The next thing that you have to do is to bear in mind that a libel in the course of a newspaper's business does not justify exemplary damages. All newspapers make mistakes. All newspapers rely on sources that get it wrong. You had a situation with Princess Anne and the baby. I wonder where the sources were and how reliable they were for that one in the *Sunday People*?

'The next point is that in exemplary damages you do not give more than you give by way of compensation unless you think it deserves more. Supposing you think that Mr Maxwell is deserving for the damages to his reputation (such as it is) but you think that the defendants should be punished. You then give Mr Maxwell £10,000 for that punishment. You should not do that if you think to yourself: "Compensation will give him £100,000; exemplary damages does not add to it in any way; £10,000 is enough." Then you do not add anything to it for exemplary damages. You may also consider whether the defendants can afford it. You heard Mr Ingrams - in fact he was criticised for saying: "We have not the money to fight libel actions all the time. We have occasionally to make apologies, and put up with making apologies because we cannot afford to litigate." You have seen their accounts. It is not for you to award some astronomical sum to put them out of business; that is not the function of a jury.

'Finally, in exemplary damages you must consider damages payable by the most innocent, the person who is least guilty. If you have got half a dozen people, all defendants in the action, and one of them has had absolutely nothing to do with it, you do not give exemplary damages in that action, because he is not guilty of conduct amounting to exemplary damages. Now, Mr Ingrams was at home. Mr Ingrams - on the only occasion that exemplary damages arise - was at home, and he gave Mr Silvester authority to deal with the matter. Now, he is a defendant in this action. So lastly, then, you come down to the situation: should you award exemplary damages against Mr Ingrams for being at home and knowing nothing about it except a telephone call? The answer is, in law, (subject to correction from his lordship) "no".

'That is all I have to say on the plaintiff's claim. I would, if I may, remind you that I only have one chance to address you. If I had more than one, I would not dream of addressing you on damages, because it is my client's case that you do not get that far; you do not get to damages. So it is only if everything else is decided against my client that you get to damages at all.

'I only want to mention one matter in the light of an indulgence from his lordship yesterday, for which I am grateful, and that is to mention these apologies. You know there was a counter-claim which has now gone, and you do not have to bother with it. We went slowly and wearily through them one after the other. Mr Ingrams, with total honesty - and I emphasise that - said: "Some of these are because we could not afford to fight the action; they are not wholly sincere and we felt some of them we were right about, but we had to apologise." There is something that seems to be thought of as discreditable in that. Members of the jury, Mr Ingrams said, and I repeat: "This is a feature of everyday life in every newspaper, including Mr Maxwell's." You do not get involved in libel actions. They are extremely expensive and extremely long - as you have reason to know, I am afraid.

'Just imagine what would have happened if Mr Ingrams had gone into the witness box and said: "Oh, yes, all these apologies were sincere." He would have been cross-examined on that television programme to show that some of them were not sincere. He has made public, in the widest possible way, the fact that they would sometimes publish apologies or retractions because they did not have the resources to prove it in court. Of course, we had a great deal of criticism of him for being that honest about it.

'The other thing is that in relation to these apologies and publications, on the plaintiff's claim, you are not here to give damages in relation to those apologies. They are put in for the purpose of attacking the credit of Mr Ingrams in the claim in this action, and in my submission that attack on his credit (that means creating a situation in which you do not believe him) abysmally fails. It was perfectly clear that he was saying what he has always said. It must have been hard for the plaintiffs, except for the fact they are a newspaper and have got a cutting room; they had to dredge back ten years in this satirical magazine to find 53 apologies in relation to a little over sixty articles, and that is out of 8,000 and more articles written. It might be said: "Other people did not sue, but they could have done." That will not do, I suggest to you. It would be quite disgraceful if it was suggested that all those other articles you must view as being false.

'Members of the jury, I am just about to leave my clients' case in your hands. I shall not have the opportunity of addressing you again. In the picture of Mr Maxwell reading the mock-up that he handed to everyone at the party, look at the back page, which, needless to say, has a picture of him on it. "You shouldn't have joined if you can't take a laugh." Mr Maxwell, you may think, can dish it out, but he cannot take it.'

CHAPTER THIRTEEN

Mr Hartley for the Plaintiff

Richard Hartley started his speech on behalf of the plaintiff, Robert Maxwell by circulating to the jury the questions they would have to answer.

They read: 'Are the words complained of defamatory of the plaintiff?' That means are the words that the plaintiff has set out in his statement of claim defamatory of the plaintiff? Do they lower the plaintiff's reputation? Then (2): "Are those words substantially true?" Have the defendants in effect justified the sting of the defamatory words? Then (3): "What sum do you award the plaintiff by way of damages?" In the second article, the first three questions are precisely the same. They have to be answered again in respect of the second article. Then you are asked: "What part, if any, of that sum, relates to exemplary damages?"

'Members of the jury, we are coming to the end of a three-week trial. I am afraid it has gone on longer than we earlier indicated and you, of course, know only too well the reasons for that. There has been legal argument during the trial which has necessitated you being absent for long periods, for which we all apologise.

'Let us go back to July 24th 1985, when the defendants told the Court of Appeal that they would justify the specific allegations that Mr Maxwell had paid for Mr Kinnock's overseas trips. The defendants at that stage were defiant - rather, you may think, like the roar of a lion. Compare that with their position now. The facts on which they rely, the alleged facts before the Court of Appeal - totally abandoned; the defence of fair comment - gone for evermore; counter claim - ignominiously abandoned; all the planks of their defence of justification broken. The roar of the lion, you may think, is now reduced to the squeak of a mouse - admittedly still quite a vicious little mouse.

'My learned friend has put up for you, I suggest, a complete smokescreen, but I trust that none of you will be fooled by it. The way that he asks you to interpret these articles, you may think, is pure Alice in Wonderland, or rather when you consider the evidence of Mr Ingrams and Mr Silvester, you may well think it more appropriate to call that "Malice in Wonderland". Let us consider facts, not fiction. The Court of Appeal would have granted an injunction if they had known that no evidence would be called as to those alleged payments for Mr Kinnock's overseas trips. The defendants knew that perfectly well then, as they do now. They knew the cost to them if they had to recall all the undistributed and unsold copies. You remember Mr Ingrams put it at £10,000, as if it were merely a case of getting back the undistributed copies from the wholesalers. He agreed with me it would be much more if they had to recall all unsold copies from the retailers - the actual shops where *Private Eye* is on sale. They did, members of the jury, take a calculated and cynical, quite deliberate decision, on the basis that it would cost more to stop further distribution of *Private Eye*, that issue, than the

RIGHT: *Mr Hartley, QC, in more relaxed mood.*

amount of damages they would have to pay Mr Maxwell if he were to go and sue them, as we now know he has. It was a risk which they realised, and they thought it would pay off. I am going to say to you at the end of my submissions that they must be taught a lesson.

'They mentioned to the Court of Appeal that they had reliable, well-placed sources. I suggest to you it is a complete joke, and we know now, though we did not know at the beginning of Mr Silvester's evidence, it is the source relying on another source. It does not matter how reliable their first source is, whether he is a Parliamentary Labour candidate, whether he would or would not have come to court. What you want to know is how reliable the source's source was. You see, it is the easiest thing in the world for a publication as unscrupulous as *Private Eye* to say that they have a reliable source and then take the sanctimonious line of a journalist's ethics that they must not disclose their sources. To suppose that *Private Eye* or Mr Ingrams or Mr Silvester have any morals in that direction whatsoever, is perhaps the sickest joke of all time. Just look at how Mr Silvester behaves. Nothing would convince him in the witness box - that blinkered man - that his so-called source might be wrong, or his source's source might be wrong. Oh, no; Mr Maxwell's evidence, Mr Kitson's evidence, Mr Timpson's evidence, Mr Clement's evidence - what did he say? "They are all lying; they are all committing perjury." Well, what value do you put on that man's evidence? Can you believe one word he says? He is obviously a bright intelligent man, but is he a truthful man?

'As for Mr Ingrams, it is pitiful to see how he tried to wriggle out of those unreserved apologies in *Private Eye*, those apologies that *Private Eye* had published over the years. He showed, did he not? his vindictiveness against those persons who dared sue *Private Eye*? Again, I suggest, it was a totally amoral stance that he was taking. There really are no depths to which *Private Eye*, under his editorship, would not sink. If someone sues him, he attacks that person again and again. Remember, members of the jury, how he treated poor Mr Kirby and his family. Now we know of course that that apology is totally valueless, as indeed is any apology that *Private Eye* publishes or any statement they make in open court, unless one has what we had in the Goldsmith action: "Oh, well, this one actually is true." Soon that will not even be believed, because they would have to put that in so many times.

'Just look at one more, the case of Ian Coulter. This was at a time when Mr Ingrams was editor of this newspaper. Can you think of anything more despicable and disgraceful than that? That is what people have to do when they are libelled in *Private Eye*; they have to go through with it and have to get damages and costs if they do not publish apologies, which they have not done in Mr Maxwell's case that you are trying; and, anyway, you wonder, having sat here, what value any apology in *Private Eye* has.

'Let us look at the first article, and it is in respect of that you have to answer those three questions on the sheet of paper I have just handed to you. You may think - and please forgive me if you do think - that this is so plain that it is an insult to your intelligence that I am making these observations, because my submission to you is that it is a perfectly straightforward allegation in that article that Mr Maxwell has made secret payments to Mr Kinnock, and in the context of the snide question at the end it is plainly suggesting that those payments, and no doubt more to come, were bribes to Mr Kinnock to get Mr Maxwell a seat in the House of Lords. I mean, can it mean anything else? Does it bear (it would be remarkable if it does) a purely innocent meaning? If it does, what is it doing there, if it bears no meaning defamatory of Mr Maxwell? What is defamatory? It is a story that is to his discredit, something that lowers his reputation amongst right-thinking persons.

'The defendants say it is not defamatory at all. They say that if it bears a defamatory meaning, it is not the meaning that I have suggested to you, of bribes or something tantamount to bribery, but it bears some lesser defamatory meaning, namely that these payments were made with the lesser improper motive of seeking to influence Mr Kinnock to recommend him for a peerage. You may wonder what all that adds up to - the lesser defamatory meaning and lesser motive. It is all mumbo-jumbo to me, members of the jury. I do not know if it means anything to you. In any event, it must be, because they are acknowledging a lesser defamatory meaning - it must be to Mr Maxwell's discredit, so presumably it is still an allegation of leaning on Mr Kinnock, getting Mr Kinnock in a position where Mr Maxwell could at any time ask for a favour in return. I do not know if any of you saw the film "The Godfather" with Marlon Brando. That is how he got people to give favours to him; he would pay them money and then many years later, no doubt, someone would tap them on the shoulder and say, "Now is the time to return that favour we did for you."

'It has been said, in a case that went to the highest court in the land, the House of Lords, how you should approach an article and how you should consider what the meaning of words is. Lord Reid said this: "There is no doubt that in actions for libel, the question is what the words would convey to the ordinary man." That is all twelve of you, members of the jury. So, you are entitled to read between the lines. You are not looking at this like a legal document. You have to put yourself in the position, if you had been a reader of *Private Eye* back in July 1985 - what would you have thought that that article meant? Would you not have said: "Wink, wink, nudge, nudge; I know what that means - a nice, cosy relationship between Mr Maxwell and Mr Kinnock, paying him money secretly for his overseas trips with the wholly improper motive that he will be rewarded by Mr Kinnock in the future and be given a peerage, a seat in the House of Lords." If that is not bribery or attempted bribery, or something very like it, I do not know what is. So please

approach that first question of what the article means - please realise that you do not have to take the words literally. You can look at the article and read between lines.

'The defendants say that it also bears a wider meaning, not just a lesser meaning than bribery but a wider meaning. It is put like this: the plaintiff has an ambition to be a peer, a member of the House of Lords, and is improperly seeking to achieve this by patronage of the Labour Party and by the self publicity which he creates through his control of the Mirror Group. Well, if you can get that out of that article, I suggest we all ought to take up conjuring, because it is just not possible. It is not conceivable. Where in that article is there anything about payments to the Labour Party at all? I suggest to you it is this cosy secret relationship between Mr Maxwell and Mr Kinnock. The Labour Party is not mentioned other than in the opening paragraph, and then it is "Labour movement". There is nothing that can for one moment suggest that he is making payments to the Labour Party; if anything, you may think it is the opposite. Where is there anything about the plaintiff's patronage of the Labour Party? Of course he has given money to the Labour Party, but, members of the jury, it is very important that we do not get confused, because at this stage we are only answering question 1: what are the meanings that you can get out of this article. Forget what possible truth there may be in any meanings that you can get out. Just think at the moment of the situation as if you had heard no evidence at all. Approach it on the basis that you simply saw that article and did not know whether it is true or false. I suggest to you that you do not get anything out of those words alone about him being a life-long supporter of the Labour Party, or him being a self-publicist, about him having made any payments to the Labour Party, even less any payments to the Boundary Commission Fighting Fund. I mean, where is there in that article anything about self publicity created through Mr Maxwell's control of the *Mirror*? If anything, the secret payments are the very opposite of self publicity of any kind, whether it be the Mirror or his standing in the Labour Party.

'Really, members of the jury, it is as though a little boy had gone to the zoo and was describing the result of his visit and said "I saw a man eaten by a tiger." And someone might say, "Are you sure you saw that?" And then it comes down to what he saw, was a boy fall down the stairs when going to buy an ice cream. It is as different as chalk from cheese. There is no tiger and there is nobody being eaten. It is a completely different allegation from the ones that my learned friend is having to put. They are forced back the whole time. They know that they cannot justify the facts in the article; they know they cannot justify the sting of the article; so they have to confuse you by saying that it bears a wholly different meaning from what you would think at first blush. I put it to you, members of the jury, that that is a farcical way of approaching this problem and the only meaning you can get out of that article (I hope you will agree) is that Mr Maxwell is so keen to get into the House of Lords that he is prepared to bribe Mr Kinnock by making these secret payments, and will no doubt go on making more until he has got what he is wanting.

'The second article - I suggest to you that the second article underlines and emphasises the sting of the first article. This article on its own is enough to show that there has been an attempt by Mr Maxwell to bribe Mr Kinnock over the "African junket, payment for which he has lamely denied". You are entitled to look at the first article when considering this one. Does it not all make it as plain as a pikestaff that what Mr Maxwell is alleged to be doing in the context of these overseas tours is bribing Mr Kinnock because he wants to be in the House of Lords? Again, can it really mean anything else? Financing Mr Kinnock's overseas trips is the bribe and the favour in return is the recommendation for a peerage. I suggest it is crystal clear. If you decide that the sting of the first article is bribery or attempted

bribery, then it is conceded that there is no defence to this action, and you would simply decide damages only. Similarly, if you decide that the sting of the second article, whether by itself alone or whether by reading it together with the first article, is bribery or attempted bribery, again it is conceded - no defence, damages only. So it is only if you decide that it bears a much less serious meaning (both articles and each article), or an altogether wider meaning, that you need consider justification.

'Let us consider justification, dealing with the first article first. The one thing that there can be no doubt about is there is no truth whatsoever in the allegation that Mr Maxwell paid for any of those overseas trips. You do not have to worry yourselves with Mr Silvester's assertion, and indeed Mr Ingrams', that they still believe their source. That has absolutely nothing to do with whether the words are true. They called their evidence. The evidence is all one way and there is no question whatsoever of Mr Maxwell having financed those trips abroad to America, Africa and Moscow.

'Now, what are the matters on which they rely? Well, can we look together at what I suggest is now becoming a very tattered defence of justification indeed. "The words complained of" - that is, the words that have been set out in those two articles "are true in substance and in fact." And then the particulars. "Mr Maxwell, who is a millionaire, is a member of the Labour Party, former Labour M.P. and an active Labour Party supporter." That we have always admitted.

'Then over the page: "Over a period of years, Plaintiff has made available, and offered to make available, to the Labour Party funds under his control, both by way of cash donations and by way of financial support for particular projects or purposes." There are two instances relied on, and two only. The first: "In 1983 the Labour Party brought unsuccessful High Court proceedings against the Boundary Commission in respect of proposed changes to the constituency boundaries. Shortly before the proceedings took place, on a date the Defendants cannot precisely particularize, Mr Maxwell met Mr Michael Foot, the then Leader of the Labour Party, and Mr Michael Cocks, the Labour Chief Whip, in the Gay Hussar Restaurant in Greek Street, Soho, handed over a cheque for £75,000 to be used in financing the legal costs of the litigation."

'We know that there was no meeting in Greek Street, Soho. We know that no cheque was handed over for £75,000. We know it was not proceedings brought by the Labour Party. Also what we know, because Mr Maxwell has made no secret of the fact, that he paid, through himself and his company, a total of £38,534.08 to the Boundary Commission Fighting Fund.

'It is perhaps worth noting at this stage, and I may well mention it again, that it has not been suggested that Mr Maxwell was flashing his cheque book or that of Pergamon Press down Fleet Street, saying: "Anybody want any money for the Labour Party or Boundary Commission?" He was specifically asked - because some of those four persons would have been financially embarrassed, gravely financially embarrassed, if they had to meet out of their own pockets the £60,000, which the combined costs were going to be - and he agreed to pay. Somehow that is regarded and seen as something improper or an improper motive. Is it really suggested that when Mr Foot and Mr Cocks and others said: "Look, we are in this terrible predicament. We would appreciate it, we are having a fund, if you could contribute", is it really suggested that at that moment Mr Maxwell says to himself: "Ah, marvellous, I can now get myself a peerage and I will give some money with that in mind"? It is ludicrous. The only other matter is again one that has been admitted: "On or about 3rd October 1984 at the Labour Party Conference, the Plaintiff made a donation of £43,000 to the Party's funds." In fact it was £44,514.

'As I say, in both instances it is Mr Maxwell who is asked to make a donation, and it is not suggested for one moment that Mr Maxwell would have contributed to the Boundary Commission Fighting Fund if he had not been asked to. I suggest that to see that perfectly generous gesture and proper gesture of saving those persons from the acute financial embarrassment I have already mentioned, to see that in the cynical and malicious way that persons in *Private Eye* have seen it, is totally unreasonable and there is no basis for such a cynical and malicious approach. I would add again, how low can you get? But when you are considering *Private Eye* and Mr Ingrams, one really feels there are no depths, as I say, to which they will not sink.

'There has been no evidence at all of any word-processor being provided for by Mr Maxwell, that again is another lie. Similarly the *Tribune* dispute, where Mr Maxwell is supposed to have offered Mr Silkin extended credit for *Tribune* amounting to over £100,000, that is another lie, that has gone. That was based apparently on a short article in *The Times*. Again extraordinary, you may think, that *Private Eye* can put into a plea of justification, which has to be done with great care, they can simply put what they have found in *The Times*, not bothered of course to check it in any way at all; they simply rely on what was put in another paper.

'Then Mr Grant. Well, I have pressed my learned friend to say on a number of occasions whether this is alive, even though it is in its terminal stages. No, it is still there. I do not know what that means. There has been no evidence called at all by the defendants to challenge Mr Grant's evidence, and you may think that Mr Grant is the person who would know the truth of that allegation, and indeed no evidence to contradict him has been called. So you are left with Mr Grant's evidence and, as I say, he plainly was telling the truth and there is nothing at all to challenge it.

'So you come back - and this is the case on paper, of course, what is important is the actual evidence that you have heard in this case - to what is on paper, and apart from what

Mr Maxwell has admitted, you may think they have got absolutely nowhere. They have proved nothing, other than what Mr Maxwell quite properly admitted. None of what Mr Maxwell has admitted is justifying any defamatory meaning at all. It is not to a person's discredit that they make payments to the Labour Party, or that they make payments to the Boundary Commission Fighting Fund, or that they are a lifelong supporter of the Labour Party, or that they are a Labour M.P., or indeed that the plaintiff is a millionaire, and that when he acquired control of Mirror Group Newspapers, he fulfilled a longstanding ambition of his to become a national newspaper proprietor. None of that is relevant to justifying a defamatory meaning. You do not justify an innocent meaning. It would have to be that these things went to some lesser defamatory meaning than bribery or some wider meaning of self-publicist, in the sense that he is doing that with the improper motive of wanting a peerage.

'You may think it is conclusive that it is the final collapse of this pack of cards of the defendants' defence, that Mr Ingrams said that he was not suggesting there was anything improper at all, no improper motive, nothing improper in Mr Maxwell making those payments to the Labour Party and the Boundary Commission Fighting Fund. If he says they are not improper, why, you may think, does my learned friend Mr Bateson seek to suggest to you there is something improper? Does that not strike you as odd, that his clients do not think it is improper but counsel wants you to think it is improper? Well, it is very odd indeed, you may think.

'What the plaintiff has got to face, this is the defence that they have put up: "The plaintiff has at all times sought considerable publicity for himself and his activities, including his political activities in supporting the Labour Party." Well, nothing wrong in that either, and that was admitted by the plaintiff. The next sentence: "When the plaintiff acquired control of Mirror Group Newspapers in 1984 he fulfilled a longstanding ambition of his to become a national newspaper proprietor." That was admitted.

'The rest of that paragraph is not admitted, and you may wonder what evidence the defendants have called to prove it. "The plaintiff has exploited his position as a newspaper publisher to seek to advance his own personal standing with, and influence over, the leadership of the Labour Party." I suggest there has been no evidence called at all on that. Secondly, "that he has exploited his control over Mirror Group Newspapers to attract for himself as much personal publicity as possible, in order to seek to create for himself a public image of an influential and respected figure in public life". For that, they rely on those pages from the *Mirror* and other MGN publications which you have got in your bundle, the defendants' bundle.

'Let me just remind you, because they were able to go through the *Mirror* cuttings library under the letter M and extract all references that they wished to rely on relating to Mr Maxwell. You remember that I got the breakdown figures which were given in evidence, and that it was a total 947 issues that were available to them of the *Daily Mirror*, the *Sunday Mirror*, the *Sunday People* - and for this purpose we are leaving out *The Sporting Life* - and that totalled some 33,668 pages. So out of those 33,668 pages you have got that pathetic amount that they are relying on to show that he is a self-publicist and that he is exploiting his control over the *Mirror* to "attract for himself as much personal publicity as possible, in order to seek to create for himself a public image of an influential and respected figure in public life". It is entirely a matter for you, but is that exploiting?

'Bear in mind that there were a number of, you may think, very worthwhile appeals that the *Mirror* conducted. I do not think even cynical Mr Ingrams would suggest there was anything wrong in having an Ethiopia Fund

RIGHT: *Apr. 10, 1977. Apology for Sir James Goldsmith.*

Appeal, in fact I think he agreed that was a perfectly worthwhile thing to have.

'Just contrast that with the funds that *Private Eye* have sponsored. The only ones that they have ever sponsored were to pay for the amount of damages and costs they had to pay to Mr Goldsmith, now Sir James Goldsmith - the Goldsmith Balls Fund - and the Kirby Balls Fund, the one in respect of that quite disgraceful series of articles over two years that they wrote about Mr Kirby. That is as far as their generosity and philanthropy goes - helping to save themselves from the damages and costs they have had to pay out as a result of their disgraceful behaviour.

'This is the criticism, this is the attack on Mr Maxwell: that he has acquired self-publicity from the Ethiopia Disaster Fund, when they flew an airplane full of goods and supplies to the starving in Ethiopia, and the Red Devils Appeal, and the Commonwealth Games. He did save the Commonwealth Games, that was not challenged. But this is something that is either to be frowned on or Mr Maxwell is to be criticised because his picture was allowed to be published alongside those appeals. It really is scraping the barrel, is it not, members of the jury? When you have thrown everything at this man, Mr Maxwell - to be left with that, it really is disgraceful.

'Then you have got the statement, the absolutely bald statement for which they have called no evidence and for which Mr Maxwell has given directly opposite evidence. "It is the plaintiff's personal ambition, to be elevated to the House of Lords as a Labour peer." It is not, and they have not proved it, and that, in my submission, goes. "The plaintiff seeks to achieve this" - so they are building on an unproved fact - "as others have done before him by patronage of a political party and by the self-publicity he can create through his control of the Mirror Group Newspapers." I suggest to you that the evidence you have heard from the man who wrote the book and what has happened in the past, all that is absolutely irrelevant. Because it could only

possibly become of any relevance, and then a very doubtful relevance, if the defendants ever proved that it is Mr Maxwell's "personal ambition to be elevated to the House of Lords as a Labour peer", and that they have not done.

'What does it add up to? What is the most you can say that the defendants have proved? As I say, it is the paragraphs that Mr Maxwell has admitted himself. What does it add up to? Well, he is in the public eye. He is a newspaper publisher and the *Daily Mirror* is a very popular, well-known newspaper. He is, you might say, the boss of two very large companies and has interests in others. He is bound to be in the news. Is he to be criticised for that? Are you to say of him that every time you read Mr Maxwell's name, that it is being done because he wants to sit in the House of Lords? It is absurd. He is proud of his achievements and is he to be criticised and pilloried by the nasty little minds in *Private Eye* for that?

'He has been responsible for the appeals for the Ethiopia Fund, and the Red Devils. Then this is to be regarded as a stick to beat Mr Maxwell with. It is an exclusive interview with Deng Xiao Ping, the leader of a quarter of mankind, the Chinese leader. "China says no to Star Wars and yes to increased trade with Britain and Europe." I will not go into that any more. Is that something to criticise, to increase trade between China, Britain and Europe? Mr Maxwell is doing something for Britain, you may think, and should not be criticised in the way that he has been. It is so easy to be destructive in life, we know it from our own lives: the one that is always carping, the one that is always criticising. It is so easy to sit back and make snide comments about people, but don't we admire those that get off their backsides to achieve something?

'Think of how Mr Maxwell has come from nothing. His family was destroyed in the Holocaust. He comes over, fights for this country and is awarded the M.C. Practically self-educated, he speaks ten languages and has built up these businesses. Of course *Private*

Eye cynically feel that that is a target, because he is a target for *Private Eye*. Well, compare, if you will, members of the jury, the destructive side of life, of *Private Eye*. "Nobody's name that appears in *Private Eye*, in the serious part of *Private Eye*, will have anything said about them other than discreditable." What an admission. They are not interested in the nice things of life or the good things of life or the things to be proud of in life. They are only interested in destroying, selling reputations for profit.

'Let's look, please, at the second article, because I have been through the particulars, and I suggest there is nothing in the particulars that would justify any allegation at all, other than of a complimentary kind. "The guest list for the glittering champagne-all-the-way party marking Captain Bob's first glorious year at the helm of the *Daily Maxwell* was awesome indeed. On it was Prince Charles, who puzzlingly, failed to turn up." No evidence given about that at all, so you can assume that that is untrue. And of course Neil Kinnock.

'Now, just bear with me when I read this next bit, that all of what I read is untrue and they have not called any evidence about it. "On the day Maxwell ordered political hack Julia Langdon to confirm with Kinnock that he would be coming, Kinnock told her that he had no intention of gracing the affair as he was concerned with more important matters of State that evening." All that, no suggestion by the Defendants that that is true.

'Compare what I have just read with how they put it in their particulars. "In July 1985 the plaintiff held a party to celebrate the first anniversary of his acquisition of Mirror Group Newspapers. Mr Kinnock was amongst those invited to the celebration. On or about the day of the party the plaintiff sought confirmation that Mr Kinnock would be attending." All that is admitted. "When the plaintiff was informed that Mr Kinnock had other commitments on the evening in question, the plaintiff threatened to withhold publicity in the *Mirror* newspapers of Mr Kinnock's tour of East Africa later that month." As you know, that is

not admitted. "Mr Kinnock duly attended the plaintiff's celebration party, and in common with the other guests was provided with a mock-up of the *Mirror* containing pictures of the plaintiff."

'Members of the jury, where in those particulars do you see anything about "ordered political hack Julia Langdon to confirm with Kinnock that he would be coming"? Looking at the article: "On the day Maxwell ordered political hack Julia Langdon to confirm with Kinnock that he would be coming. Kinnock told her that he had no intention of gracing the affair as he was concerned with more important matters of State that evening." None of that is even in the particulars. "The fat man's response was typical: 'Tell him,' he boomed, 'that if he does not come to my party, the *Mirror* will not be reporting his African tour'." It is in respect of that, that Mr Maxwell told you of how he made that remark in jest.

'You have been asked by my learned friend to regard Mr Maxwell as about the most unreliable man on his oath that you can imagine. If that were so, would it not have been very easy for Mr Maxwell not to have referred to that at all? Because there has been no evidence called by the other defendants, of this incident or indeed of any of the other incidents. He need never have referred to it. He could have simply left it for the defendants to prove if they could. You may think he is an honest man from the fact that he said: "Yes, I did make a remark not like that but, you know: 'If he does not come to my party, I will not come to his,'" and you can understand, members of the jury, how you might make a remark like that as a joke, and look how it has been puffed up and put into this article. No joke here, this is being said to have been a very nasty threat.

'"Kinnock was furious. 'You tell him,' he stormed, 'that I will not be bribed'." Where is there any reference to that in the particulars? Of course there is not. It is another made-up story; it is a piece of fiction. The source for this is supposed to have been a mole inside the

HIS MASTER'S VOICE (see Street of Shame)

'His Master's Voice'

Mirror. Again you may think it quite remarkable that this unnamed source, this mole in the *Mirror*, is allowed simply to put in an article like that on his say-so. Not one word apparently was changed. It was written in that form and put in in that form. You may think that quite remarkable, and you may think it shows the evil motive of the defendants, the malicious motive that they believe anything about Mr Maxwell; any dirt which you have got on Mr Maxwell, take to *Private Eye* and they will publish. They will not bother to check it, they will publish it.

'"Mindful of His Master's Voice, Kinnock duly turned up. Maximum publicity for the African junket, which Maxwell lamely denies financing, was promised." Well, again it is entirely a matter for you what those words mean: "which Maxwell lamely denies financing". But you bear in mind that in the very same issue of *Private Eye* as that article, you have got the strongest possible denial by Mr Maxwell and Patricia Hewitt. One must never forget that it is in the same issue of *Private Eye* as the article I have just been referring to. What further denial - and categorical and complete denial - can one

make? "Dear Mr Ingram" - and you remember how Mr Ingrams was so incensed by the 's' being left off, although his own counsel forgot to put the 's' on the end (you may remember that amusing episode). It is incredible, you may think, that Mr Ingrams is so sensitive in that respect when he is plainly so insensitive in every other department of life - "Dear Mr Ingrams," or Ingram, "There is not a word of truth in the allegations published in the 12th July issue of *Private Eye*, alleging that I am acting as paymaster of Mr Kinnock's trip to East Africa, nor that I subsidised Mr Kinnock's trip to Moscow, nor that I picked up the tab for Mr Kinnock's Central American tour." Pausing there, what more can you do than to start off by saying: "There is not a word of truth"? Is that not a complete denial.

'"Finally, the disgraceful allegation that I provided Mr Kinnock with freebies, which presumably is intended to mean bribes, for the purpose of securing for myself a peerage recommendation. This is as insulting as it is mendacious. I call upon you, your printers and publishers, to withdraw these allegations unreservedly, and to publish prominently in the next edition of *Private Eye* retractions and suitable apology, a draft of which I enclose herewith, and to pay £10,000 to the *Mirror's* Ethiopia Appeal Fund. Failing which I will issue proceedings for libel and damages against you, Pressdram and the printers without further notice."

'So it is quite clear, is it not? that that letter is saying: "There is not a word of truth in your allegation, it is totally untrue. Also I am incensed by the disgraceful allegation that I give bribes or I bribe Mr Kinnock, quite untrue." He is also making clear that unless they withdraw and "publish prominently in the next edition … a retraction and suitable apology", that proceedings will be started. They know that. What more can one do? What stronger denial can one have than that? Yet we get, if you look at the article, "Mr Maxwell lamely denies". I think there has been some suggestion that it may have been based on the *Mirror* article, which again, I suggest to you, could not possibly imply that that is in anyway a lame denial. "*Private Eye*," - you remember it well, I know, - "*Private Eye* or Public Lie, as it ought to be called, last week alleged that the Mirror publisher Robert Maxwell is paying for Neil Kinnock's trip to East Africa this week and financed Kinnock's trip to Moscow last year. Not so." Well, again is that a lame denial? I suggest to you quite the reverse.

'So, I suggest to you that the articles, both articles, each article, plainly mean bribery or something so near to it that you need not worry about shades of bribery; that, secondly, the defendants have not come within a million miles or light years of proving the sting of that allegation, that Mr Maxwell had an improper motive in making those payments or in allowing his picture to adorn the pages of the *Mirror*. It would have to be with the improper motive all the time that he is, quite against his own evidence, seeking to be a member of the House of Lords. Everything is done with his eyes on that goal. Again it is ridiculous. You have heard him say that it just never was his ambition at all. He has got other ambitions, ambitions which he has achieved. You remember what Mr Ingrams says about ambitious people. In general. he does not approve of them, and particularly ambitious politicians. So, I suggest that the answer to the first question in each case - "Are the words defamatory of the plaintiff?" - is yes. Are the words substantially true? The answer is no.

'Really, you may think that we have all taken far too long on what really is a case solely for consideration of how much money the plaintiff should recover to restore his reputation, and whether, on top of that, and on top of the injury done to him and his injured feelings, there should be an additional sum to punish the defendants because they knew or were reckless, at the time that they told the Court of Appeal that they were justified, they were reckless as to the truth of what they were publishing and calculated there was more to be gained by not recalling the unsold copies than they would have to pay to Mr Maxwell.

'One thing that is being urged upon you is that you should take into account - I do not quite know how my learned friend suggests you do take it into account - at any rate, you should take into account the payment by the *Mail on Sunday* of £5,000 to the *Mirror's* Ethiopia Appeal Fund. You see, to make any sense of it at all one has to look at what their original article was, in the *Mail on Sunday* published on July 14, 1985: "When help can be dangerous. I was surprised by a story that Neil Kinnock may let *Mirror* publisher Robert Maxwell fund his trip to Africa next Thursday, just as he did for Neil's Moscow visit in November. It was precisely to avoid the need for this sort of private funding that the taxpayer now hands over £400,000 or so a year to the Official Opposition pocket. But if it won't cover overseas trips, Parliament should be asked to amend the Act and reassess the grant. Of course I am sure that Maxwell money could in no way influence Neil as Opposition leader or as Prime Minister, but he should not give anyone the slightest reason for thinking he might be in someone's pocket."

'Now contrast that with the two articles in *Private Eye*. There is nothing there, I suggest, that spells out as clearly as the first article, and indeed the second article, in *Private Eye* that Mr Maxwell is bribing Mr Kinnock to get a peerage. There is no mention of a peerage at all. What is said in that article is that it is a mistake for Mr Kinnock to be beholden to Mr Maxwell at all. Indeed, it does not go as far as that: "He should not give anyone the slightest reason for thinking he might be in someone's pocket."

'You may think it is a completely different animal, and going back to the mouse and the lion, you may think that this is a mouse-like article compared with the lion of *Private Eye*. It is just not the same. There is nothing there about bribing and there is nothing there about peerage.

'You will see that the *Mail on Sunday* did put the record straight and how different that is from this case. "I am sorry that an item in my column last week about my old friend *Mirror* publisher Robert Maxwell and Mr Neil Kinnock seems to have been misunderstood. Of course, not for a moment do I now believe, or have I ever believed, that Mr Kinnock is in Mr Maxwell's pocket or anyone else's. Both Mr Kinnock and Mr Maxwell tell me, however, that this is how the paragraph might be construed, so I must put the record straight, because of course I accept that neither Mr Kinnock's trip to Ethiopia nor his trip to Moscow was funded by Mr Maxwell. The real point I was seeking to make is that the Government is still too mean in the grant it pays to the Leader of the Opposition. I believe it is wholly desirable that every Opposition Leader should travel, but this often overstretches the miserly budget we provide for them. As a gesture of goodwill to Mr Maxwell we are paying £5,000 to the *Mirror's* Ethiopia Appeal Fund."

'You may recall that Mr Maxwell took precisely the same view about the funding of Mr Kinnock's overseas trips. He said it was quite wrong for that to be done in the way in which it was suggested had been done in that article in *Private Eye*. The articles are completely different. You have got a quite different article, making a much less serious allegation. You have got Lady Falkender and *Mail on Sunday* immediately, or reasonably immediately, because it is in the very next edition of the *Mail on Sunday*, putting the record straight, and they pay £5,000 towards the *Mirror* Ethiopia Fund. For some reason, which is not, I am afraid, clear to me, you are being asked to say that that somehow helps you to reduce the amount of money which should go to Mr Maxwell. In my submission, it should have precisely the opposite effect: it should show you that the defendants have behaved in a totally different way, by not only not apologising, not putting the record straight, but of actually justifying, and the hurt to Mr Maxwell is having a plea of justification persisted in right to the very last moment. Not even now, when there is nothing left, is that plea of justification withdrawn. Not a bit of it,

it is still there, it limps on. Well, how different from the way the *Mail on Sunday* dealt with it.

'It would have been the easiest thing in the world for *Private Eye* to have published an apology such as Lady Falkender did in that article. They could have said: "It has been drawn to our attention by Mr Maxwell and Mr Kinnock that the article suggested that Mr Maxwell was in some way bribing Mr Kinnock. Of course we never intended that, and of course we acknowledge that there is no truth in any such allegation." They could have done that. They did not, and they have not apologised to this day. Quite the reverse.

'I suggest to you, this again is something you can take into account - and I am dealing now with damages - that this is something that you take into account when assessing the hurt to Mr Maxwell. Of course, look at the articles themselves. You think of the seriousness of the libel. You think of the circulation of the newspaper, over a quarter of a million, read by probably four times that amount, a million readers. No apology, quite the reverse, persistence in the plea of justification, and in this court the remorseless and relentless attack on Mr Maxwell. It has continued right until the end of my learned friend's speech. You remember yesterday he referred to Mr Maxwell as "ruthless and vindictive", and today accused him of bribery, as set out in that second article. That perhaps is the most shaming of all: saying that is an allegation of bribery. And for that, of course, they have given no evidence at all. You would have thought they would have said that the allegation of bribery made in that second article is of course withdrawn. Not a bit of it.

'So how can Mr Maxwell - if they won't apologise, if they won't withdraw - how can he clear his name? The only way that this country allows - because you cannot go out and fight a duel or murder Mr Ingrams, you cannot do that, it is not allowed. The only thing you can do is to bring an action for libel. The way it works is this: your award of damages should be seen to nail the lie, so that Mr Maxwell can point to the sum that you give him and say, if anyone were to repeat that allegation again: "Well, I have been awarded a sufficiently large sum by the jury to show the baselessness, the untruthfulness of the allegation."

'There is a very brief passage from a case which reads, "Not merely can he recover the estimated sum of his past and future losses", well, there are no past and future losses, that is of the financial kind, I am not dealing with that - "but in case the libel driven underground emerges from its lurking place at some future date, he must be able to point to a sum, awarded by a jury, sufficient to convince a bystander of the baselessness of the charge." That is a proper way of assessing damages in this case.

'Now, my learned friend has said more than once that he imputes on behalf of his clients an improper motive to Mr Maxwell in bringing this action at all, or at any rate criticises him for the conduct of the action, because he says in effect he (Mr Maxwell) is trying to swat Mr Ingrams like a fly.

'Published in August 1975 is a story which I think I can summarise as follows: it is suggesting that Mr Maxwell is wanting to take over the *Observer*. The fact is false, as they had to acknowledge later. Mr Maxwell had not got even enough money to take over the *Scottish Daily News*, they said, that he would have to borrow £10,000 from two journalists. I am sure you remember that well. You see the letter that the two journalists wrote. They made it perfectly plain Mr Maxwell was not pressed to raise the £25,000 in cash, and he did not need to borrow £10,000 from two senior news journalists, nor was he involved in any way in delaying the repayment. You remember the original article said that he had taken three months to pay the money back.

'Now, what does *Private Eye* do with the letter? You remember Mr Silvester rather piously said: "Whenever we receive a letter we publish the letter without any comment." Well, that is a load of eye-wash, as you can see, because on this occasion you see below: "The only inaccuracy in our story was the suggestion that Maxwell had paid back the £10,000 to the two authors of this letter." I put it to Mr Ingrams, that is just adding insult to injury. Their constant theme, if you write to them, if you complain to them ... they do not like you doing it, they will kick you again. That is precisely what they have done. Not just kick you again on the same allegation: they will add another. There is no value, then, in that letter from Mr Chard and Mr Saxton at all, as regards clearing the matter up from Mr Maxwell's point of view, because the editor, Mr Ingrams, is sticking by his story, but adding the gratuitous insult that Mr Maxwell has not even paid back the money. A fresh allegation, because in the earlier one it said he paid it back, but after three months. Then the further allegation of 3rd October 1975. They will not leave Mr Maxwell alone. There is the allegation that Mr Maxwell is lying about the circulation figures.

'So we come to the statement in open court, which was accepted by the defendants, that there was no truth in any of these allegations. The settlement of that libel action - does that suggest to you that at that stage, at any rate, Mr Maxwell was intent on swatting Mr Ingrams like a fly? I suggest not. He had been libelled outrageously in those three separate publications and the defendants paid up and apologised.

'Then, we come to the Kray twins. It has been said, and indeed it was said at the very end of my learned friend's closing speech, Mr Maxwell cannot take a joke: he can dish it out but cannot take it when it is dished to him. Just consider please: Kray Twins. Picture of Ronnie Kray and Mr Maxwell switched around. "Have any of your readers noticed a remarkable likeness between Robert Maxwell, Chairman of BPCC, and Ronnie Kray, the famous East End gangster?" If it had ended there, there might just be a cause for saying: "Well surely, Mr Maxwell, you can take a joke." But the next sentence has been reserved for Mr Maxwell and Mr Kray and for nobody else, it has not appeared in any other issue of *Private Eye* with these look-alikes. "I wonder if they have anything else in common." Now, what does that mean? Of course it means, does it not? "I wonder if Mr Maxwell has some of the attributes and character of Ronnie Kray, the famous East End gangster, who, we all know, was a murderer as well." Cannot take a joke?

'How did Mr Maxwell react on that? You see that they published an apology, and you know how this has been described as going over-the-top, and *Private Eye* do not mind publishing over-the-top apologies, because they know no one will take them seriously. If that is so, why did they not publish the apology that Mr Maxwell asked for in this case? They cannot have it both ways. March 1983, they give an undertaking: "We shall not hereafter publish offensive material defamatory to Mr Maxwell." We know how quickly they broke that. They actually say: "In recognition of this profuse apology and undertaking, Mr Maxwell has generously agreed not to seek damages." Well, does that not indicate to you, that far from Mr Maxwell's intent to close down *Private Eye* or to swat Mr Ingrams like a fly, he was doing absolutely the reverse? He was letting them off with this apology and a belief that their undertaking was sincere. We know now that belief was cruelly misconceived.

'The "look-alike" feature began very soon after the March 1983 apology to Mr Maxwell and an undertaking not to refer to him in defamatory terms again. You know, do you not? that on 2nd December 1983 there was this disgraceful and highly hurtful look-alike, purporting to have been written by Mrs Maxwell, comparing the Duke of Edinburgh to Adolph Eichmann. "Have any of your readers noticed the remarkable similarity between the Duke of Edinburgh and Adolph Eichmann, the Nazi war criminal?" To be fair to Mr Ingrams - if one can ever be fair to Mr Ingrams - he did say that of course he now regretted that that was put in, because of course he appreciates and accepts that that would have a devastating effect on Mrs Maxwell and on Mr Maxwell, bearing in mind the unhappy events that surrounded Mr Maxwell's family in the war.

'I just want to remind you how unfair the line of cross-examination of Mr Maxwell was on President Zhivkov. "Well, is that really something the *Mirror* readers want to read? Is that the most important matter that day?" President Zhivkov: the photograph with Mr Robert Maxwell. He talked about the miners' strike. Well, you remember I showed you the very issue of the *Mirror* which has that champagne speech on one of its centre pages, has at the very beginning, "The bitter end, the end of the miners' strike", so you may think that was a very unfair line of cross-examination.

'Going back to damages, Mr Maxwell, as you know, and Mr Ingrams concedes, has been a favourite target of *Private Eye* over the years, and I suggest to you that *Private Eye* have had their malicious fun at Mr Maxwell's expense and the day of reckoning has finally come. I am going to read you a short passage from one of the textbooks: "The jury, in assessing the damages, are entitled to look at the whole conduct of the defendant, from the time when the libel was published down to the very moment of their verdict. They may take into their consideration the conduct of the defendant before action and after action. Quite obviously the award must include factors for injury to the feelings, the anxiety and uncertainty undergone in the litigation, the absence of apology, or the re-affirmation of the truth of the matters complained of or the malice of the defendant."

'All these matters, I suggest to you, are present here. You know how they behaved to Mr Maxwell before the action - that is the libel in *Private Eye* for which they had to apologise in a statement in open court. The Kray twins look-alike - all this is evidence of their malice against the plaintiff, and naturally the effect it has on his feelings is something which you can take into account when arriving at what sum to put in the damages scale.

'Factors for injury to the feelings, the anxiety and uncertainty undergone in the litigation ..." - well, you can imagine that, members of the jury, over the last sixteen months. "The absence of an apology" - well, there has been no apology. "The re-affirmation of the truth ..." - that means the repeating of the truth of the matters complained of, stating that it is true, which is what you have got here, and "the malice of the defendant". All those are matters which you can properly take into account in deciding what sum you can give Mr Maxwell. And at this stage in my submissions I am not on exemplary damages at all. I am talking about what is sometimes referred to as aggregated damages. As I say, you look first of all at the articles themselves. In this case you have to look at each article separately, because you are going to give a damages award on the first article, and a damages award on the second. You have to look at the first article, see how seriously you regard the allegation - no apology, persistence in that it is true; the malice of the defendants towards Mr Maxwell - and you arrive at a sum. And you do precisely the same with the defendants' second article. As I say, all this is on compensation.

'It is not just that it is persistence in a plea of justification; it is the persistence in a plea of justification which they have known for months that they had not a hope in hell of making good. They have known that, at least since the end of last year when they knew that the so-called source would not be willing to come to this court and give evidence. Would you not have thought that at that stage - they have lost their source, no question of being able to call anybody to say that the matters are true, and in the face of Mr Maxwell's evidence, Mr Kitson's evidence, Mr Timson's evidence and Mr Clements' evidence - would you not have thought that *Private Eye* would say even now, "Well, obviously we got it wrong and we are sorry"? Because that would lower the damages, if they were even to say it at this 11th hour and 59th minute - but they have not. Not a bit of it. Quite the reverse. What do they do? They accuse Mr Kitson, Mr Timson and Mr Clements - quite apart from Mr Maxwell as well, of course - of lying. Mr Ingrams and Mr Silvester prefer the evidence

of their unnamed source or sources to that of the evidence that you have heard in this court.

'Mr Kitson - do you remember how at first, when it was suggested, and I said to him, "Is there any truth in it?" and he said, "It is a complete lie"? And then how he was recalled, in view of the fact that he is apparently alleged to be one of the sources' sources, and he said, "It is quite untrue"? Would you not have thought that a fair-minded person, a man whose word you can believe, a man Mr Ingrams would have you (or his counsel would have you) consider him, would you not have thought at that stage he would appreciate, "The game is up, I really haven't got a leg to stand on. The honourable thing I can do is to apologise"? Not a bit of it.

'The question of how you deal with sources has been put in the case of Hayward v. Thompson. It is dealing with assessment of damages and I stress again we have not reached the exemplary damages stage, it is still the compensatory damages. This is what Lord Denning, of whom some of you may well have heard, said in the Court of Appeal, when Master of the Rolls: "So long as journalists insist on keeping secret their sources of information ... I think they must take the rough of it together with the smooth. They cannot expect the jury to believe they got their information from a trustworthy informant, on whom they were entitled to rely, when they refuse to give his name. They cannot expect the jury to believe that it was not solicited or not paid for or rewarded by them, when they will not disclose how they got it. They cannot expect the jury to be sympathetic to them when they lose their notebooks so they cannot be disclosed to the court. Assessment of damages is peculiarly the province of the jury in an action for libel. They take a poor view of the conduct of any of the defendants, be it journalist, sub-editor, editor or proprietor. They are entitled to fix whatever sum they think fit in aggravation of damages, without distinguishing between them, so long as they do not wander off into the forbidden territory of exemplary damages."

'The important point in that passage I read to you is that they have to take the rough with the smooth. They cannot have the best of all possible worlds. They were able to go on saying, "We believe in the source", but they won't disclose the source, so we cannot check it to see whether in fact it is somebody who was in a position to know what was going on inside Mr Kinnock's private office; or whether in fact it was a person who could never have had access to that sort of information. So how can you be expected to believe that the person was a trustworthy informant on whom they were entitled to rely, when they refuse to give his name? I suggest to you, it is asking you to swallow an awful lot. As I say, all that goes to compensation.

'Now what my learned friend is seeking to do on behalf of his clients, is to say - and you know they called Mr Hird - that Mr Maxwell has a general bad reputation as a self-publicist and a bully. You remember that Mr Hird did not in fact use the world "bully" at all, but when asked about the manner in which Mr Maxwell treats his employees, Mr Hird answered that the general reputation is that he deals with them in a rough-handed way. That is one person who has been called. You know I put it to Mr Ingrams that they had been trying to drum up witnesses to come and give evidence of bad reputation against Mr Maxwell, and how they had singularly failed, and he said, "Well, I don't know anything about that. It is something my solicitors may or may not be doing." They have come up with this one person. Mr Hird agreed with me that in the field of Fleet Street a time for change has come, and you know it from reading newspapers yourselves, how drastically Fleet Street has changed, quite dramatically, and how Mr Hird mentioned Mr Eddie Shah. Indeed, we know that Mr Maxwell in the *Mirror* said, "The gravy train has hit the buffers. The Fleet Street party is over."

'That maybe did ruffle some feathers, and maybe some people did not approve of losing their fat salaries, for very little work in some cases. So, do you really think it helps you to have heard Mr Hird's evidence? Do you not think it is just another example of the scraping of the barrel to try and avoid your giving a substantial sum - which I suggest is the appropriate sum here - for the damage that they have done to Mr Maxwell's reputation? On the question of "bully", you may think that is a word they bandy about fairly frequently.

'There it is. You may think that that evidence of general bad reputation completely misfired, because it in fact entitled me to then call evidence of his general good reputation. You heard Lord Elwyn-Jones give his evidence about his friend, Mr Maxwell. There is nothing to be ashamed of, that he is a friend of Mr Maxwell. He had seen him when Mr Maxwell was in the House of Commons, was a Member of Parliament for those four years. I am sure there would have been a lot of opportunity to have assessed him as a bully, if he in fact had been a bully and he did not, of course, give any such evidence. And you also heard the evidence from a union man - a man who had direct dealings with Mr. Maxwell - and again you may think his evidence is a much truer guide to the general reputation of Mr Maxwell than Mr Hird's evidence ever was. If we look at our own lives it would be remarkable, I think we would all agree, if we had not rubbed somebody up the wrong way at some time or other. I suggest you do not attach any importance to Mr Hird's evidence at all. You may think that the only relevance of his evidence is as a guide to how he in fact teaches would-be journalists to check their stories. You remember that is one of the things he does, teaches would-be journalists to check their stories with the persons they are writing about. You remember Mr Ingrams does not do that, he does not believe in that,

RIGHT: *A Royal tribute to the 'Self-publicist'.*

PALACE OF HOLYROODHOUSE

31st July, 1986

Dear Mr Maxwell,

The Queen has asked me to send you
her warm thanks for receiving her at the
Meadowbank Press Centre yesterday, and
for the splendid Royal Wedding souvenir
book with which you were kind enough to
present her. Her Majesty will treasure
this, and it gives her addition pleasure
to know that sales of the book will make
a significant contribution to meeting
the deficit of the Commonwealth Games.
The Queen sends you her congratulations.

Yours sincerely,
Kenneth Scott

Robert Maxwell, Esq., MC.

because he knows they will just deny it. Mr Ingrams, *Private Eye*, do not check with the person they are about to defame whether there is any truth in the allegations they are going to make against them. Also he agreed with me, did Mr Hird, that when you are relying on sources you have to be very careful indeed to check on those sources.

'As I say, I am dealing with and finishing with the compensatory damages, reminding you again that they seek to reduce those damages by virtue of what the *Mail on Sunday* did. Bear in mind the articles are quite different. There was nothing about how many more freebies will Maxwell have to provide before he is recommended for a peerage, in the Lady Falkender article, and the sting is quite different. Yet the *Mail on Sunday* honourably apologised, or put the record straight, promptly in their next issue.

'Exemplary damages arise in this way. If by the time you consider what damages to award in the second article - it only applies to the second article - if you decide that that sum, however large, is still not large enough to punish the defendants, to deter them from publishing stories which they know to be false or reckless, whether they are true or false, in the future, you are entitled to add a further sum as penalty. But you only do that if you are satisfied that they did know that the words were false, or reckless as to whether they were true or false, and not that they sat down at a table with a calculator but they did have the intent that it would be worth their while to resist the injunction and thereby not have to call back undistributed copies of *Private Eye*, because the cost of paying out Mr Maxwell whatever sum they might have to pay him in compensatory damages would be less than the cost of retrieving those unsold copies of *Private Eye*.

'We are not seeking exemplary damages from the moment that the second article was written, but only at the time when they told the Court of Appeal at two o'clock on the Wednesday afternoon that they were going to justify. It is from then on that we say they had this knowledge or state of recklessness, and it was then that they made the calculation. We are not suggesting that they calculated at an earlier time than two o'clock on the Wednesday. What we say is they knew that Mr Maxwell was denying it strongly. They knew that Mr Kinnock, through Patricia Hewitt, was denying it strongly. And yet, in spite of knowing that their allegations were false - or at any rate reckless as to whether they were true or false - they chose to repeat the libel by publishing that second article and cartoon is as eye-catching a manner as possible. We are only asking for exemplary damages in relation to the unsold copies of *Private Eye*, the ones that were unsold on that Wednesday afternoon. They could have got them back. It would have cost them money, but they calculated that they would pay out less to Mr Maxwell than they would incur in costs if they did that.

'What more could Mr Maxwell or Patricia Hewitt on behalf of Mr Kinnock, do than they did do to try to convince Mr Ingrams, Mr Silvester, that the first article - and indeed the second article in so far as it repeated the first article - was untrue. As I say, they wrote those very strong letters. Next morning - not that afternoon but the next morning - was the confirmation telex from Mr Kinnock which we see at 19B in that same plaintiff's bundle. It is very short, two-and-a-half lines: "Mr Robert Maxwell - this is to confirm that at no time has he offered or contributed finance as alleged by the article in *Private Eye* ..."

'What is it that the defendants say? They say, and it is really all they can say, "We relied on our source." But in fact, we know that it was a source upon a source. So it would not have mattered at all how reliable the source was, because that would not have helped them at all. Because we know that the source himself the Parliamentary Labour candidate, was himself, relying in part on what Mr Kitson had told him - although we know that Mr Kitson denies that, that is plainly untrue - and on another source privy to what goes on in Mr

Kinnock's private office. Can I just remind you how Mr Silvester put it in evidence when examined by my learned friend, Mr Bateson? He was asked "Where did you obtain the information about various matters?" In his evidence-in-chief - that means when he was answering my learned friend's questions - he never once said that there were two sources of that first article. One source, highly respected within the Labour Party, was a prospective Parliamentary candidate. "He was also privy to what went on in Mr Kinnock's private office. In other words, he used to occasionally advise members of the office about various matters." It became clear when I questioned him that that was plainly wrong.

'It is clear, is it not? that it was not just a source, a reliable source in the Labour Party as Mr Silvester said at first. That is quite wrong. Indeed, I suggest to you, when you look at Mr Silvester's affidavit, that he must have been referring to then was what we have discovered in the course of this trial - there was a separate source for the second article. That, you remember, was a mole inside Mr Maxwell's Mirror Group. So the sources he is talking about, I suggest what he meant by that was the one source for the first article and the one source for the second article. As I say, we know now that it is the source for the first article relying on another source. So it does not matter how reliable that first source is that Mr Silvester spoke to. What you want to know is how reliable the source's source was. Or, indeed, whether there ever was a source's source. I certainly do not concede that. And you will recall how his lordship put to Mr Silvester and Mr Ingrams that if *Private Eye*, who knew the names of the sources back in July 1985, realised that the sources then were waiving any right not to have their names disclosed because their evidence was being put forward on the basis that they would of course have to give evidence at the trial - so they had waived their anonymity, their right, as if it were, to remain nameless and faceless - the defendants could, if they had wished, have subpoenaed them. That means they could

have ordered the witness to come to court and to give you the help that you may think you need if you are to believe anything that the defendants say. What we say is that they did not just sit down and make a mathematical calculation, but that they did realise the cost if they were to recall those unsold copies. You remember Mr Ingrams, as I have told you already, calculated it at about £10,000, but it would be considerably more if he had to get them all back.

'I want you to look very shortly with me at the accounts. And I know you will find them as difficult to read as I do. There are only two lots of figures that I want you to have in mind. If you would put a ring around £1,202,511, and also a ring around the comparable figure for 1982, £1,059,994. Those are the turnover figures. If you go to "Creditors", you see "Provision for libel costs and damages". Put a ring around £364,924 and £312,600. What I am suggesting to you is that those figures make it plain that on a turnover in 1983 of £1.2 million-odd, £364,900-odd goes in libel costs and damages; and for 1982 a slightly lower figure for turnover and a slightly lower provision for libel costs and damages. In other words, it comes out at around 30%. And you see how much the creditors were for 1984, a figure of just over one million. You see that the figure for 1983, £767,000-odd, and we know of that £364,924 is in respect of libel costs and damages. So again that figure is nearly half the amount in the way of creditors, and I was suggesting to Mr Ingrams that the figure for libel costs and damages of the million figure in 1984 could be something approaching half that, and he said, "I leave it to Mr Cash," who, you remember, is the aptly-named man who deals with the accounts.

'The point I am seeking to make is that you may think that it is a reasonable description of *Private Eye* and Mr Ingrams to say that they do sell reputations for profit. They never ever write about anybody, in the serious part, other than to be rude about them. Quite unlike any other newspaper that you and I are ever likely to read, I suggest. And it is part of their stock in trade. Whereas the larger newspapers have plant and machinery and gifted and well-paid journalists and printers and all the rest to pay for, in *Private Eye* their main overhead (or 30% of their overhead) is provision for libel damages and costs. So it is in that background, and it is in the background of the threat from Mr Maxwell, which by two o'clock on that Wednesday afternoon is more than a threat - the writ is being issued, and indeed he is trying to get an interim injunction; and he would have got that interim injunction, he would have been able to call back those copies, if *Private Eye* had not maintained, on the basis of their so-called source, that their facts were true.

'It is also important to bear in mind that if you think it is unfair that someone should get an injunction that way, if when it came to the trial Mr Maxwell had got an injunction - in other words, all these unsold copies of *Private Eye* came back and had to be destroyed and the defendants had to pay the costs as a result of bringing all those copies back - if at the trial of the action Mr Maxwell had failed, in other words if there had been no libel at all because those alleged payments to Mr Kinnock for overseas trips had been true, well, then, Mr Maxwell would have to have paid all those costs of bringing back *Private Eye*. It is an undertaking you have to give when you are getting an injunction in those circumstances.

'My learned friend has said there is really no difference between *Private Eye* and the *Mirror* when it comes to apologies. I suggest there is all the difference in the world. You heard Mr Maxwell say that he was embarrassed by, and much regretted, the untrue story about Princess Anne. That does, you may think, rather contrast with no protestations of embarrassment or apology by Mr Ingrams or Mr Silvester. Have you heard any genuine expression of regret from Mr Ingrams in any story he published? You may think that during this trial the defendants have wasted no opportunity to throw any dirt that they can at Mr Maxwell. There is nothing - there is no stone that they have left unturned. If they can find anything, you can rest assured you would have heard about it. They have scraped the barrel until there is very little left of the barrel itself. You remember what they tried to suggest at one time - and that is how all this discovery, all this question of trying to get at Mr Maxwell's chequebooks and Pergamon's accounts - you remember how they were suggesting there was something wrong with the way it had been dealt with in Pergamon accounts? They concede now that there is no point that they can take on how it was dealt with in Pergamon accounts, or whether it was proper for Pergamon to make those payments, and they keep alive "so long as they were made with no improper motive" - that "improper motive' there, of course, is the only one they allege, of wanting a seat in the House of Lords. You remember that Mr Ingrams has conceded that it is not suggested that either of those payments were made with any improper motive. So you might well think what was left of the defence of justification, in shreds as it was, had then completely gone.

'It is a serious case. It is a very important case. I often think a good way of testing it is to say how would oneself enjoy reading what was said about Mr Maxwell being said about oneself, and also how would one like to have been a plaintiff in this court for the last three weeks, having to listen to the malice and abuse that Mr Maxwell has had to undergo? As I say, it is a serious case, an important case, and one in which you may well feel that a very substantial sum should be given to Mr Maxwell to compensate him for this injury to his reputation, so that he can hold his head up high and say, "Well, I have nailed that lie once and for all", and that it will not be published again. As I say, however large a sum you think he should have in respect of compensation, when you come to the second article I do invite you to say that it was quite cynically, callously and determinedly done when they came before the Court of Appeal. They were going to rely blindly on their source, full well knowing the danger of relying on a source, how he may change his mind, may be unwilling to come to court - and remember always that Mr Maxwell had denied it, Miss Patricia Hewitt on behalf of Mr Kinnock had denied it, and in a telex Mr Kinnock himself had denied it, and they - *Private Eye*, Mr Silvester and Mr Ingrams - had taken no steps whatsoever themselves to check the story out. They simply relied on the source, who himself was relying on another source.

'So, members of the jury, I do invite you to say they were desperate to prevent the bringing back of all those unsold copies of *Private Eye*, and they were prepared to go the the Court of Appeal saying, "Well, it is true", reckoning that it was worth the candle to them because they would not have to pay out to Mr Maxwell as much as they would incur in loss if they had to get those copies back.'

Mr Robert Maxwell, Prince William and the Prince of Wales watching the Red Devils.

CHAPTER FOURTEEN
The Judge Sums Up

Mr Justice Simon Brown started his summing up mid-afternoon on the third Wednesday, the thirteenth day, and finished early on the Friday morning. As Mr Hartley sat down after his speech the judge asked the jury: 'Do you want five minutes before I start? Or you might just like to proceed straight on? Is anybody desperate for five minutes?' There were no takers.

'Members of the jury, sixteen months ago in July of last year *Private Eye* published two articles, a fortnight apart, about Mr Robert Maxwell, the plaintiff in this action. Later this week, and more probably Friday than tomorrow, after a long, and a hard fought, and a much interrupted trial, you and you alone will decide whether either or both of those articles were defamatory of the plaintiff; and, if so, whether the substance, the gist, the sting of the articles were true. And if either or both articles were both defamatory and untrue in substance, then you will decide the damages that should be paid by *Private Eye* to the plaintiff.

'There are two defendants here, as you know: Pressdram Ltd - they publish *Private Eye*; and Mr Ingrams, who, as you remember, was editor for no fewer than I think 24 years, from 1962 until just last month. The fact that there are those two defendants really matters nothing. You will decide this case on the basis that both the defendants, both the publishers and the editor at the time, were jointly and equally responsible for the publication. And if you decide the defendants are liable in damages, then do not trouble yourselves with the fact that there happen to be two

defendants. That is subject to one word only, as Mr Bateson rightly told you. If and when you get to the question of exemplary damages, why then, you decide those on the basis of the least guilty defendant. And if you think Mr Ingrams would be less guilty than the publishers themselves in any matter relevant to exemplary damages, why then, you decide them on the basis that the award will be against him.

'I am bound to say that from time to time during the course of this trial, I have wondered what you have made of this not quite every day story of newspaper folk. From time to time it seemed to me you must have found an awful lot of it wholly unintelligible, and I would have great sympathy with you in that. Do not worry if parts of it have, so to speak, gone over your head. It would be surprising were it not so. I will do the best I can to explain it to you.

'In summing-up this case to you I have really three main tasks. First, I have to tell you all that you need to know about the law that you must apply in this case. Counsel have already told you a good deal about the law - and, indeed, told you perfectly accurately - but that unhappily does not relieve me of my duty to direct you as to the law, and those directions you must faithfully accept from me. And if I am wrong about them, why then, the party who complains can go, yet again, to the Court of Appeal. It would be the third time in these proceedings.

'My second task is to identify and explain the questions which are for your decision. Now I say for your decision, and I mean for your decision; because, members of the jury, all questions of fact in this case are for you and you alone. That, as I told you over two weeks ago when you were first empanelled, that is your essential and crucial function in this trial. I am the judge of law. It has been my duty to control the case, the way the evidence has come up, matters of that sort, to rule on procedure and all that sort of thing, but you are the twelve judges of fact, and no one can tell you what you decide to be the facts of this case. Mr Bateson cannot tell you. Mr Hartley cannot tell you. And I cannot tell you. They are your decisions.

'The third function I have, is to remind you of some of the evidence in the case and to try and relate it to the issues which you are going to have to consider. Let me make one or two things very clear at this early point. I am certainly not going to be reminding you of all, or even most, of the evidence in this case. That would take hours and hours and hours, because, of course, it all took hours to emerge. So I am bound to be highly selective in what I remind you of in the way of the evidence, although I shall try and remind you of what you may think are the more important, more salient aspects of the evidence. I shall, in being selective, hope to be fair to both parties. But remember, you decide the case not merely on the evidence that I remind you of, but on all the evidence that you recollect, that you regard as relevant to the issues in accordance with the directions that I give you. And so just because I might very well omit part of the evidence when I remind you of the evidence, I might omit it because you have heard it so often that I do not believe it is necessary for you to be told about it again. On the other hand, I might omit it because I forget it, or because it does not seem to me to be of great importance, or for some reason like that. Just because I do not remind you of it, if you remember it and think it important, well then, it is important, because it has got all the importance that you attach to it. Equally, if I remind you of evidence that you do not think is helpful or relevant, or you do not accept it, do not give it any special weight just because I mention it. Do you see?

'During the course of summing-up I shall suggest to you from time to time possible views that you might take about various of the questions and issues that arise for your decision in this case. Indeed, I might at any rate appear to you to be indicating my own view of some particular issue. All of that I shall be doing in the hope that it may assist you to arrive at your own views. But bear this very clearly in mind: as I have said, and cannot say too often, you alone are the judges of fact in this case. If you agree with my views, all well and good. But if you disagree, then of course it would be your clear duty to reject any different view I might suggest to you. Because otherwise you would be substituting my view for your own, and that would never do - that would be surrendering to me the exclusive province that is yours: namely, to decide the facts.

'Let me next suggest to you one or two golden rules as to how you might approach your task as the judges of fact in the case. First, this (and really I have said it already):

decide the case on the evidence that you have heard, and to some extent of course that means having evaluated, having judged, the witnesses who gave that evidence. You have to weigh them up, decide who you can rely on, decide whether anybody is trying to mislead you, decide what inference is to be drawn - matters like that. You decide the case in accordance with my legal directions, but on the evidence you have heard in this court. You do not decide it on counsels' speeches, however eloquent they were, to whatever heights of hyperbole they aspire. Decide it on the evidence. Of course counsel make valuable points, points worth hearing and listening to, and give those points such weight as you think they deserve. But decide the case on the evidence.

'Secondly, use your common sense. That, members of the jury, is the ultimate purpose, the great value of having a jury. You are twelve men and women of the world, from different professions, activities, backgrounds and the rest. You pool your experience of life. You use your common sense. You apply a sense of balance, a sense of proportion and you add all that up and apply all that, and you will not go far wrong in this case. We lawyers are all very well and fine and useful in our way, but members of the jury, sometimes we do rather tend, do we not? to overcomplicate things and see the wood for the trees? We lose sight sometimes, you may think, of the obvious.

'I am afraid that this summing up is bound to be a little long; it is bound to be, at least in places, a little involved. Listen to the detailed points, as you have throughout this case. Listen to the detailed directions that I give you. But, at the end of the day, do not get bogged down when you finally come to reach your decision, in all the minutiae, all the details of the evidence. If you stick, at the end of the day, to the essentials, to the obvious, use your common sense, use your sense of proportion, you will get it right. This action has been fought out, has it not? keenly, passionately, from time to time, you might

even have thought, venomously? You may think that the parties - and I really here refer to the main protagonists on both sides - displayed a conspicuous lack of charity to one another and a great deal of heat. You, however, as the jury, will decide the issues here coolly, dispassionately. I do not know - you may have sympathies, you may have predilections for either side, or neither side, or both sides. I do not know what your general view is of business magnates and press barons, on the one hand; or satirical, investigative journalists on the other. but whatever your predilections are, really you must put them aside. The reputation, of course, of both sides is to some extent, you may think, at issue in this action. But fairness, truth and justice are far greater goals by far than the interests of the individual parties to this case. You decide what you believe to be right, without worrying overmuch about who loses, or to what extent anybody loses; somebody always has to lose in an action like this, as I am sure you realise.

'With those general observations, I come to the first issue, and the first issue, as you know and indeed can see, from the questionnaire that has been put before you, in regard to each of these two separate articles, is: "Are the words complained of, defamatory of the plaintiff?" The first direction of law that I must give you as to that is about what lawyers call the onus and standard of proof. In this case, on this issue, it is for the plaintiff to show that in respect of whichever article you are considering - and you have to consider both - that the words are defamatory of him. I will tell you in a moment what that means, but the burden is on the plaintiff to establish that the article defamed him. Just in case you did not know, let me tell you at this stage that if it did, it is called a "libel". A libel is anything that is written down, like these articles. It is also in fact what is broadcast, but we are not concerned with that. It is a slander if you just say it in the pub to somebody. Maybe you did not know that difference. They are both defamatory, but the permanent sort, written down: libel; the other: slander. The standard that the plaintiff has to establish is the balance of probabilities. He has to satisfy you on the balance of probabilities that this article defamed. That means he has to make you satisfied that it is more likely than not. It is quite a different standard to that which you might well have heard of in criminal cases, when you have to establish things, prove things, beyond all reasonable doubt. Do you see the difference? All he has got to show, is that it is more likely than not - 51 per cent. Criminal case, well, we do not do it, of course, this way, but 90 plus per cent. Do you follow? So we come to ask this question: does the plaintiff show, has the plaintiff shown, you that the published words here are defamatory? And it is a question you have to ask separately of each of the two articles.

'Before we look at the words of the articles, let me just point out to you this - it has probably occurred to many of you. The question: "Are the published words defamatory?" itself really breaks down into two other questions. One, what do the words mean? What imputation do they bear? What is it that they are actually saying about the plaintiff? Secondly, giving the words the meaning that you decide they have, the implications you decide they bear, are they defamatory of the plaintiff? We can put those together, or leave them apart. But just bear in mind that there are really the two aspects of it: what do they mean, and then, given that meaning, is that something defamatory of the plaintiff - to his discredit? What defamatory means is really just that.

'Essentially it means that it is to someone's discredit. Whether or not it is true is immaterial for this purpose. It is defamatory whether it is true or false. If it is true, when we get to that, consider that, at a later stage, with question two: "Are those words substantially true?" Truth is not something, at the first stage, that we are concerned with; we are asking: "Is it defamatory?" And the question you ask yourselves when answering question one is, "Does the article lower the plaintiff's reputation in the eyes, in the estimation, of

right-thinking people generally?" It is a phrase you have heard both counsel use; quite rightly. It is perhaps rather a pompous, lawyer-like phrase, but what it all comes to is really this: would ordinary, decent people think the less of the plaintiff, think the worse of the plaintiff, as a result of reading the published words?

'In deciding what the words mean and in deciding whether they are defamatory, you have to bear in mind certain basic rules, and these are legal directions that I have to give you as to the proper approach to the question. First, it is wholly irrelevant what the author or publisher intended the words to mean, and whether or not he intended them to be defamatory. That all becomes very relevant to the question of damages, if and when we get to them. But it has got nothing to do with question one. Two, it is equally wholly irrelevant what the plaintiff or, indeed, any other readers of these articles understood the words to mean. That, too, only becomes relevant if and when we get to the question of damages. Three, and this is the final direction on this part of the case, what is all important is how the words would reasonably have been understood - and I am going to take this a little slowly because I can see that one of your number, if I may say so, very sensibly is writing these basic directions down - by people of ordinary intelligence and experience of worldly affairs. You ask yourselves in what sense would the words have been reasonably understood by such people, what meaning and inference would naturally have been drawn by such people, by reasonable and intelligent people reading the article? Bear in mind, members of the jury, that ordinary, reasonable people are neither unusually suspicious, nor unusually naive.

'In considering the question: "What do these words mean? Are they defamatory?", although it is essentially your view, the twelve of you, as ordinary people, whose view we seek, you are entitled to bear in mind the sort of people for whom the words are being published and who therefore would have been going to read them; in a word, the readers of

Private Eye. You have now seen a number of publications of *Private Eye*, including two whole copies, the copies containing the two articles complained of, and the people who read *Private Eye*, from all you have seen and read in this case, you may think are, or would be likely to be, people with a marked interest in, and general knowledge about, political affairs and matters such as, at least, what is involved in getting a peerage, being a lord. With those directions and considerations in mind, can we turn to the first of these articles and consider what view you might take as to the meaning of the words of that article, what imputation they bear, and more particularly, whether they bear a defamatory imputation? Would they reasonably be understood by right-thinking people, in such a way as to make them think less of the plaintiff.

'First, let us take a quick gallop through the five paragraphs. As to the first, very little to be said: "de rigeur" happens to be misspelled, there should be another "u" in the middle, but that does not very much matter. It means no more than "in". So you read it: "But he's definitely 'in' with Party Leader, Neil Kinnock." Paragraph two, the words that you might think you need to concentrate on are "though she won't be revealing that Maxwell is acting as paymaster". The clear implication of that, you may think, is at least this: that the payments are intentionally not being publicised; putting it perhaps no differently, that they are being kept secret. Third paragraph, the longest and, it is right to say, the least to do with this plaintiff. All about Mr Kinnock, is it not? and nothing about Mr Maxwell at all. Fourth paragraph, what it says, in effect, is that this plaintiff paid for two earlier, foreign trips by Mr Kinnock: those to Moscow and Central America. And so to the last three words, which, heaven knows, we have looked at often enough: "How many more Kinnock freebies will Maxwell have to provide before he is recommended for a peerage?" It is of course the critical paragraph. Though you must read it in the context of the article as a whole, what

inference, what imputation, does one draw from it? What comment, what statement, what assumption, underlies the question posed in the paragraph, reading between the lines, as of course one counsel, I think Mr Hartley, rightly told you one must do because readers do, read between the lines, do they not?

'Before I make one or two comments upon those paragraphs, let me tell you what, as a matter of law, I must direct you, are possible defamatory meanings that you might ascribe to that first article. What I am going to do is to tell you the six views you could take about that first article, that there are in fact six possible meanings variously contended for by the parties. First, that although there are six, there are two pairs, and they are paired for this reason: that ultimately they depend on whether or not you think it improper to do what that meaning indicates was being done. And the other thing I will tell you in advance of setting them out for you is that some of them, you may think, really do stretch the language to breaking point and, perhaps, beyond breaking point. So I am not suggesting to you, at the end of the day, when you retire you are all going to be saying to each other, "Well, it really might be any of these." The chances are you will have already formed a view which will rule out at least some of these possibilities as being the real meaning of the words. This is what the plaintiff says the article means. You can perhaps jot that down in shorthand as, "The plaintiff was making payments for Mr Kinnock's overseas trips and was thereby guilty of bribery or attempted bribery." Second - and you might like to put in brackets "lesser defamatory meaning" - "The plaintiff was making these payments for Mr Kinnock's overseas trips, in the hope, and with the improper motive, of being recommended for a peerage." Three - and you might like to put in brackets "non-defamatory" - as in two but, substituting for the word "improper", "entirely proper". Four - and you might like to put in brackets "wider defamatory meaning" - "The plaintiff has an ambition to be a peer and is improperly seeking to achieve that by patronage of the Labour Party and by the self-publicity which he creates through his control of MGN" - you do not need to write it out in full; I am sure you all know it is Mirror Group Newspapers. Fifth - again, you might put in brackets "non-defamatory" - as in four but, substituting for the word "improperly", "entirely properly". Sixth and last - again in brackets "non defamatory" - "The plaintiff will go on making payments with the result that in the end he will become a peer, a lord," - it does not matter which word you use - "no imputation that the payments were in any way related to that end."

'Just let me say one or two things about that collection of six at least theoretically possible meanings that the first articles could bear. As you know, the plaintiff's primary case is that meaning one, which is bribery or attempted bribery, is what anybody reading the words would immediately realise was being alleged, and if you accept that, that is an end of the case, except for how much, because plainly the defendants are not saying, indeed, Mr Bateson has said from first to last that they certainly are not seeking to contend, that there is any truth in an allegation of that sort.

'Before I look at the two pairs in the middle, the last one that I gave you is what Mr Bateson has said from time to time, including in his address to you yesterday, is what the words mean. They mean no more nor less than that. It is a matter for you, but you may have some difficulty in reading them quite like that. That may have been how they were intended by the authors, but that does not matter. For this purpose it is how they would read, and you may think that is a difficult construction for the words to bear.

'When deciding, as you will have to, between those six candidate possibilities - some perhaps more promising candidates than others - you will, I hope, be assisted by these observations. Some of them owe their inspiration to Mr Bateson, some to Mr Hartley, others, no doubt less inspired, are mine. First this: There is nothing in the first four paragraphs, as Mr Bateson points out,

about bribery in any shape or form. Mr Bateson says there is nothing wrong with making payments to political parties; this sort, as here set out, or any other sort, and indeed that fact is an admitted fact within the proceedings, at least in regard to payments to the Labour Party and the Boundary Commission Fighting Fund, and you may think that there would not be anything improper - indeed, Mr Maxwell accepts that there would be nothing improper - in making payments to Mr Kinnock's private office to enable him to travel overseas. Although, as eventually I shall have to remind you, Mr Maxwell of course says that he not only did not make such payments but would not do so as a matter of principle.

'Mr Bateson further says that there is nothing wrong, of course, in having the ambition to become a peer, and whatever anybody, like Mr Ingrams, might feel to the contrary, you may agree that there is indeed nothing wrong with that. Mr Hartley says that when one reads between the lines, one in fact must read, can only read, the article as asserting bribery, even though nothing in the first four paragraphs suggests it, and it is not to be found in the last.

'"Bribe" is defined by at least one dictionary as "money offered to procure action or a decision in favour of the giver", money offered to procure what is often an illegal or dishonest action or decision in favour of the giver, and clearly it is implicit that the briber is acting dishonestly and corruptly himself. He is seeking to buy what he could not otherwise expect to get, or at least, he is seeking to get it quicker than otherwise he could expect. Mr Bateson suggests that the allegation of bribery necessarily carries with it this: that the briber is seeking to obtain an actual agreement to profit from his payments, that it involves, therefore, an allegation of bribery, that in this case Mr Maxwell has actually spoken to Mr Kinnock about getting a peerage as a result of giving these moneys. If you think that in order for the allegation to be one of bribery it involves necessarily that, then it is a matter for you, but you may wonder whether the article does indeed go as far as to allege bribery.

'The article as a whole says a number of things, perhaps, about the payments, which give some flavour, some colour, to the basic nature of the transactions which it says took place. I say "which it says took place" because, as you very well know, there is no question now of the payments having been made. For the purposes of this action the one thing you can take as absolutely plain and axiomatic is that the defendants are not asserting that there is any truth in the suggestion that any of these payments for trips were made or were being made. They recognise that there is absolutely no question of them being able to show that, and you must decide this case on the basis that none of those payments were made or were being made. I am sure you have all picked that up. The great question we are now considering, of course, is how you would read the article, and, as I suggest, there are a number of things about the article as a whole which perhaps tend to throw some light on what was being said to be the consequence or relevance of the payments it was there setting out. First, that the plaintiff was acting as paymaster. Second, that Patricia Hewitt would not be revealing that fact; in other words, that the payments were being intentionally unpublicised or kept secret. Third, that the trips were freebies. And, fourth, that the payments were being made on a continuing basis.

'As far as the word "freebie" is concerned, Mr Bateson is quite right in saying that it means no more nor less than that something is provided free of charge, and you may well disagree with and reject what Mr Maxwell suggested about that, namely, that a freebie is necessarily a relatively small amount, £100 or so, and that anything around £1,000 - and you may be quite sure these overseas trips would have cost a good deal more than that - would constitute, says Mr Maxwell, a bribe, and you may think that that is really putting it far too high, quite an impossible view. But you may think that a freebie does at least connote this:

that what is being provided free of charge is being provided as a favour. In its overall context, you may think that the final paragraph may be paraphrased in this way. It is a matter for you. How many more of these continuing, secret favours will Mr Maxwell have to provide to Mr Kinnock before Mr Kinnock recommends him for a peerage? If the words do bear that meaning, then you may think that the six possibilities I have given you shrink to three: namely, one, two and three. Even though the article may be read as being directed essentially against Mr Kinnock for associating too closely with somebody who the article presupposes is bad company for Mr Kinnock and better kept at arm's length - that of course is how Mr Ingrams and Mr Silvester said they intended the article to be read - that last paragraph, you may conclude, must inevitably be read as something of a jibe or dig or comment, not so much upon Mr Kinnock but upon the plaintiff. The words, in particular "have to provide", you may think imply that the plaintiff himself, acting in a calculating fashion, intended some relationship between the payments and the suggested end product of a peerage.

'There is not within the article any suggestion that the plaintiff was making payments to the Labour Party generally, as opposed to Mr Kinnock personally. There is not any suggestion at all of self-publicity, which is again said to be within this wider meaning; self-publicity created through controlling the Mirror Group. On the contrary, as Mr Hartley suggests, you may think that making secret payments is really the precise opposite to seeking to achieve your end by self-publicity. And so you may think it difficult, though it is for you to decide, to spell out of the article the wider meaning, whether defamatory or non-defamatory, that are possibilities four and five. I repeat, although I think it is implicit in what I have already told you, you must certainly not feel obliged to agree with the plaintiff's interpretation as set out in the letter that he wrote, having read that article. You do not have to agree with that interpretation. How the plaintiff read the article does not matter; what matters is how it would be read by ordinary, sensible, reasonable people, given the sort of political interest and knowledge that readers of *Private Eye* would have. And equally, of course, you do not have to agree with the defendants' suggestion as to what they intended the article to convey and what they contend that it means.

'Very often one's first impression, one's first reading, or at any rate, one's second or, just possibly, one's third reading, of an article like this is actually the best guide to what it really means and what imputation, if any, it really bears. It really gets, if anything, more difficult rather than easier, the more you read it, to realise what it means and how it would have struck - because this is actually what we are concerned with - how it would have stuck the readers who did read it on its initial publication in *Private Eye*, and you have got to do the best you can, I think, to get back at least in part to the impression you had when you did first read it and, certainly, you must not look at it too artificially and you must not, because you have read it so often, give it artificial interpretations one way or the other, whether favourable to the plaintiff or the defendants.

'Now, as between the lesser, or, indeed, the wider, defamatory meaning, all depends on what view you take of somebody who makes payments in order to influence the beneficiary to recommend him for a peerage. Is it improper or is it not? If it is improper, then, assuming at this stage you have rejected meaning one, it is either meaning two or meaning four, as those are the other two possible defamatory meanings. Is it improper? Would you think the less of somebody for making payments, which in themselves are perfectly proper, in order to secure a peerage, bearing in mind it is a perfectly legitimate ambition to want to be a peer? Mr Bateson says that it is not enough that some people may disapprove of making payments with a view to, in order to, influence others to make

you a peer. It is not enough that some may disapprove; in order for you to find it defamatory, that must be the general view of society as a whole, of the reasonable reader of *Private Eye*. You may think that the reasonable reader of *Private Eye* would realise, perhaps, something of both aspects of the evidence given as to how peerages can be acquired. The average, reasonable reader of *Private Eye*, you may think, would appreciate that in these days, sixty years on from the scandals of the Lloyd George era when peerages really were bought, that certainly is not how it is meant to happen. On the contrary, as Mr Foot, who, after all, was himself the Leader of the Labour Party from 1980 to 1983, told you, the Leader of the Opposition, indeed of either Opposition party, is entitled to nominate people with a view to their then being put forward by the Prime Minister to the Queen to be raised to the peerage, made a lord, ennobled - you can use all these funny words but it is the same end. And what Mr Foot told you was, that the Leader of the Opposition, if he is the person recommending the honour, has to state that there have been no improper payments of money, that there have been no payments made which would affect the nomination of the candidate for recommendation, and apparently the recommendations go, and have for many years now gone, to a committee established in order to investigate the recommendations, in order to try and ensure that there are not again the abuses of the system of getting people into the House of Lords that, as I say, used to obtain in Lloyd George's day. And I think you perhaps should bear in mind this: going to the House of Lords is not just, so to speak, all very nice if you happen to like to go along to your butcher's and tell him you are Lord X. The House of Lords is one of the legislative chambers, it is a part of the legislative process, as I am sure you know. In order for anything to become law it has to go through, not only the House of Commons, but also the House of Lords. So if you are in the House of Lords it is very important. You do not get there just by paying money, because it is important to have people of repute and ability and value as well.

'I suggest, the average readers of *Private Eye* might very well be thought to realise that the system is designed to ensure that you cannot simply buy your way into a peerage. But, equally, the readers of *Private Eye* might very well be thought to have some idea of how, and maybe quite rightly, it appears that the system works in practice and there is in fact, as a number of the documents, in particular the extracts from Mr Walker's book before you, show, apparently some striking or significant correlation between those who have themselves, or as directors of substantial public companies, made significant payments to a political party, and those who eventually obtain honours. Honours, of course, includes both knighthoods and peerages, and you will remember what Mr Smith, Man of the People, wrote in December of last year. You may think that that is putting it perhaps a little simplistically, cynically and, indeed, inaccurately. But it may be that the phrase "for political services rendered", or something of that sort, which tends to be the explanation for the making of certain people peers, can, and indeed perhaps can perfectly properly, include services in the way of assisting a political party in its proper dealings by making financial contributions. I just remind you of this: the plaintiff himself, although recognising Mr Smith to be an outstandingly able reporter, says that on that occasion, although exercising the right to freedom of expression in our free society, he was expressing a totally inaccurate view and one that Mr. Maxwell says is totally alien to the view generally held in Fleet Street. I suggest the average reader of *Private Eye* might, you may think, know something at least of both those attitudes: what certainly ought to happen, and what certainly some people believe in practice does happen, and certainly has happened in the past.

'Just assume that that is the position; even if in the past and, perhaps to a degree still, people can, by paying money, obtain, or at any rate, hasten their peerage, you may think that it by no means follows that you would not think the worse of somebody if they sought to climb on that particular bandwagon and follow that particular route to a peerage. So, even assuming that a reader would realise that this is sometimes how it works, you may think, if you regard the article as meaning either two or three, or four or five of those possible meanings I have set out, that it may be that the article is indeed suggesting what people might regard as impropriety, that they might take the view that it is, despite whatever the practice may be, nevertheless an improper motive, to pay money in the hope and with the intention that it shall influence somebody towards giving you a peerage.'

After adjourning for the night, the judge returned to the words of Michael Foot and John Smith the next morning.

'Let me emphasise the significance and the relatively limited significance that that evidence has in your approach to the first question. What you are concerned to do in answering the first question is to decide what ordinary, reasonable readers of *Private Eye* would have understood by that first article, reading between the lines of the last short paragraph of it - what imputation would they have thought it to bear. The relevance of the evidence that I have just mentioned is only this: that you may think that the ordinary readers of *Private Eye* would perhaps have some general appreciation of both those aspects of the matter. They would probably, you may think, know how the system generally was intended to work, namely not by people being able to buy honours, but they may well also have some appreciation of the fact that payments might tend in practice - not alone, no doubt, but coupled with other things - to improve one's chances. So remember that the readers of *Private Eye* of course have not heard Mr Foot give evidence, and they may very probably not have read Mr Smith's article and not read Mr Walker's book. So do not, so to speak, assume that they would know all that in the sort of detail that you now know it, but all you would have in mind is that they might have some general appreciation of those matters. With that in mind you would then decide how they would understand that first article.

'The second article, and again, question one is: are the words complained of defamatory of the plaintiff? So again you ask: what meaning does it have? What would it convey to the ordinary, reasonable reader to whom it was directed, the people who read *Private Eye*? The plaintiff's contention is that it bears exactly the same defamatory meaning as the first article, namely that the plaintiff was bribing or attempting to bribe Mr Kinnock to recommend him for a peerage. Mr Hartley says that that is perfectly plain and straightforward, and can it mean anything else? These lesser and wider defamatory meanings, he suggests, are, to use his term, mumbo-jumbo.

'Except for the mention in the last line in the second paragraph of "African tour", there is nothing about the payments for Mr Kinnock's foreign trips or any ambition that Mr Maxwell might have for a peerage or anything of that sort at all. The crucial paragraph here is the last one, and the crucial words in it are the words "which Maxwell lamely denies financing". You might even underline the three words before "the African junket", because that is, of course, what it is that it is said Mr Maxwell "lamely denies financing".

'What the plaintiffs assert, and you may think rightly assert, is that those words involve the reassertion of the truth of the first article, insofar as the first article said Mr Maxwell had paid for that trip. Indeed, there really is not any dispute about that. Mr Ingrams and Mr Silvester both said that the phrase was indeed intended to show that the magazine was standing by its first story. Neither Mr Ingrams, nor Mr Silvester, nor Mr Bateson suggest that Mr Maxwell's denial was a lame denial, a half-hearted denial. They both agree - you may think obviously rightly agree - that the denial was in fact a strong denial. But what Mr Ingrams and Mr Silvester say is that they

regarded it, although strong, as essentially unconvincing. That is what they were seeking to convey by use of that phrase "which Maxwell lamely denies financing". They are therefore saying, are they not? "We repeat what we said before about that; we don't accept Mr Maxwell's strong denial; nor indeed do we accept Patricia Hewitt's denial printed just below Mr Maxwell's letter."

'Let me indicate what the plaintiffs are not alleging about that second article, because it is important you should bear this in mind. The plaintiffs are not alleging that the story about the party is defamatory. You are not being asked here to award damages for the first two paragraphs on the basis that they themselves bring discredit on the plaintiff; nor is the plaintiff saying that you should regard the assertion that his letter of denial is untrue, as a libel on him. They are not saying: "Look here, *Private Eye*, in the phrase 'which Maxwell lamely denies financing' is saying that my letter of denial is false and untrue. That is defamatory on me. That brings discredit on me. Give me damages for that." They are not saying that. What they are saying is that those words constitute a clear reiteration, or repetition, reaffirmation, of the truth of the first article, and therefore it is the same defamatory meaning that you should give to those words in that article as you should be to the first article.

'But, says Mr Bateson, even assuming that the second article reasserts the first article, it only does so as to the allegation that Mr Maxwell was paying for the African trip. That, suggests Mr Bateson, is insufficient to import into the second article the sting of the first article, the last paragraph, or with any imputation you may think that has. Mr Bateson says there is nothing therefore in the second article that on any view could be regarded as itself an allegation amounting to bribery or attempted bribery. Mr Hartley says that, on the contrary, there are features of this second article which positively underline and emphasise the sting of the first article. He says you must read the article in its context, and that of course is indisputably right. The context includes the publication in the same issue of the plaintiff's letter. That is right too. The second paragraph of Mr Maxwell's letter reads: "Finally, the disgraceful allegation that I provide Mr Kinnock with freebies (which presumably is intended to mean bribes)..." For the moment, ignore entirely whether you yourself, reading that first article, would think that that was a fair assumption or not. The fact is that that assumption is contained in this letter which *Private Eye* then are publishing in the same edition as the article which simply calls that letter a "lame denial". The defendants do not say in that issue, do they? "Gracious me, we never intended the first article to mean bribes or anything like that," and they did not say, "Nobody could possibly, let alone reasonably, have understood the first article in that way." Rather, they published the letter without comment, save only to comment that it constitutes a "lame denial of financing the African trip". So, suggests Mr Hartley, even if you do not conclude the first article would have been understood as alleging bribery, when you read the second article in context, then you could and should.

'The next topic I must direct you about is justification. That is an issue that only arises if you have found either or both of the articles defamatory, and indeed, for reasons that I must explain, the question of justification even then only arises if you find either or both articles defamatory because they bear the wider meaning, meaning No. 4. In order to succeed in a plea of justification, the defendants have to prove the truth of all the adverse imputations conveyed by the words, all the inferences that would ordinarily be drawn from them. When you ask the question: are the words substantially true? that means: are they true in all the respects that matter? If you decide that the first article bears meaning No. 1, which is the bribery or attempted bribery meaning, then there is no question of the defendants justifying the substantial truth of that allegation. Mr Bateson has told you from first to last that if you decide it bears

meaning No. 1, then the defendants accept without more ado that it is not true, not justified; so there is no question of justifying that meaning.

'But if you decide that the first article bears the second meaning, that is the lesser defamatory meaning "that the plaintiff was making these payments for Mr Kinnock's overseas trips in the hope and with the improper motive of being recommended for a peerage", then equally there is no question of the defendants proving the truth of that allegation. It is only if the defamatory meaning is meaning No. 4, the wider defamatory meaning, only if, in other words, you regard the actual details of the payments set out in that first article as immaterial, that there is anything left in the defendants' case of justification, anything left in the pleaded particulars of justification which could conceivably support that meaning. Let me just point this out to you. If you decide that the words bear meaning No. 4, it follows that you have decided that the gist of the libel, the sting of the libel (as it is sometimes called) is simply this: that the plaintiff is trying to achieve an ambition to become a peer improperly in various ways, without it mattering very much which ways. You will have decided that nothing is added to the sting of the first article by the details set out, nothing, that is, that cannot be justified by reference to other payments or other aspects of the plaintiff's conduct. So you will have accepted that the defendants are right to say, as they do say, that it really does not matter that the first article was wrong in saying that these payments were being made for Mr Kinnock's overseas trips, whether secretly or otherwise, whether as personal favours or otherwise, and whether on a continuing basis or otherwise. None of those particular features of the first article, the defendants contend, add to the sting of the libel. If you accept what Mr Bateson says as to all that, if you agree that none of those particular features of the first article add to the sting of the libel, why then it may well be that the wider meaning is indeed the meaning to be attached. As I have directed you, that is a view that you are entitled to take as to the meaning of the first article. It is a matter for you. It is perhaps not a conclusion which you would altogether readily arrive at.

'Let me try and illustrate the position briefly by reference to a case decided a year or two ago about a very well-known rugby player. I will not name him because there is no good reason to do so. You might have heard about it. What was alleged by the publication in that case - he sued for libel just like Mr Maxwell - basically that the plaintiff was a "shamateur". Do you know what that means? It means he was an amateur, playing rugby as an amateur, which requires that you are not paid anything at all for playing or anything like that, but in fact he was being paid in certain ways and therefore was a "shamateur". That carried with it a charge of hypocrisy and deviousness, which was obviously defamatory of him. The point was that the actual article supported the charge of shamateurism by saying that he had infringed his amateur status by contracting with a publisher to be paid for a particular book all about rugby; in other words, that he was cashing in on his fame as a rugby player in order to make money, by writing a book. That would indeed have affected his status as an amateur and justified the allegations that he was a shamateur.

'In fact, all that turned out not to be so at all, but the defendants said: "It is true we cannot prove that, but what we can prove is that the plaintiff was regularly taking cash payments from a well known sports supplier called Adidas, for wearing their boots in rugby matches." I am sure you would easily see that if he did that, that was at least as serious an allegation and at least equally justified the charge that he was a shamateur. So it was held that in that case the article bore that wider meaning. It did not need to be supported by the truth of the actual allegation to which it was tied in the article, namely that he was getting money from a publisher. You could prove it, justify it, by reference to quite other, but similarly serious, misconduct, which in fact

meant that you were not properly an amateur.

'Really, that is what the defendants seek to say in this very case. They say that here, as there, nothing is added to the sting of the first article by reference to the particular payments made, secretly, on a continuing basis, personal favours - as you may read that first article - to Mr Kinnock, and that it is just a general allegation which, if defamatory at all, is to the general effect that here is somebody who one way or another will improperly pay money and do other things in order to become a peer.

'Assume that you do indeed accept, as the defendants urge you should, that if this article bears any defamatory meaning, it is that wider one, meaning No. 4. As I have told you, it is only then that you have to consider the plea of justification. Look at it therefore on that basis, and everything I am going to tell you now assumes you find meaning No. 4. The onus is upon the defendants to prove the defence of justification, prove that the words are substantially true. The standard to which they must prove them is the same standard that I mentioned before, when I told you what the plaintiffs had to prove to establish a defamatory meaning, namely the balance of probabilities - more likely than not. So the defendants have to show first that the plaintiff was ambitious for a peerage, and second that the plaintiff was improperly seeking to realise that ambition by patronage of the Labour Party - that means payments to and support of the Labour Party - and by self-publicity. I have summarised it. It is self-publicity and exploitation of his position as publisher of the Mirror Group and all that.

'We ought to look briefly at what is left of the pleaded case of justification. You had a great deal of evidence indicating that there is not, you may think, one shred of substance in the suggestion Mr Grant was unpopular with Mr Kinnock, that there was some risk or likelihood of his dismissal, that that would have cost a lot of money and embarrassment to the Labour Party, and the plaintiff in effect took Mr Grant off the Labour Party's hands. You may think that is in fact a thoroughly unpleasant slur on Mr Grant. Mr Grant was called, Mr Maxwell was called, Mr Clements, the executive officer in charge of Mr Kinnock's office was called; he said there was no truth whatever in the assertion that Mr Grant was unpopular. I am not going to go through that evidence. You may have not the least hesitation in rejecting totally and utterly that paragraph. You may indeed be surprised and perhaps rather saddened that it has not, if not long since, at least by now, been conceded by the defendants to be properly struck out, as the paragraphs ahead of it. You may think it brings them little credit to leave that slur on the pleadings without their calling one word of evidence in support of it.

'At the very heart of this case of justification, the paragraphs that actually say that the original story in the first article about Mr Maxwell paying for these overseas trips, was true - those paragraphs finally bit the dust, again, you may think, a good deal later than they should have done - after the end of the plaintiff's case. Not one single word of evidence has been called to support the truth of those matters. It is conceded that you are bound to regard them as wholly and utterly untrue.

'I come back to the two matters that the defendants have to prove in order to support the plea of justification for meaning No. 4, if that is the meaning you decide on. First they have to show the plaintiff was ambitious for a peerage. Well, the only direct evidence on that point, of course, is the plaintiff's own evidence, which of course you do not have to accept - it is not decisive on the matter but it is perhaps not uninteresting. He said that it is not his personal ambition to be a member of the House of Lords. When he was asked, as the very first question in cross-examination, whether, if he were offered it, he would not accept it, his answer to that (which may perhaps have disappointed Mr Bateson) was that no, he would not, and indeed, he had twice refused a peerage. He told you that a few years ago during the time when Mr Foot was the Leader of the Party, which means

therefore 1980-83, he had been asked by the late Lord Goronwy-Roberts, who was a senior Labour Party member of the House of Lords, whether he would allow his name to go forward to be recommended for a peerage. That he refused because he said he could not support the defence policy of Mr Michael Foot, which was unilateralism, and then he told you he was again asked whether he would allow his name to go forward last year by the Deputy Leader of the Labour Party, Mr Roy Hattersley, and on that occasion, without any explanation as to precisely why, he says he simply declined. Mr Bateson says you should reject that; you should reject the plaintiff's assertion that he has no such ambition. Mr Bateson argues that here is somebody who enjoys being in the public eye and he says that you should not accept the plaintiff's evidence; you should regard him as unreliable in his disavowals of this sort of ambition. He invites your attention to "Forward with Britain". This is the day Mr Maxwell assumed control of the Mirror Group - in the second paragraph: "I am proud to be the proprietor of this group." Mr Bateson says that is not what he was at all. He was its publisher. You may actually note that in the middle of the page under the headline "Forward with Britain" by Mr Robert Maxwell; there indeed he is said to be the publisher. Mr Bateson says there is a paragraph saying: "Mr Maxwell confirmed his undertaking to safeguard jobs and honour all union agreements," and such evidence as there is is not to the effect that he did not - and again Mr Bateson says that you should not accept what this plaintiff says. Those are all very much questions for you. Whose evidence you believe is absolutely a question of your assessment. You have seen some of these people give evidence for a considerable time and it is up to you what evidence you accept.

'Perhaps whether or not the defendants establish that here is a plaintiff ambitious to become Lord Maxwell is something that is not quite as straightforward as: do you or do you not believe the plaintiff? Consider this matter. Mr Bateson has asserted repeatedly that this particular plaintiff can take a peerage whenever he wants to. That indeed, Mr Ingrams told you in evidence, was his view. Mr Ingrams supported it by saying: "After all, as the plaintiff himself told you, he has been offered a peerage more than once." So here is somebody, by common consent - and indeed as part of the defendants' case - a very obvious candidate for a peerage. He has really got all the right qualifications, you may think. He is a press baron, and as you have seen very often they go to the House of Lords. He is a benefactor of the Labour Party. Again, it is part of the defendants' case that that eases the journey. He is a Labour Party activist and supporter, and you may well think that he is the sort of person who could in any event properly contribute to the debates and the processes of the upper legislative house, which, as I told you yesterday, is what the House of Lords is. And if all that is so, which you may think is indeed very convincing, well then, you may ask yourselves, "Why on earth should Mr Maxwell have been reduced in July of 1985 to having to continue patronising the Labour Party with payments and self-publicising himself in order to achieve the ambition that could be achieved at the asking anyway?" In short, if Mr Maxwell is, indeed, ambitious for a peerage, well, then, why has he not simply taken it? Mr Bateson says "Well, one can understand his having refused it in Mr Goronwy-Roberts' time, because he would have then, in the House of Lords, had to vote in support of Mr Foot's unilateralist policy, and he would not have been able to do that conscientiously." Well, if he is that conscientious then are you to believe that he is nevertheless prepared to make improper payments, which is at the heart of this case of justification?

'That is, you may think, something of a difficulty in the defendants' path - to prove the first of the two points, namely that this plaintiff was ambitious for a peerage. But even if he was, and you are sure of that, they still have to satisfy you that he was improperly seeking to achieve that - to become a peer - by making these improper payments or by self-publicity, things like that, and we ought therefore to have a brief look at those other obstacles to the defendants' path to a successful plea of justification. Let us first look at the payments that we know are accepted to have been made. First, the payment of £44,500 to the Labour Party. All you might care to know about that payment is that, unlike the payments alleged in the first article, it is not a payment personally to Mr Kinnock's private office and for his use for overseas trips, it is to Labour Party funds generally. Secondly, so far from being secret, you may think it was very well publicised indeed; and thirdly, he was, of course, asked for it - you remember the evidence of Mr Kitson, who I think was then the member of the National Executive Committee charged with launching this financial appeal, and he was asked to respond to it. I turn to the payments to the Boundary Commission Fighting Fund. You may certainly agree with Mr. Bateson, first that there is no material difference between the beneficiaries of that, that is to say the plaintiffs in that particular losing case - Mr Foot, the Leader of the Party, Mr Cocks, the Chief Whip, Mr Mortimer, the Treasurer and Mr Hughes - all very top officials of the Labour Party, even though they brought the action privately, and the Labour Party. As Mr Foot told you, it was entirely for tactical reasons that the challenge to the Boundary Commission was not by the Party as such, but by these senior officials. So you will no doubt agree with Mr Bateson that there is no magic in that distinction, and equally you may very well agree with Mr Bateson that, at the end of the day, although they got the facts wrong about how much money — £75,000 was what their mole had told them and as to where it was handed over, namely, this Soho restaurant, the Gay Hussar. Again, nothing turns on that. And so you have got to look for differences of substance, if any. You may think that there are, indeed, such differences - but consider, when you are deciding whether there is any difference, really, between the actual payments alleged in the articles and the payments that had been made to the BCFF, these two matters: first, the Boundary Commission Fighting Fund payments were, were they not? once for all payments. They were not - and this, you may think, is a very different kettle of fish to what the article was alleging - ongoing or continuing payments. They were to meet a particular liability that was finally met with the payment of the balancing figure of £8,500-odd, which was over a year before the Private Eye article and, in fact, the balancing figure was paid at the time when Mr Foot, one of the beneficiaries, had ceased to be the Leader of the Party.

'The other aspect of it when you are deciding whether it is as good a candidate as these freeby payments that were not made as a candidate, so to speak, for an improper purpose, is that you may think the BCFF payments were made as an act of personal friendship and, indeed, charity. The plaintiff was approached by, in particular, Mr Cocks, who told him that he carried the main burden of raising this £60,000, he had had a number of sleepless nights and it was all a very great worry to him. It was not the case of the plaintiff, so to speak, foisting himself onto these people and seeking to make friends and influence people in that way - you may think he merely responded generously to a personal plea. And so you ask, "Were these payments really all done improperly to secure a peerage that, in fact, the defendants say he could have had at any time and that he had already, as we now know, refused?" And you may think you cannot ignore Mr Ingrams' own evidence, where he recognised there was nothing in the least improper, no ulterior motive, in the plaintiff making these payments to the BCFF.

'What about the other basis on which the defendants seek to justify that the plaintiff is guilty of self-publicity - the exploitation of his position as controller of the Mirror Group? Well, I am not sure that I sufficiently followed some of Mr Bateson's points under this head and may be, therefore, unable to do justice to them. I am a little unsure as to how any of this aspect of the case assists the defendants to show that the plaintiff was in some way misconducting himself in order to get a peerage that he did not want, or, if he did want it, that he could have got in any event whenever he wanted it without misconducting himself. I mention the party - the *Mirror* party. Mr Bateson relies, in some way, on Mr Maxwell's having said, "Well, if he will not come to the *Mirror* party we will not go to his African party", and, says Mr Bateson, here is the plaintiff holding a big stick, using his power, his position and payments, to exercise an influence over the Labour Party. Well, it is a matter for you, members of the jury. I do not think I can assist further in trying to explain the circumstances in which the plea of justification would arise and whether or not you should accept the defendants' case as to that.

'I pass to the final aspect of this case - the issue of damages. Now, I do that on the assumption that you find one or both of these articles defamatory of the plaintiff and untrue. Of course, as I am sure you have gathered, if that is not the position, then the defendants will have succeeded, and you do not arrive at the point of considering damages at all. So everything I say from now on assumes that you find that the articles, or one of them, unjustifiably defame the plaintiff. I am going to have to tell you, I fear, a good deal about damages - it is a difficult question, it is the issue in the case to which most of the evidence given, in fact, goes. I say that for this reason, as I am sure you realise: on question 1 really there is not much evidence - that is how the original readers of *Private Eye* would have read the article - and, as I have told you, it does not matter what was intended, it does not matter how, in fact, Mr Maxwell read it. And so very limited evidence, do you follow? goes to that first issue. On the second issue that I have just been dealing with - justification - really, there is not a great deal of evidence, you may think, that goes to that. Most of the evidence, as I say, for reasons I shall come to in a moment, goes to the question of how much money, assuming damages here are to be awarded.

'Basically, there are two quite different kinds of damages that you have to consider in this case - first, compensatory, second exemplary - and in a nutshell the difference between them is this: compensatory damages, as the name suggests, are to compensate the plaintiff so far as the law and money can, for the injury done to him by the published libel. It is for the injury to his feelings and reputation and to vindicate his good name. I will come back to that and tell it to you again in rather more detail to try and put it in enough different ways so you really have the full flavour of it. Exemplary damages are completely different. They are only very, very rarely awarded and, again briefly, it is only when the defendants have behaved quite disgracefully and in certain narrowly defined circumstances, which I will tell you about shortly. And when, of course, you award exemplary damages that is not to compensate the plaintiff - if he needs compensation that has already been taken care of by the compensatory damages - it is rather to punish the defendants additionally and to deter them and others like them from behaving so disgracefully in future. Exemplary means, as I am sure you know, to make an example of the defendants.

'If you pass an exemplary prison sentence it means to make an example of that defendant - to the people as a whole. And it follows, of course, that exemplary damages are, therefore, what you might call a windfall to the plaintiff - he is getting more than compensation requires - and the reason for it is, of course, that exceptionally there is a public interest in adding to the defendants' punishment. The punishment that is in effect there already by paying compensatory damages, it is adding to that, to mark the public's view of the defendants' conduct and to emphasise that it should not happen again and to deter others.

'Now, basically you cannot award exemplary damages unless three conditions are satisfied: first, that the defendants had published the libel knowing it was untrue, or reckless as to whether it was true or not; secondly, that the defendants did that because they thought it would pay them to do so; and, thirdly, that the damages required to compensate the plaintiff for the wrong done to him would be insufficient to deter and punish the defendants and so you need to add more.

'Compensatory damages - I come back to those. It will not comfort you when I tell you this, but perhaps it is more difficult to assess damages in a defamation case than really almost any other sort of case. Take a breach of contract case: somebody has promised to do some work or sell something or see that the car is in good order - something like that - and they break the contract. They are sued, and damages are really quite straightforward. You just ask how much the other party is out of pocket as a result of that breach. Sometimes it is quite tricky to work it out but at least it is clear what you are aiming at - to compensate the plaintiff for the actual loss he has suffered. Take a case, a negligence case, where somebody is hurt at work in a factory or run over on the roads. Maybe he breaks an arm, he is out of work for six months, he has got various nursing expenses, he has broken his watch - you just calculate all those things and then, of course, you have to add for what is called pain and suffering, the loss of the ordinary enjoyment of life through having your arm in a plaster. That is something that happens quite often. There are well-known figures that you tend to get for this sort of injury. Judges try the cases, who are very experienced, and counsel, or the barristers, are allowed to tell the judges that there was another case decided last year about just such an injury and in that case the judge awarded x thousand pounds. It is all really fairly straightforward.

'But in defamation it is not so easy, and it is one of the very few cases, in fact, in the civil process where one person is seeking damages against another. We still have juries and so it is your unhappy fate to be involved in the assessment of damage in perhaps the most difficult type of case.

'It is a little more difficult than that, too, because I am not allowed by the law to suggest any figures to you at all - I cannot even give you a bracket. I can tell you that the lowest award is the lowest coin in the realm, which I think now is 1p, and the highest is, you might say, the sky, but it has always got to be sensible and reasonable. All I can do is to direct you as to the factors to take into account, and to tell you that your award should be not too much and not too little. Not, you may think, terribly helpful. It is not, and it cannot be, a scientific exercise - it is an exercise of good sense and judgment. And that, no doubt, members of the jury, is why we are all happy, in this sort of case, to leave it to you and not be professional judges. Just let me say this before I explain more of what the damages are designed to compensate the plaintiff for, and the sort of considerations you should have in mind: I repeat, I am not permitted and I am not suggesting, figures for your consideration but I cannot suppose that you will not have noticed that once or twice in the 53 instances that we have in our papers of retractions and apologies, sums of money are mentioned as representing the damages agreed in those cases. Let me show you what I have in mind and where, because I must then say a word or two about those matters. The Harold Evans case: you see in the headline ;"Private Eye to pay £1,000 libel damages". Then the headline "Eye pays £20,000". I am not asking you to look at the details of the articles, certainly at the moment.

'Now go to "Libelled Wilcox wins damages". "TV Producer, Desmond Wilcox, won £14,000 libel damages yesterday over allegations in *Private Eye* he was involved in sharp practice with BBC money. It must also pay an estimated £80,000 costs for the 15-day hearing."

'What I must say about all that is only this - two things: first, that you may think it is really very difficult to get much, if any, help from any of those figures in those quite different contexts. You simply do not know enough about precisely what the libels were, precisely how widely they had been disseminated, precisely how they had affected the plaintiff, precisely how the defendants had behaved. You do, of course, know in respect of some of them, though not in Mr Wilcox's, that often they were part of an overall deal whereby the defendants withdrew the allegations, apologised and all the rest of it, which are not features of the present case. That is not so, of course, in Mr Wilcox's case - that is an award on a contested allegation, but you still do not know very much, if anything, about that case and therefore you may find that it is misleading rather than helpful to pay regard to any of those matters. So far as the figure for costs is concerned, my direction to you is this - it is simple but it is very firm: you must totally ignore all questions of costs - that is a matter wholly and solely for me at the end of the case.

'One final matter in this context about figures. I will come back to the *Mail on Sunday* article that Mr Bateson was inviting you to have regard to, because they paid £5,000. You may not think it is terribly helpful to have that fact at the forefront of your minds when you are deciding on compensatory damages in this case. As Mr Hartley pointed out, there were really very strikingly different considerations in that case.

'Now, as I have told you, compensatory damages are to fulfil two real purposes: they are both to vindicate the plaintiff's reputation and to console him for his injured feelings, and again I will tell you more about that later when I explain to you what considerations are capable of aggravating the damages and why. This particular plaintiff happens to be a millionaire - no doubt a multi-millionaire. That, however, I suggest should have no effect whatsoever upon your award one way or the other. I suppose in one sense it might be said, "Well, here is somebody who is as rich as Croesus and he really does not need the money anyway, so there is no point in giving him any." That would, of course, be quite wrong. Equally one might say, "Well, here is somebody who is so rich that the only way to bring a smile of satisfaction to his face and to vindicate him is to award some vast sum that will mean something even to him." But that, again, would be a wholly wrong approach, and so I suggest you put totally out of your mind the consideration that here is somebody who actually already has plenty of money. What he says, in effect, is, "I have got plenty of money but I have only got one reputation, and it is that that is damaged here and I should have damages for it."

'One starting point when you consider what damages to award is to ask yourselves these two basic questions: one, how serious a libel was this? And two, how widely was it published? As to the first, how serious - well, really I have said, I think, all I can to help you on that. It is for you to consider. Obviously if you conclude that meaning one is the meaning of the words there - an allegation as extreme and serious as bribery or attempted bribery - then it is more serious than one of the lesser defamatory meanings, which is an improper motive for making payments and so forth, but nothing like as serious, you may think, as bribery.

'Mr Bateson says, of course, that it is not a libel at all, but even if it is, bear in mind that it is not a libel to make the payments to Mr Kinnock. Of course, they were not made, but even the allegation does not allege a libel simply by making the payments. It is not a libel to say somebody wants a peerage and even if we put the two together and then we get an imputation of impropriety, that is not a very serious libel. Well, those are all considerations for you. As to the extent of publication, there is an agreed figure of, in effect, 230,000 - that is the circulation of *Private Eye* at the relevant time - although everybody seems to agree the actual readership is three or four times as much, so that is whatever it is, three-quarters of a million upwards as the numbers who would read *Private Eye*.

'That is only the starting point, because the law recognises that in assessing compensatory damages there may be a number of factors which may tend to mitigate the loss and so reduce the appropriate award; and equally there may be other factors that tend to aggravate the injury and so call for a larger award, and I will consider them briefly.

'Let me take matters in turn. First, the publication of the letters from the plaintiff and Miss Hewitt. Generally speaking, of course, it would mitigate the injury to a defamed plaintiff if, when he writes correcting errors in the publication, you print that letter, even if you do not accompany it by an apology. Mr Bateson suggests that that is the effect of the publication of these letters here. You may think that rather than mitigating the plaintiff's loss, more realistically it aggravates it, because what happens is the letter is published without the apology that the published letter itself denies and instead of being accompanied by any such apology it is accompanied by the second article which describes it sarcastically as a lame denial which, in other words, says of it, "it is an untrue denial which we, *Private Eye*, do not accept". And Mr Hartley suggests the effect of publishing it in the context of the article is rather like the editor's comment under the letter "Hacks fight back", all those years ago when the plaintiff was first libelled. In other words, instead of reducing the sting you may think it increases it.

'The next point Mr Bateson takes is that some mitigation is to be found because here is the plaintiff jointly writing with Mr Garth Gibbs, the *Mirror* Diary, and with the 12 million-odd circulation of the *Mirror* able to take a lot of the sting out of the *Private Eye* article by a very widely published correction, such as is set out. In other words, this is not a plaintiff like you or I would be, without our own means of publishing a correction, without our own means of setting the record straight; at least he has, and took, the opportunity of making his position widely clear and telling his public that the *Eye* had lied about him and had been guilty of "Another Whopper". You may think there is more in Mr Bateson's point that that affords at least some mitigation that in the

Eye's publication of the plaintiff's letter of denial to them.

'I come next to Mr Bateson's point that you should regard the payment by the *Mail on Sunday* of £5,000 as mitigation. Mr Bateson relies on what Parliament has enacted to this effect. "A defendant may give evidence in mitigation of damages, that a plaintiff has received compensation in respect of publication of words to the same effect as the words on which his action is founded" - I have paraphrased so far as relevant to what the law is. In other words, here is a provision - a very sensible provision you may think - which is designed to ensure that a plaintiff does not recover in respect of basically the same damage, twice, or more often, against various different publishers. It is to ensure that he is not over-compensated by getting, in respect of the same amount of damage to his reputation, £5,000 here, ten here, twenty there, etc. etc. - do you follow? "But," says Mr Hartley, "that really is a million miles from the situation here." If you look at the original *Mail on Sunday* article the reference in the first line to a story, Mr Bateson agrees, is the story as it appeared in the first article in *Private Eye*. But see what part of the story is, in fact, picked up in the Marcia Falkender article - it is really in the last two short paragraphs: "Of course, I am sure the Maxwell money could in no way influence Neil as Opposition Leader or the Prime Minister, but he should not give anyone the slightest reason for thinking he might be in someone's pocket."

'What Mr Hartley says is that as an allegation that is, so to speak, a mouse compared to a lion - there is no hint or imputation or suggestion of bribery or making payments improperly or anything like that in order to realise an ambition to become a peer. And, indeed, if you turn on [in your bundle] you see the less defamatory meaning that is there recognised as possibly to have been given to the article on the previous page. And it is in the second paragraph: "Of course, not for a moment do I believe now or have I ever believed that Mr Kinnock is in Mr Maxwell's

pocket or anyone else's. Both Mr Kinnock and Mr Maxwell tell me, however, this is how the paragraph might be construed, so I must put the record straight, because, of course, I accept that neither Mr Kinnock's trip to Ethiopia and nor his trip to Moscow was funded by Mr Maxwell."

'And so there it is accepted that the article might - the *Mail on Sunday* article the previous week - have been regarded as defamatory, although, of course, not defamatory in the full sense that the plaintiff alleges here. So one big difference, you may think, is how defamatory the *Mail on Sunday* article was compared to this article, assuming you accept this article was defamatory, the *Private Eye* article. So there is a comparison as to the different seriousness of libels.

'The other important comparison, you may think, is that here is the *Mail on Sunday*, not like *Private Eye* asserting month after month the truth of what they said and trying to justify it, but rather immediately, in the very next edition one week later, putting the record straight, making an apology, doing all they could to undo the hurt, the injury to reputation, the injury to feelings, and in those circumstances paying what Mr Hartley would suggest is the relatively modest figure for their libel of £5,000. And you may think that it would not be right to regard that £5,000 as, so to speak, something which should compensate Mr Maxwell for the quite different injury and the continuing hurt to his feelings that *Private Eye*'s more serious libels, if you accept they are libels, have caused. I will come back in a moment to the allegation that Mr Maxwell has a generally bad reputation though that, you might note, is the fourth matter relied on by the defendants in mitigation. The fifth and final matter relied on by the defendants in mitigation can be put under this head: any facts which tend to negate or disprove malice on the part of the defendants. Now, those would be facts which generally suggest the defendants ought not to be viewed too critically for having libelled the plaintiff - facts, that is, which are favourable to the defendants because they indicate that they were not, at least, being malicious towards the plaintiff, they were not intending to damage his reputation without good reason, or anything of that sort.

'Another mitigating circumstance would be if the defendants themselves genuinely did not regard the publication as defamatory and did not intend the publication to be defamatory. It is important to know what was their intention - whether they were acting maliciously - when it comes to deciding how much damages should be awarded. But, of course, the other side of this particular coin - the coin which says on one side "facts negative in malice reduce the damages" - is the principle that facts which tend not to disprove, but rather to establish, malice on the part of the defendants, aggravate rather than mitigate the damages. In other words, favourable, good conduct by the defendants reduces the award, but misconduct by the defendants increases the award, and that what the plaintiff says is the position here. The plaintiff says that far from the defendants being able to rely on their conduct to mitigate damage, rather their conduct aggravates the damages, and I am now going to tell you what the plaintiff relies on in the word "aggravating". Bear in mind when you are considering what aggravates, these are factors that cause additional injury to a plaintiff - additional hurt to his feelings; it is not the function of compensatory damages to punish the defendants. And so aggravating features only aggravate compensation - only increase the award of compensatory damages - if they have caused greater concern, worry, hurt, insult to the plaintiff. What the plaintiff relies on by way of aggravation are various aspects of the defendants really from first to last. You are entitled, when you consider your assessment of damages, to look at the whole of the defendants' conduct from the time of the original publication to the very moment of your vote.

'There are several aspects of the defendants' conduct which the plaintiff draws to your attention and which I simply tell you are capable, depending on your view of them, of aggravating the award. First, that it is suggested there was no sufficient basis for the original publication; not least, the defendants could and should have asked the plaintiff for his comment in advance of publication; not least in the light of the Kray apology two years earlier, when in the final paragraph, the defendants undertook "not hereafter to publish offensive material defamatory to Mr Maxwell". Secondly, says Mr Hartley, this is compounded by the time of the second article because by then at least there are clear and strong denials from the plaintiff and Miss Hewitt and yet, apparently, no further checking of the truth of the story was done - certainly none of any value. Thirdly, this carelessness as to the truth, says Mr Hartley, is compounded yet further by the time of the Court of Appeal hearing at 2 o'clock on the Wednesday, the day of publication, 24th July, and Mr Hartley says all the defendants had is the essentially flimsy evidence of their source - they are reliant on a source who, in turn, is reliant on other sources, whom the defendants never contacted. As to that, the defendants say that they obtained the assurance of the source, both that his story was true and that he would, in due time, give evidence in support of it. Fourth, there was never any apology for the untruths - indeed there still is not. Rather, despite the denials, despite the back-tracking of the source as to his willingness to give evidence, there has been instead a plea of justification persisted in to the very end, with a repeated avowal of the truth of the original allegation. Fifth, it is a well-established principle that justification, like fraud, should not be pleaded unless there is clear and sufficient evidence to support it. Here, says Mr Hartley, even accepting that on the material available to the defendants there was a basis for pleading justification, certainly by the end of last year when the defendants knew that all three of their sources were unwilling to give evidence, the only honourable thing to do would have been to withdraw it. Instead they kept the allegation as part of their case until their own evidence began, knowing that they were going to refuse to reveal their source; they nevertheless persisted in the allegation, hoping to find material from somewhere to support it.

'Sixth, and finally, not only did the defendants behave lamentably by persisting in their assertion that the allegation about these payments was true, but they had the effrontery to counter-claim against the plaintiff to allege that he had defamed them by saying their allegation was a lie.

'I have set out for you the main aspects of the defendants' behaviour on which the plaintiff relies in asserting that this calls for a substantial award of damages, or aggravated damages, as sometimes it is called. Certainly if you were to conclude that the defendants have acted here with malevolence or spite so as to injure the plaintiff's feelings of dignity and pride, as it is sometimes put, if the defendants' conduct has made you indignant on the plaintiff's behalf at the injury done to him, then certainly you are entitled to award generous damages. Putting it slightly differently, if you conclude that the defendants have been high-handed, oppressive, insulting in their conduct in such a way as to increase the hurt to the plaintiff, if you think the plaintiff has suffered additional insult and injury through behaviour that you regard as disgraceful or monstrous, then it would indeed be proper to award very full compensation.

'Remember the other object of compensatory damages, besides consoling the plaintiff for the hurt to the feelings and reputation, is to vindicate his reputation. Mr Hartley read you a passage from one of the cases that went thus: "In case the libel driven underground emerges from its lurking place at some future date, he must be able to point to a sum awarded by a jury sufficient to convince a bystander of the baselessness of the charge." Now I remind you of some of the evidence in the case. There are really two basic aspects of the relevant evidence. So far as it concerns the plaintiff, what general reputation did he have

in the relevant area of his character which was attacked by these publications? How far did he feel injured and insulted by these libels and the defendants' conduct? And how also has the plaintiff himself behaved? Is there anything of significance to criticise in his behaviour? Because any misconduct by the plaintiff in the course of the proceedings will also operate to mitigate the damage in the case. I am not sure if I mentioned that as one of Mr Bateson's contentions, but if I did not, I should have done. If you think the plaintiff has been guilty of misconduct, then that mitigates the damages.

'Secondly, I shall turn to the evidence concerning the defendants. Have they or have they not behaved disgracefully? In particular what did they intend by these publications? And how do they seek to explain their attitude to the plaintiff and their publications and the continued avowal of the truth of these allegations?

'First the plaintiff and the evidence concerned with his reputation, behaviour and the like. Obviously so far as the plaintiff's own evidence is concerned, and indeed the plaintiff himself is concerned, you will ask yourselves: well, now at the end of the day, at the end of three weeks, what do we think of plaintiff? Do we regard him as somebody with a worthwhile reputation that he is entitled to protect? Is he somebody essentially genuine, or is he, as Mr Bateson suggests, ruthless and vindictive with a vast ego. Someone who did not like the pricks of a satirical magazine? You will want to ask yourselves: did Mr Bateson have a field-day with the plaintiff when he cross-examined him? Do you remember, all those days ago, he said he was going to, and I suggest it would be for the jury at the end of the day to decide whether he had succeeded in that. Did he? Did he show the plaintiff up as somebody not meriting any significant award of damages in this case? So far as the plaintiff's own evidence is concerned, I remind you only of a very, very small part of it. He is, as you know, a man of 63, happily married with seven children. He is undoubtedly a high-profile public figure, member of the Labour Party twenty-five to thirty years, MP for Buckingham 1964 to 70. For the last two years or more chairman of the Mirror Group Newspapers. He is chairman of two substantial public companies, including Pergamon Press. He was born in Czechoslovakia in 1923. His family having been destroyed by the Nazis on the continent, he came to the United Kingdom in September 1940 as a soldier from France, served with obvious gallantry and was awarded the M.C in the field, as Lord Elwyn-Jones told you.

'As to these particular publications, the two articles with which this action is concerned, he took them, he says, very seriously indeed. He regards it as a monstrous lie to allege that people get peerages as a result of financial contributions. He says that goes to the heart of the political process, that nothing has done more damage to our public life than the suggestion that peerages can be bought, and he brings these proceedings for the protection of his reputation and the reputation and integrity of the political system. He regards these libels as accusing him of bribery. You know the interpretation he put upon them. He regarded the libels as gravely damaging to him and the Leader of the Opposition, destructive of the body politic of the country, could not be left on the record, gross allegation and lie, and he has been, he tells you, wholly shocked and distressed that the defendants have persisted in their allegations against him, and indeed at one stage said that he found it offensive, as do millions of people throughout the country.

'You may think that at least in part that constitutes something of an over-reaction. You may think that the body politic is not so fragile that it cannot withstand such a slur upon it as was constituted by these publications. You may think that it is a rather over-egged case as to the extent to which these publications have damaged his reputation. As to the extent to which they have injured his feelings, that is for you. It may be that some are more sensitive to hurt and insult than

others, and if that is right it may be that his feelings were more damaged than others would have been. But you may think anybody would indeed have felt a growing hurt as the words, now at last agreed to be untrue, the assertions about the payments to Mr Kinnock having been made, that those were persisted in for so long and the assurances given to the Court of Appeal that they were true and would be justified, and matters of that sort.

'Mr Maxwell told you that in fact not only did he not, as it is now agreed, make such payments, but he would not have done so. He was invited to make just such payments at the time of Mr Wilson's premiership. He was invited to contribute to Mr Wilson's private office, but he specifically refused to do that because he takes the view that the right course is that the Leader should get such finances as he needs from public funds, or at the very least from public bodies, like trade unions, and not from individuals specifically, because he himself says that it damages public life, that that can then in turn raise the suspicion that peerages are for sale. He has been, he says in short, most disturbed and troubled by the continuing course of these proceedings and the insults which the defendants have lost few opportunities of aiming at him.

'As to the plaintiff's general reputation, let me just tell you this. It is only relevant for your assessment of damages to the extent that it related to the same aspect or area of the plaintiff's character as is impugned by the libel. If a libel alleges bribery, then it is irrelevant that a plaintiff might have a thoroughly bad general reputation as a philanderer, as an adulterer, and if a libel were to allege of a woman that she was a prostitute, well, it would be quite irrelevant that she was also widely known as a confidence trickster. Do you see? Because it simply would not relate to the same sector of the person's reputation as the libel goes to, and that is why it would not be relevant in mitigation of damage.

'What is said of the plaintiff here, is that he is an ambitious self-publicist and a bully. Even if all that was made good, even if it was his general reputation, you might regard that as very much at the borders of relevance to the libels that are alleged here.

'Mr Bateson took the plaintiff, and indeed the rest of us, through what we call the defendants' bundle and there is no question at all but that there is a great deal more about Mr Maxwell published in the *Daily Mirror* than one usually finds about the proprietor or publisher in his daily paper. That was one matter which Lord Elwyn-Jones, the witness of immense distinction and matchless charm, you may think, told you about. He said that he had noticed Mr Maxwell's picture fairly frequently in the *Mirror* and he does not by any means hide his light under a bushel. He also, Lord Elwyn-Jones, you may think, offered a glowing testimonial to Mr Maxwell generally. I shall not remind you of it in detail. He has been a friend of the plaintiff and his family for some thirty years. What he said is that he has been particularly struck by the plaintiff's moral and physical courage.

'It was put to Mr Maxwell that on the very day, I think I am right in saying, the miners' strike came to an end, look how half the centre page of the *Mirror* appears devoted to publicising the publisher Mr Maxwell with President Zhivkov. Mr Hartley procured the rest of the paper and you may think that the criticism is perhaps less than wholly fair, because other pages, as I recollect the first two pages of that issue of the *Daily Mirror*, gave full and ample coverage to the ending of the miners' strike. But the second aspect of that article which was the subject of evidence was this: Mr Ingrams contends that Mr Maxwell has indeed exploited his position in the *Mirror* to advance his own personal standing and his own business interests. He uses that article as an illustration, because what he says is that he seeks to secure business advantages by writing propaganda for the leaders of these foreign governments. He says of this article: here is President Zhivkov, a dictator of the worst type, a murderer, and that it is a thoroughly undesirable thing for this sort of propaganda,

for such an odious regime, to be included in the *Mirror* in order to advantage the plaintiff in his general business interests with the government of that country. By all means have some regard to that, but bear in mind this: this libel is not about, you may think, that aspect of Mr Maxwell's conduct or activities. It may be that the defendants could publish a quite different article. They could say: "Mr Maxwell behaves quite outrageously, giving propaganda to obvious, murderous, foreign dictatorships." If so, then we would need to look at that article very closely indeed and decide just exactly whether that is the true interpretation to put upon that article and its place in the *Mirror*. But that is, you may think, rather on the fringes of this case.

'I pass to Mr Hird's evidence. He has been a journalist for ten years. His particular area of interest is financial and political investigative journalism. He says that he has known of the plaintiff's general reputation for some eight years in those circles. He tells you that that reputation is essentially that the plaintiff controls the *Mirror* for his own personal and, more particularly, business interests to a far greater extent than other publishers do. Further, that he has a general reputation for dealing rough-handedly with his employees. He agreed, when he was cross-examined, that Mr Maxwell, when he took over the *Mirror*, inherited a very substantial problem of overmanning that had to be coped with, but said that it did not need to be dealt with as it was by confrontation, and that there was a solution available by negotiation with unions, but he suggests Mr Maxwell chose to impose rather than to negotiate a solution. I remind you of one other aspect of it which goes to a rather different question at a rather later stage, because he not only practises investigative journalism, he teaches it too. Mr Hartley asked him about what he taught, and he said he teaches journalists to check their sources, that is very important. "What you must really try and do is to try and check independently with another source or with documents." He also said it is his policy to confront the person about whom you are going to make a critical statement, to give that person an opportunity to deal with it.

'As to what he said about Mr Maxwell's dealing rough-handedly with employees, Mr Bateson would suggest that that is very much all of a piece with the answer that Mr Maxwell gave to the Anglia interviewer, and you remember that was back in May 1984. During the course of a long interview he was asked by the interviewer: "One of your senior executives said to me the other day that he thought you were, to use a lovely phrase, as tough as old boots, the toughest man he has ever met." To which Mr Maxwell replied: "Really? I wonder why he said that. He had been kicked too many times, perhaps." Lord Elwyn-Jones said he regarded that as, on the face of it, bad staff relations, but perhaps one knows altogether too little to know quite what was meant by all that. Mr Bateson would suggest too, I think, that it is also all of a piece with the sort of hectoring or perhaps the sort of stance he adopted towards the news that Mr Kinnock was not coming to his party, namely: "Tell him if he does not come to my party, we will not go to his Africa party." Again something of the arrogance of success, of having one's own way perhaps too often in life.

'Against the view of the plaintiff, not only is there Lord Elwyn-Jones, who speaks volumes for him as a friend and as a remarkable success in life, but also Mr Young's evidence. He was, I think, the very last witness called. He was the general secretary of BALPA, that is the airline union, has been for a dozen years, and he has known the plaintiff for that period. He has got experience of the plaintiff in these industrial negotiations, and one particular contact was negotiating the move of British International Helicopters from British Airways to the plaintiff's own Group. He said he found the plaintiff very pro-union, 'a very, very tough negotiator, a man who focuses very clearly on his objectives and makes it very clear where he stands. He takes into account, however, the interests of the other side. He wants to ensure that the other side also reaches their goal, and once the principal deal is settled, then he is very generous with the small print, which is also important to unions.' The small print being of course the details of the deal. He said that before that transaction he told a number of senior trade union figures, who had closer relationships with the plaintiff, that he was going to be negotiating with the plaintiff, that all these senior trade union figures advised Mr Young that he was a tough man but on the whole all his companies prospered; he provided security of employment and created fresh employment. His own experience of the plaintiff is that he has kept his side of the bargain absolutely, and he for his part does not believe the plaintiff has a general reputation as a self-publicist. What does all that come to? You may think it is plain that the plaintiff does indeed have a driving will and perhaps a fairly relentless ambition to prosper and succeed in life and become a substantial public figure of influence and standing, both in the Labour Party and the affairs of the nation generally. No doubt on occasions all that makes him act immodestly, unpleasantly, on occasions ruthlessly and even threateningly.

'On the other side of the coin, as Mr Hartley says, you have got a man who, some may think to his considerable credit, has pulled himself up by his boot straps and has done well not only for himself but his companies and his country, a creator of employment, a creator of profits with British business. How far any of that really assists you in this case by way of mitigation or aggravation of damages is of course entirely for you. Nobody of course suggests that Mr Maxwell has a general bad reputation for seeking to realise ambitions, like to become a peer, by improper financial inducements, let alone a general bad reputation for bribery or anything akin to that. If you are looking for knights in shining armour, you may doubt whether you will find them on either side of this court.

'Mr Bateson criticises the plaintiff's motives for bringing this action. He invites your attention to the extract from the May 1984 Anglia TV interview. I will not read it again, but the crunch lines are, "I am one of those that he" - that is Mr Ingrams - "knows that if he steps out of line he will be swatted like a fly, that's it." Then the last answer: "I did it not for myself but for many hundreds of other people who have been hurt and have not the ability to hit back, I do it for them." So Mr Bateson says that there you have two wholly improper reasons for bringing libel proceedings against *Private Eye*, and certainly reasons which detract from the plaintiff's avowals that he is much injured in his own feelings: one reason being to swat Mr Ingrams like a fly, the other being to avenge many hundreds of others who cannot avenge themselves. Mr Bateson also reminds you, as I already have, of what the plaintiff said about how he was seeking to protect the political system, the reputation of the body politic. I have already suggested that that might be thought to be a rather farfetched and unnecessary object, and Mr Bateson says that you should accordingly conclude that the plaintiff is not entirely genuine as to his assertions as to the extent of his hurt and injury in the case.

'Another criticism that Mr Bateson advances against the plaintiff, and particularly as to his conduct of these proceedings, is the plaintiff's strenuous efforts through counsel to enforce here the disclosure of the defendant's sources. Mr Bateson says that for one newspaper proprietor to do that against another is unthinkable, it is disgraceful, and indeed I think I rightly recollect that Mr Hird expressed the opinion that it was disgraceful that the plaintiff should have sought to get the defendants to disclose their sources. Mr Bateson says that it is a measure of the plaintiff's vindictiveness and of his hatred of *Private Eye* that he should have done all that.

'Mr Hartley, on the other side, describes Mr Ingrams' stance, and no doubt Mr Silvester's stance too, in regard to non-disclosure of sources, invoking that ethic of the journalist's profession, as sanctimonious.

'You may think perhaps the epithets of both sides are rather extreme. One knows how sensitive journalists are to the protection of their sources, and you may think that sanctimonious is putting it too high as a criticism of that stance. But equally, you may think, that Mr Maxwell, albeit a newspaper proprietor, when his own personal reputation is at stake is entitled to avail himself of the proper processes of the courts, which is all he was doing, in order to seek to persuade the court that justice in the action could only be done by a ruling that the defendants should disclose. In fact the court very narrowly, I may say, disagreed with that, but is he really to be regarded as having misconducted himself for making the applications?

'I come then to the defendants' evidence, as to how they have conducted themselves and obviously particularly Mr Silvester, and yet more importantly perhaps, Mr Ingrams. Let us take Mr Ingrams first. He was editor, as we all know, for twenty-four years until last month - I think almost from the very start. He told you about the policy and aims of *Private Eye*. Perhaps I can paraphrase it thus: to puncture pomposity and expose hypocrisy. He said that it is a satirical magazine, it makes fun of public figures, it attacks those set in authority over us, it is concerned to expose humbug and indeed to expose more serious misconduct than that. It has no political affiliation. It has to its credit a number of exposures involving political figures and public scandals. He mentioned two: the Jeremy Thorpe case, and the architect, the Poulson, case. Many of us might well think that there is indeed a place in our society, in Fleet Street, for such a magazine, and we might well be prepared to look with some considerable indulgence upon it. It fulfils perhaps a valuable function and has made some notable contributions to upholding values and exposing corruption. Mr Ingrams says that the contents fall into two basic categories: first, jokes, teases, political satire, humour of one kind and another; secondly, the stories, by which he means of course these various exposures and criticisms of various sorts. Perhaps one of the problems is that the categories are not as distinct as they might be. What in one section may be intended as a joke, may all too easily be taken seriously by a reader and understood in a libelous sense.

'Mr Ingrams tells you that *Private Eye* has never deliberately published an untruth, if one puts to one side the various expressions of retraction and apology that Mr Ingrams says were insincere and inaccurate. Sometimes, he said, what were intended as jokes were taken seriously; sometimes *Private Eye*'s sources, or indeed the sources' own sources, got things wrong, perhaps on occasions even made things up, but *Private Eye* for its part, and he for his part, believe all that they print. So far as the position generally goes, you are entitled to bear in mind the picture which emerged from consideration of the defendants' counter-claim, even though of course it is now abandoned and dismissed. That counter-claim brought to light fifty-three instances over ten years of apparently a total retraction and apology in respect of published libels, what Mr Hartley in opening this case to you called a litany of lies.

'Let me say a word or two about that counter-claim. It was brought, Mr Ingrams accepted, as a tit-for-tat in response to the plaintiff's claim. Now, it is a matter for you how you regard the bringing of such a counter-claim, and indeed the persisting in such a counter-claim until so advanced a stage of the proceedings. It was abandoned, was it not? I think last week. But you would be entitled, to regard it as a thoroughly ill-judged impertinence, and you may think that it was wholly misconceived, based, as it was, on the untenable proposition that because a lie is a deliberate untruth, therefore an article in *Private Eye* is not a lie, unless Mr Ingrams himself, or just possibly one of his more regular staff, actually knows it to be untrue. You may have thought, from first to last, that a lie is a lie is a lie, and what starts as a lie is not in some mystical way purified by its appearance in *Private Eye*. It does not cease to be a lie because it is fed down a chain of informants, sources or gossips, to the point where Mr Ingrams himself may well be misled into believing it and publishing it. Well now, of course the counter-claim has gone, none too soon, you may think. As to that, I suggest that all you should infer from the abandonment of the counter-claim is the defendants' own final realisation that it was a nonsense for the reason that I have just sought to explain.

'What significance, then, is left in this aspect of the case? You will remember that a great deal of the very long cross-examination to which Mr Ingrams was quite properly subjected went to the counter-claim, to show that the plaintiff was quite justified in saying that this particular article was another whopper and that *Private Eye* should be called Public Lie. Indeed, it is up to you to decide, not only did Mr Bateson have a field-day with Mr Maxwell, but did perhaps Mr Hartley have a field-day with Mr Ingrams? But the relevance of all that, those very many hours of cross-examination, really is this: that it goes essentially to Mr Ingrams', and to a much lesser extent Mr Silvester's, credibility, their credit, that means their reliability in your minds. It can affect the extent to which you think you can rely upon them as witnesses of truth.

'Of course the fact that *Private Eye* published defamatory untruths 53 times in ten years - no doubt considerably more often when one takes account of the many people who of course do not sue - does not mean that they know that they are publishing, and intend to publish, libels and lies. You have to look, of course, at the history of these libels in the context of ten years of publishing, that is to say, of some eight to ten thousand pieces of the sort which attracted these fifty-three claims. A large number of those eight to ten thousand articles would, as Mr Ingrams made plain, themselves have been critical to the point on many occasions of being defamatory. So look at it in context which dilutes, does it not? the effect of those earlier libels, and it is clear of course that by no means all of those involved in any misconduct on the

Defendants' part, let alone that they knew that they were publishing untruths. Mr Ingrams says, on the contrary, the paper depends for its survival on the confidence of its readers, and if it publishes too many untruths then that confidence is lost. No doubt there is some truth in that, but of course you can also bear in mind that readers from time to time enjoy reading material to someone's discredit, and no doubt some of these many articles are bound to prove inaccurate and this, says Mr Hartley, is clearly a high risk publication which devotes no less than 30% of its revenue to paying libel damages and costs.

'You are certainly entitled to have regard to the fact that some of at least 53 apologies appear to indicate, you may think, clear misconduct by the defendants in the past. I am certainly not going to go through those articles again. From time to time you may think it is pretty plain that *Private Eye* pursues a campaign against somebody. The Harold Evans apology refers to a campaign of malice and denigration. The Ian Coulter apology refers to what, as Mr Hartley describes it, was the despicable and disgraceful feature that the magazine published Mr Coulter's private telephone number after he pointed out the falsity of the allegations, and unsurprisingly, no doubt inevitably, malicious people made phone calls to the great distress of his family. You may think that was a wholely shocking way for the defendants then to have behaved.

'From time to time, also, *Private Eye* actually admit to failing to make the checks that they could and should make to verify the accuracy of their articles. One such is the Lord Goodman apology. "We published both these references to Lord Goodman without making any of the checks we could and should have made to verify their accuracy." Another is the Penelope Keith apology. The paragraph just over halfway down it: "Despite the serious nature of the allegation it was accepted that no attempt had been made to verify it before publication." From time to time also the defendants have to admit to publishing for a wholly improper purpose. Lady Havers, an

apology: "A complete fabrication, and its purpose" - I am reading from the second paragraph - "its purpose was moreover to embarrass the Attorney General. It should never have been published."

'Of course Mr Bateson is right to say, and I emphasise, that you must on no account award damages to the plaintiff in this action for misconduct and libels committed against others in past years. Really these articles and the whole cross-examination over the days that it took go as I have said, to the defendants' credit. In so far as you regard their explanation of all these matters in the witness-box as being wholly candid and truthful, well, that no doubt reflects well to their credit so far as their reliability as witnesses in this case is concerned. But just reflect on this one other aspect of the evidence adduced upon the counter-claim: the advertisement taken in the *Evening Standard* by way of an apology to Sir James Goldsmith, and the reference to Mr Ingrams having said on BBC television, as he said in this court: "*Private Eye* would sometimes publish apologies or retractions not because what it had originally published was untrue but because *Private Eye* did not have the resources to prove it in court." One may add: not only on occasions they did not have the resources, but on other occasions they could not persuade the sources to prove these allegations for them. No doubt it is perfectly correct and not ultimately in any way to the defendants' discredit to say that from time to time apologies, by the facts of life - certainly the facts of publishing life - have to be made insincerely because the defendants have no option. They simply cannot afford to fight the case or cannot persuade the source to give evidence, and that one cannot properly in any way hold against the defendants. But you may think that Mr Ingrams and Mr Silvester were, perhaps, surprisingly and somewhat unattractively ready to believe their untested sources in preference to the powerful denials that these criticisms, that these defamatory articles, have attracted from the defamed subjects. You may think that the defendants are all too prone to prefer the evidence of their sources, untested in court, often unrevealed sources, and give too little weight to what others may say which is more to the credit of those defamed.

'Now let me turn to *Private Eye*'s publications in so far as they directly concern this plaintiff. The 1983 libel, the Kray twin libel. You will remember that Mr Silvester said that the plaintiff was the only person who ever complained about a look-alike, which has been a very long-running, a ten-year feature in *Private Eye*, and, said Mr Silvester, "These are jokes and the plaintiff simply could not recognise it." The suggestion is that his humour is wanting. But you may think it right to bear in mind also that, as we now know, this particular look-alike, unlike any of the others over the ten years, had in the last line of the joke letter: "I wonder if they have anything else in common?" Every other one of these look-alikes has the last line: "I wonder if they are by any chance related?" This one, you may think has that sting in its tail, a sting peculiar to that particular look-alike and, accordingly, you may think it rather less surprising that the plaintiff took strong exception to it, although of course Mr Silvester and Mr Ingrams regarded the apology as being if not a joke, at least likely to be regarded by many readers of *Private Eye* as so far over the top as to amount to a joke.

'I turn, fleetingly, to the Eichmann/Duke of Edinburgh look-alike. You saw the plaintiff's reaction to that. It is a matter for you as to whether or not you regarded him, as I suggest you must have done, as having been in obvious distress at that, and you may think that, even these many years on, it is really perfectly understandable for a sensitive person after the dreadful early history of his life. But really that has nothing, repeat nothing, to do with this case. You will clearly not, if you decide to award damages here, add one penny piece for that. That is not the subject of these proceedings, and I do not doubt you would accept Mr Ingrams' evidence that he had no knowledge of Mr Maxwell's early life and that

he most assuredly would not have published any such article, any such piece, had he appreciated that or appreciated the distress it would cause. As for these various look-alike articles which pretend to have been sent in by Ena B. Maxwell from the plaintiff's Oxford address: again, you may think that they are really of precious little importance. No doubt they were intended as teases and a minor sort of sting to the plaintiff, but you may think that they are essentially pretty innocuous.

'I come, therefore, to the first of these two articles. How did it come to be written and with what intention? Remember, those are important questions from the point of view of damages - as to whether the damages should be less or more. They have got nothing to do with whether the article is libellous. Mr Silvester wrote the article. He, I will remind you, is a young man. He was 27 last week, I think. He has been a political correspondent for *Private Eye* since June 1983, having previously, from time to time, contributed freelance articles, and having previously worked for a non-political, in-house Parliamentary magazine. He got the information for this first article from what he called a "highly-respected source" within the Labour Party, a prospective Parliamentary candidate who was privy to what went on in Mr Kinnock's office, and who used occasionally to advise members of that office on various matters. And so far as that source was concerned, he told you, you may think, essentially consistent things about him, although Mr Hartley you heard criticise that evidence. He said that the source told him that he in turn had two sources: one was Mr Kitson, who told him how the payments were arranged, how Mr Maxwell channelled the funds through Mr Kitson's own union; and the other source was himself within Mr Kinnock's office. He told you that Mr Kitson had told his source that he, Mr Kitson, had got Mr Maxwell to organise and subsidise the Moscow trip. You may think that not only are you bound as a matter of law to treat all that as untrue, but that little could be clearer than that it is untrue, and you will remember that Mr Kitson was recalled and in fact said he never spoke to the plaintiff about these trips, ever, and, what is more, Mr Kinnock was in Moscow before he, Mr Kitson, ever knew he was even going there. So you really may think that this has to be, as it is accepted to be, a thoroughly false story. But I am at the moment reminding you of how Mr Silvester indicated it came to be written.

'That is how it came to be written, in reliance on that source, who, in turn, was reliant on his sources. Mr Silvester did not intend to suggest bribery or anything like that. He regarded it as a fact of modern political life, that people who make donations to political parties receive honours, and he made the comment he made in the final paragraph, bearing in mind his general knowledge of the Honours system. He knew generally of the plaintiff's contributions to the Labour Party and, indeed, of some payments to the Boundary Commission Fighting Fund, and he said that all affected his view of the matter. But he told you when he was cross-examined that the last paragraph was not intended to suggest a bribe, that the intention of the article was simply to draw attention to the relationship between the plaintiff and Mr Kinnock, which he regretted. He said that he believed that all the plaintiff's conduct is improper, in the sense that it exploits his position to his own advantage and to advance himself in the world. He believes the plaintiff was seeking a peerage. He believes he is a very cynical man. He believes that the plaintiff is acting for the improper motive of trying to obtain a peerage. He indeed, despite all, is not prepared to apologise. He believes to this day in his source. His source, he said, has been consistently reliable over the years, and he has every reason to believe this source, and so you may think he is, in effect, re-asserting the truth of the article even though he has not spoken to the source's sources and, instead, is dependent on the single source.

'As to the second article, so far as Mr Silvester is concerned, he had no personal responsibility for it, or the cartoon. He told you that the second article was written by a freelance, that is to say, it was sent in as a completed article by a move in the plaintiff's own *Daily Mirror* offices and it was simply published, although he, Mr Silvester, knew in advance that it was going to be. We are not sure who was responsible for including the phrase "which Maxwell lamely denies financing", but you may think it more probably somebody in *Private Eye* than the mole, because it would be somebody in *Private Eye*, you may think, who would be having in mind the letter which Mr Maxwell wrote by way of that denial.

'Mr Ingrams' evidence about the first article was that he would have seen it before it was published, and discussed it with Mr Silvester. He regarded it as a convincing sort of story, likely to be true. He did not regard it as of great importance. He was aware that Mr Maxwell had been a long-time benefactor of the Labour Party and it did not seem to him at all remarkable that he had made those payments. He had always thought of the plaintiff as a sugar daddy to whom the Labour Party could turn if it was a bit short of cash, and he said that both stories really were attacks on Mr Kinnock rather than Mr Maxwell, and Mr Kinnock was being presented in a poor light as associated with an undesirable such as the articles presupposed the plaintiff to be. And all it was saying about the plaintiff was that he was doing what he always did, which was to be a sugar daddy. He said that there was no suggestion intended or implicit in the article, so far as they were concerned, as to an impropriety, an improper motive, on Mr Maxwell's part. He did not intend to defame the plaintiff; rather, the article was directed at Mr Kinnock because it was in Mr Kinnock's interest, as he, Mr Ingrams, perceived them, to keep Mr Maxwell at arm's length. Mr Maxwell had had a "checkered career" as he described it, was a strong opponent of the printing unions, had a bad image in the Labour Party and was somebody Mr Kinnock would have been well advised to keep at a distance. He said - and you may remember this rather throwaway line in his evidence - "The only thing the plaintiff has done well was in regard to Oxford United Football Club. Nothing else springs to mind." You may think perhaps all three of the main witnesses - Mr Maxwell, though perhaps - it is a matter for you - more obviously Mr Silvester and Mr Ingrams - spared few opportunities of taking a cheap point, making a jibe in the opposite direction, that little charity was displayed, little thought was afforded to anybody else's reputations that might be at issue. Mr Ingrams says that he was not intending to suggest, and indeed still does not suggest, any improper motive in the plaintiff at all for making these various payments.

'As to the second article, Mr Ingrams himself suggested the image for the cartoon, and again, although he regarded it as a much more interesting story than the previous one because he thought it highlighted the relationship between the plaintiff and Mr Kinnock and again it seemed convincing, he did not regard it as a story of any real importance.

'As I have told you, Mr Silvester persists in asserting his belief in the truth of the story. Mr Ingrams, likewise, continues to assert the truth of the story. He says that the source has always stuck to his guns and has not backtracked. He believes the story is still, to this day, in substance correct. He thinks it an obligation that he should come to court and contest the action on that basis: he believes his source to be a man of principle. What are you going to make of all that? As I told you, for the purposes of this action you are bound to treat the story as untrue. It would be for the defendants to prove its truth, and there is not one single word of evidence before you which supports it; on the contrary, there is a great deal of evidence which indicates that it is wholly untrue. You remember all the early witnesses were called specifically to show that it was a false story. Mr Kitson himself; Mr Timpson, the Executive Financial Secretary of the Transport & General Workers' Union,

who said that it was absolutely impossible for any payment to have been channelled through that union; Mr Clements who, likewise, told you, as the executive officer in charge of Mr Kinnock's office, that the plaintiff, to his knowledge, has paid no funds at all, whether directly or through the Transport & General Workers' Union, and that the story which the defendants also particularised, about there being some unspent surplus from Moscow, was again simply a falsity.

'The defendants have chosen not to reveal the source. That is their right. Their right, as I ruled upon it and as the Court of Appeal ruled upon it too, although a fairly borderline decision. There is, as we know, this well recognised journalistic ethic which enjoins against the disclosure of sources lest they dry up. But of course the result of all that is that it is quite impossible to test the accuracy of Mr Ingrams' and Mr Silvester's assertion that this source is indeed reliable, as well placed, and as much a man of principle as they assert. You may think it is all too easy to assert all that, and then hide behind the refusal to name them.

'On the defendants' evidence here, the source gave an assurance that he would give evidence on their behalf in support of their plea of justification. He then, on the defendants' evidence, changed his position on that at the end of last year, together in fact with the two other sources - the sources for the second story, the Party story - and yet this is a source who you are asked to accept as one who has never wavered or backtracked. He certainly wavered and backtracked as to his preparedness to give evidence, did he not? It is very easy for the source to assert this, that and the other on the basis that he will not be required to emerge from his cloak of anonymity and face cross-examination in open court, as the plaintiff and his witnesses have done. Whatever you think of the refusal to name the source, what really may surprise you is less that the defendants have refused to name him, even though he might be thought to have exonerated them from keeping his identity a secret when he assured them, according to Mr Silvester, at the time when the matter was before the Court of Appeal last year, that he would give evidence. At that stage he appeared to be prepared to emerge from his burrow. Despite all that the defendants still will not name him, still apparently prefer his account, wholely untested as it is by cross-examination, and dependent as it is, at least substantially, on the reliability of yet another source. They prefer that, nevertheless, to the evidence that you have heard from all these various witnesses called. And on that basis they actually go as far as to say, "Mr Kitson is a perjurer. All these others are perjurers." They still believe their witness.

'It is all very well to run a high-risk business, as you may think *Private Eye* is, and to accept, as *Private Eye* does, from freelance journalists stories that their own newspapers regard as too risky to run, but their policy is publish and be damned. You may think it requires that they should follow two other principles too. They should accept two other cardinal rules of responsible journalism. First, they should check their sources. I have reminded you of what Mr Hird said about that: "Did they do that, do you think, sufficiently here?" Secondly, because inevitably, high-risk or not, mistakes are going to be made and untruths are going to be published, they should retract and apologise, correct the mischief as soon as possible. You will remember weeks ago Mr Foot said he was all in favour of good, strong, satirical journalism, but even satirists get their facts wrong on occasions and, if so, they should print an apology and retraction. The simplest way is, if mistakes are made as is inevitable, to correct them as soon as possible. Did the defendants follow those tenets, or have they, as the plaintiffs suggest, high-handedly clung to their belief in their hidden source, in much the same way as they have continued to put question marks over a number of other libel victims who thought that they had been completely vindicated by the apologies you have seen? Is that perhaps all of

a piece with the question mark that they have put over Mr Grant? Not a word of evidence called to support that part of their case.

'I move much more briefly to the second article. By the time of the second article the plaintiff and Miss Hewitt had written their own strong denials. In the first place, he did not like his name being misspelled. One can very well understand a moment of pique, but for it to colour, as Mr Ingrams said the misspelling of his name did colour, his whole approach to that letter might betray, you might conclude, the sort of vanity and self-importance that Mr Ingrams would have been all too alert to puncture in another. What else did Mr Ingrams say about this letter? Why in the face of it did he publish the second article, containing, as it did, the re-assertion of the truth of the first, as he accepts it did? Because, he said, he regarded Mr Maxwell's letter as "huff and puff", but also as a threat that he would sue, and so he, Mr Ingrams, or *Private Eye*, returned to the attack to demonstrate to the plaintiff that: "We were not going to be threatened. To stand up to the bully boy. To show that we were not going to be silenced by him." And when asked what he thought of that letter and the enclosed apology, you will remember, he regarded them as Mr Silvester did too, as containing wholly outrageous demands. Mr Silvester said that he thought that the demands for damages and costs, £10,000, was outrageous. He thought it was outrageous to suggest that "freebies" meant "bribes", and he thought it was outrageous to attempt emotional blackmail on *Private Eye* by citing the Ethiopian Appeal fund.

'I suppose one reaction that the letter could have elicited, but clearly did not, was, "Dear Mr Maxwell, your letter was quite outrageous. We did not for a moment intend to suggest bribery or any other misconduct, and you are quite wrong and oversensitive to suggest that we did. £10,000 is a ludicrous amount. We would be prepared to pay £500 or some other such sum, if any, and call it a day." But that was not the course here chosen.

'I pass then, finally and yet more shortly, to

the additional facts that you need to be reminded of as to the, so to speak, third stage of publication, the hearing before the Court of Appeal at two o'clock on the Wednesday when that second article came out. Mr Ingrams, we know, was in the country and, substantially, was entrusting the conduct of the injunction proceedings to Mr Silvester in London, though you may think that they would be likely to have kept in very close contact and Mr Ingrams does not, I think, suggest otherwise. Mr Silvester swore the affidavit. Mr Silvester tells you - it is entirely for you whether you accept it - that between the date of the original publication and the affidavit he checked with the source, who gave him those additional details, re-affirmed the truth and reliability of the story and said that he would indeed be prepared to give evidence in support of it. By this stage, as you know, not only had the plaintiff written his letter of denial but he had of course issued the writ, which is a necessary start to any such proceedings. Even if exemplary damages, to which I shall come in an instant, are not appropriate in your judgement in this case, you will have to consider whether and to what extent the defendants' conduct of the Court of Appeal proceedings, their decision to resist them in these terms, their decision to ensure by that that the rest of the issue was published, went out to the readers - to what extent, if at all, that all tends to add to the insult, increase the injury and inflate the damages.

'Before you consider exemplary damages at all, decide, I would suggest to you, how much compensatory damages to award, assuming, as all my directions on damage do assume, that you get as far as question three. I have already told you a certain amount about exemplary damages and, not least, that they are only very rarely awarded. It is only most exceptionally that it is both possible in law, and appropriate in fact, to award them. And there are, as I mentioned, the three basic conditions that have to be satisfied. First, that the defendants knew that the article complained of was defamatory and untrue, in other words, that it

was an unjustified libel; or were reckless whether or not that was so. By "reckless" I mean this: that the defendants shut their eyes deliberately to the truth, or, suspecting that the article was defamatory and untrue, deliberately refrained from taking obvious steps which, if taken, would have turned that suspicion into certainty. The second condition is that the defendants published because they took the view that, in a broad sense, it would pay them to publish and to risk the consequences in terms of a libel action and a damages award. And, third, that the sum that you have decided upon as compensatory damages is not sufficient to punish and deter, so a larger award is necessary. So you would then add to the compensatory damages enough to make the total award - that is compensatory and exemplary damages - large enough to make an example of the defendants for such monstrous misconduct. As Mr. Bateson says, and I remind you again, it is a Draconian measure and it is anomalous in that the money, the additional money, goes to the plaintiff because there is nobody else for it to go to.

'Remember when you consider those questions - and particularly requirements one and two - you must bear in mind that they are serious allegations and you should look for a high standard of proof. The plaintiffs must prove a standard commensurate with their seriousness. You should then look for clear and cogent evidence. You ask yourself: are the facts such that you are driven to infer that those conditions have been satisfied, that the defendants really have behaved in that way? I have aleady ruled that the only publication in respect of which you would here be entitled in law to conclude that those conditions had been satisfied and that exemplary damages should be awarded, is the publication resulting from the distribution of the rest of the second issue of *Private Eye*, that is to say, the copies still undistributed when at two o'clock on the Wednesday afternoon in the Court of Appeal the defendants successfully resisted the plaintiff's attempt to get an injunction. So you ask yourselves: as at that time did the defendants either know or - because I do not suppose for a moment you could be satisfied that they knew the articles at that stage were untrue - were they reckless as to that as at the time the matter was before the Court of Appeal? And ask yourselves also: did they nevertheless resist the injunction because they considered that in the long run it would pay them, that they would save more by fighting off the injunction and saving the remaining copies, allowing them to be distributed and sold, than it would cost them when the day of judgment, the day of reckoning, arrived on the plaintiff's libel action?

'If you think Mr Ingrams is less guilty, misconducted himself less than Mr Silvester, it is Mr Ingrams as one of the defendants who is entitled to the benefit of that. You decide exemplary damages, as I told you yesterday, by reference to the least guilty defendant. Mr Bateson suggests that at the highest you should conclude that Mr Ingrams or, indeed, Mr Silvester were careless and that they should have taken more care, and if that is all, that falls short of recklessness. But Mr Hartley says that uncertain circumstances what otherwise might only be carelessness, becomes recklessness if those circumstances cry out for the most thorough and obvious checking, which is not done. It is up to you to decide whether here it was done. Bear in mind that by the time the matter at any rate was finally decided by the Court of Appeal on the Thursday morning, not only were there the letters from the plaintiff and Miss Hewitt, there was also the telex from Mr Kinnock. That had arrived by the time the Court of Appeal gave judgment on the Thursday. Secondly, not only of course was the plaintiff asserting that these articles were untrue, the story about personal payments to Mr Kinnock were untrue, but he had actually issued a writ and he was prepared to give, as all such plaintiffs who try and get an injunction in the courts are required to give, a cross-undertaking in damages. This means: he was very much putting his money where his mouth was, because if he had succeeded in the injunction, if in the result those further copies of *Private Eye* had not gone out and so had cost the publishers a great deal of money, and if at the end of the day the publishers had justified the libel and won the case, then Mr Maxwell would have been bound, pursuant to that cross-undertaking, to pay that loss to them. And so at that stage you may think that he was very much backing, by that undertaking, his denial and it could not be regarded just as a bland denial, a gagging writ, or anything of that sort.

'As to the second requiremnt, as Mr Bateson rightly told you, the calculation, the attitude that it would in the long run save money, that in a broad sense it would pay them to get the rest of the issue out and pay damages, does not have to be a mathematical calculation; it is a broad calculation only. Remember what the position was as to the state of publication at two o'clock on the Wednesday. Mr Ingrams' evidence about that was that *Private Eye* is sent to the printers - put to bed - on the Monday. On the Tuesday, it is sent by the printers direct to the wholesalers, except for the, I think, 40,000 odd copies that the printers send to *Private Eye*, who themselves, send those out to the actual subscribers. And as at two o'clock on Wednesday, Mr Ingrams tells you that the bulk of the copies would already have been on sale but some would still have been with the wholesalers, not sent out to the retailers, and others would have no doubt been recoverable from retailers. He has since discovered - although of course he would not have known it at the time, nor would Mr Silvester, and so this is only the very roughest guide to the sort of calculations, if any, that might have been running through their minds - that had the injunction been given, it would have cost *Private Eye* about £10,000 in undistributed copies, but that would exclude such copies as might have been recoverable unsold from the retailers. And if and to the extent that copies from the retailers could have been recovered, then the cost to *Private Eye* would have been considerably more.

'Mr Silvester's affidavit set out the distribution pattern. In fact apparently 47,000 subscription copies; those would of course all have gone out. "Distribution of the wholesalers' copies will have been completed by six-thirty on the Thursday morning." So that is by first thing on Thursday morning all the wholesalers would have got rid of their copies to the retailers. What evidence is there about any such calculation? Very little direct evidence. What you have to consider, of course, is Mr Silvester's and Mr Ingrams' state of mind. They both told you that they were not resisting the injunction in order to ensure the further distribution of this issue of *Private Eye*.

"The plaintiff will contend [this is the top of that page] that in resisting the said application the defendants were concerned solely ..."
- I hope you wrote in the words "or mainly" -
"... to ensure the further distribution of copies of *Private Eye* even though they knew the said words to be false or were reckless as to their truth or falsity."

'Mr Hartley shows you what the turnover of the publishers was in the years 1982 and 1983, something over £1 milliom; and you see "Provision for Libel Costs and Damages", and the figures are given: something over £300,000 in each of those two years, representing in each case about 30 percent of the turnover. To a limited extent it seems to be on a rising scale, and what Mr Hartley says is that the defendants are not only a high-risk publication but they are selling reputations for profit. Whether or not that is generally a fair criticism is not really the critical point. The critical point is whether you think that is what the defendants were doing here. Are you satisfied, bearing in mind you really ought to be very sure of it before you award exemplary damages, that the defendants were in truth getting out the rest of this issue, effectively selling the plaintiff's reputation?

'Even if you decide that the defendants were acting in that sort of disgraceful way and therefore should be punished, then bear this in mind: it may be that the compensatory damages you are awarding will be punishment enough, and that is why the questions in respect of this second article, which is the only one that could attract an exemplary damage award, are framed as they are. Questions three and four - if you just look at the questions with me. "What sum," says question three, "do you award the plaintiff by way of damages?" Four: "What part, if any, of that sum relates to exemplary damages?" Because even if you decide that punishment is required, you may decide that the amount necessary for proper compensation of the plaintiff is sufficient and that therefore nothing is needed to be added by way of an additional exemplary damage award.

'But let me add just this: when deciding whether or not any exemplary damage award is needed, even if punishment is deserved, bear in mind not only the compensatory damage award for the second article, but also the compensatory damage award for the first article. Do you follow? Because basically it is the same general sting that the plaintiff asserts in these proceedings, and, in any event, bear in mind that even if you do add anything by way of an exemplary damage award, what you add must not be excessive. It is not an occasion to go, so to speak, through any roofs.'

After summing up for a complete day the judge adjourned to Friday morning.

He continued then:

'Members of the jury, would you be kind enough to take your question sheet. Now, it would, I think, be helpful if one or more of you write down a number of things after each question. Do you see the first question: "Are the words complained of defamatory of the plaintiff?" Write in there, I suggest: "If no, proceed no further. If yes, proceed." Those words in fact you can put after the first question for both articles. The second question: "Are those words substantially true?" I suggest you write down: "If yes, proceed no further. If no, proceed." Again, equally with the second article as the first. Now, after question three for the first article simply jot down: "Compensatory damages only." Now, for the second article, I suggest you bracket questions three and four. Luckily you have got a bit of space at the bottom of the page, because I suggest you write down these half dozen or so lines that I am going to dictate. I suggest this approach: decide first compensatory damage, then, taking into account the punitive affect of whatever compensatory damages you award for both articles, decide if any more should be added by way of exemplary damages. If so, decide how much more. Calling this additional sum, your answer to question three will be the sum you decide as compensatory damage for the second article plus, and your answer to question four will be. If you decide this is not a case for exemplary damages — this is the last sentence — then the answer to three is the sum you decide as compensatory damage and the answer to four is nil.

'Of course you approach all those questions in accordance with the full directions that I gave you yesterday and in part the day before, you appreciate that. That, members of the jury, is I believe all the help that I can give you in this case. If after you retire you think I can help any more, whether by reminding you of any of the evidence in the case, or by repeating or further explaining any of the direction that I have given, if you want any help at all beyond that that I have given you, well, then do not hesitate to write down what you want in the form of a question, send it out through your bailiff, it will come to me and we will bring it back into court and I will give you all such further help as I can. I do not suppose you will need it, but if you do, I am here and available to give it. Remember that.

'Take with you when you retire all your various bundles and documents. There is, I think, one loose document that it has been agreed shall go, that is the copy of the *Daily Mirror*, I forget the date, but you know when it is. You have got various copies of *Private Eye*. Take anything of that sort that you have had with you. If you have not already elected from amongst your number a foreman, be it a lady or a gentleman, I suggest the first thing you do when you retire is to do just that. There are really two objects in that: first, the foreman or forelady can, so to speak, organise your discussions, make sure anybody who wants to have a say has a chance to be heard, and generally give some order to your debate and consideration. The second function of the foreman of forelady will be when finally you return with your decisions, then the foreman will in fact on behalf of all of you answer these various questions.

'Some of you may have heard about what are called majority verdicts. If so, I would urge you to put aside all thoughts of any such verdicts, at least for some considerable time. This case, as Mr Hartley said, and Mr Bateson would not quarrel with this, is a serious and important case and it is very desirable, if possible, and there is no reason that it should not be perfectly possible, that all twelve of you agree upon your decision on all these questions, reach therefore a unanimous verdict, and I hope very much you will be able to do that. If not, well then the time may come when I will ask you to come back into court and I will give you further directions about that. But it would be some considerable time before I would think it right in a case like this to consider anything other than a unanimous decision.

CHAPTER FIFTEEN

Day 15

The fifteenth and final day dawned. The anxiety obvious on faces of both sides was beginning to diminish. There was lighthearted talk of relaxing weekends, drinks whatever the result, and a general sense of gratitude that Court Eleven at the far corner of the Law Courts would soon be someone else's concern.

Mr Justice Simon Brown welcomed the jury at the start of their big day. The six women had all decided it was an occasion for 'Sunday best' while two of the men broke the habit of three weeks and wore ties. The judge, his summing up behind him, made the issues clear: 'I suggest one or two of you write down what I am about to say so your task will become easier,' he said, knowing that much of the legal language of three long weeks had gone over their heads.

The first question they had to answer was: 'Are the words complained of defamatory? If your answer is No, proceed no further.' The second question: 'Are those words substantially true? If your answer is Yes, proceed no further.' Depending on the decisions, then would come the question of compensatory damages, only for the first and second articles. The judge went on: 'Then taking into account the punitive effect of whatever compensatory damages you award for both articles, decide if any more should be added by way of exemplary damages. If you decide this is not a case for exemplary damages, then the answer to question three is the sum you decide as compensatory damages and the answer to question four is nil.'

With that, he asked the jury to retire, taking with them the mountain of folders, magazines and documents they had been given. Immediately there was a loud interruption from the rear of the court, packed at that time with media people eager for the result. The jury members were stopped in their tracks. The judge was rendered speechless. For Stuart Holmes, champion of the Smoking Kills campaign, the moment he had planned had come.

Throughout the case there had been over a dozen people, mostly elderly men, who appeared to have season ticket status for the libel case in Court Eleven. Many of them, obviously retired, are regulars at the Law Courts and are very knowledgeable about legal matters. They enjoyed listening to the argument on the days the Appeal Court was brought into the action as well as the juicy evidence from witnesses. Although the 'Court Full' sign was never posted on the outside doors it was a case of standing room only on each day, with the regulars lining up before the court was opened. Stuart Holmes was one such regular. Ever since the Labour Party conference in the summer he had haunted Robert Maxwell over the advertising of cigarettes in his newspapers. For weeks he had encamped during daylight hours on the front steps of the *Mirror* building at Holborn. Each day of the court hearing he sat at the back in the same brown check overcoat, with an attache case full of handouts and his lunch in a paper bag.

Holmes chose the crucial moment of the retirement of the jury for his outburst. With his speech written on a minute scrap of white paper he shouted: 'Mr Maxwell is guilty of crimes against humanity. He is personally the cause of two thousand British deaths every week and is being bribed to keep this holocaust a low-profile issue. In referring to tobacco advertising and payments it would be wrong and insulting for a court of justice to turn a blind eye to a crime of gigantic proportions against the well being of a nation, while one of the culprits spends three weeks here progressing relative trivia.'

He managed to complete his message as he was hustled from the courtroom by a bailiff, the judge's clerk, and court ushers. The jury had to wait while the bailiff calmed matters in the corridor. Then they were on their way, the judge assuring them that such outbursts were not uncommon and should be ignored totally. It was 10.50 a.m.

Holmes was ushered back into court to face the wrath of Mr Justice Simon Brown. He was given three choices: Stay in court but promise not to utter one more word all day; leave the building and not return; or go to prison. He chose the first but refused, on the judge's request, to apologise for his outburst. The choices were then cut to the latter two. 'For how long?' he asked, when prison was mentioned again. 'That's it, I am not bargaining with you, you must leave the building immediately,' the judge commanded.

With Holmes outside in the cold, chatting to the photographers and television crews, for both sides inside the long wait began. Mr Maxwell returned to his office less than a mile away to await a signal that the jury were ready to return. *Private Eye* people - major shareholder Peter Cook, managing director David Cash, political writer and major witness Christopher Silvester - adjourned to the coffee shop in the crypt of the famous building. A small media circus followed them, to collect background notes for their stories and reports, once the jury's verdict was known. The man with his hands on the magazine's purse strings, the appropriately named Mr Cash, revealed there would be no Maxwellballs Fund to raise necessary money in the same way the Goldenballs Fund had allowed readers to help

Private Eye counter legal battles with Sir James Goldsmith some years earlier. The plan was a bumper Maxwell edition before Christmas which would sell at £1 a copy. With a slight increase in circulation from the publicity from the trial, perhaps £250,000 could be taken in sales alone.

A chain smoking Andrew Bateson led the return to Court 11 at 12.30, obviously with lunch in mind. The judge's clerk brought from Chambers the news that the jury had ordered food, so there would be no movement before 2.00 p.m. Lunch could be thirty minutes longer than usual.

The afternoon wait was clouded for a time by thick smoke, which darkened the long stone corridor. Had Stuart Holmes, the man who hates people inhaling smoke, got his own back by setting fire to the place ? No, some rubbish in an annexe had caught fire, but there was no cause for alarm. With so many satirists present there had to be the comment that the colour of the smoke might indicate the jury's mood — white for Maxwell, black for *Private Eye*. Peter Cook showed off his shirt, covered with coloured sketches of fish and such questions as: 'Do fish have lips?' Mr Bateson took this as the cue to explain in detail his love of, and expertise at, hunting, shooting and fishing. He did not hide the wish that he would prefer to be out in the cold with a gun in his hand rather than to be waiting for a jury which could well shoot him down in flames.

Forecasts of possible damages ranged from £20,000 by Cook and Cash, to £65,000 from the man from the *Daily Mail*. At 3.00 p.m. Peter Cook left, complete with small blue overnight bag, to spend the weekend with his mother in Hampshire.

Mr Bateson complained of being referred to in print as the Rumpole of the High Court. 'Could sue for defamation,' he said with a twinkle in his eye, bringing some light relief to the growing tension.

RIGHT: *Peter Cook after the action.*

At 3.35 p.m. the judge called counsel back to court to explain that news had filtered through that the jury had ordered tea. So what was to be done? he asked. Arrange, if possible at that late hour, hotel accommodation for the weekend? Sit late that evening in the hope there would be a result? Or call them back and explain that a majority verdict, preferably 10-2, would be acceptable? Both counsel

BELOW: Comment on the case from The Independent *immediately after the verdict.*
RIGHT: Peter Cook in original belligerent mood.

That's enough Private Eye lawsuits — New Ed.

Jane Ellison on the effects of the magazine's libel reverse

AT £255,000 costs and damages, *Private Eye* has just lost the most expensive libel action in the history of the organ.

Maxwell v Pressdram will certainly be the *Eye's* last great battle in the courts: not because the settlement has imposed any intolerable financial strain on a magazine whose libel fund stands at nearly £400,000; but because the *Eye* has changed its editor since the Maxwell case began.

No one doubts it has changed its character, too. Ian Hislop, successor to Richard Ingrams, regards libel payments as an unnecessary and expensive waste of money.

The wretched hacks of Carlisle Street are already reeling under the tiny supremo's new peremptory orders: "Check the facts". For 25 years no one has ever heard anything like it.

Richard Ingrams has always enjoyed an obsessive, uneasy fascination for lawyers. In *Who's Who* he lists litigation as his recreation. During his period as editor of *Private Eye* the magazine undertook some historic legal battles against Harold Evans, Desmond Wilcox and — most famously — Sir James Goldsmith.

In the latter case the *Eye* nearly went bankrupt. Staff worked for half their salaries to keep the magazine alive — unthinkable now in the *Eye's* new age of profit.

Did Ingrams know he would lose the Maxwell case? Almost certainly. The story turned out to be impossible to prove as Ingrams knew it would be. Why then did he go to court and turn down Maxwell's offer to settle the case half way through the hearing? Why did he print the story at all?

Ingrams has always believed that he has an instinct for the truth of a story however defamatory and however insubstantial in terms of the facts. If it sounds right, he will print it.

Facts, as *Eye* hacks often laughingly observe, can really spoil a good story. And even if the facts prove the story wrong...if it sounds right, there must be something to it. Ingrams believed that

Mud in the *Eye*: Cecil Parkinson and Sir James Goldsmith.

he could sense whether a story was "true" or not. This attitude often induced a sense of heady exhilaration in his toiling hacks. "Richard, I just can't manage to stand this one up," one would say. "But I'm absolutely sure it's right."

Ingrams would study the story and, after a few moments of concentration accompanied by a paroxysm of facial contortion, utter the famous reply: "Put it in." And sure enough, it would appear.

Many times his hunches were absolutely right. The risk paid off. It was the *Eye* which broke the story that Cecil Parkinson's secretary, Sarah Keays, was expecting

Unlike others on the *Eye*, Hislop checks his facts

the minister's child. The information turned up at Carlisle Street on press day, perfectly and professionally typed on a sheet of beige notepaper. The anonymous correspondent set out the facts in a cool and dispassionate manner. Was it true? Attempts were made to check the story but no one could confirm the facts. Ingrams decided to run it in the Grovel gossip column. It is a measure of his genius as an editor that he was absolutely right in his judgement. The next day Parkinson was on the radio, making an official statement. Has Hislop got that sort of nerve? Most people would say no. He is not a journalist and regards the hacks as lazy, expensive and dispensible. Unlike ev-

eryone else at *Private Eye* he is punctilious in checking his stories. Only one of his pieces has ever received a libel writ. Hislop provided so many affidavits that the plaintiff's case collapsed. Libel payments, to Hislop, are a nuisance and a waste of money.

Is he right? A great majority of the employees of the *Eye* would agree with him.

These days the organ is vastly profitable, through its steadily increasing circulation of around 250,000, its lucrative income through *Private Eye* books, and its comfortable ownership of the freehold of the listed Carlisle Street Georgian building.

Directors pay themselves around £40,000 a year; staff contribute to a pensions scheme. Hacks and contributors benefit from a yearly profit-sharing scheme after deductions for libel have been made.

In spite of a recent disastrous libel settlement for £240,000, staff enjoyed "bonus payments" of double their salary for 14 issues of the magazine.

But there is another argument which says that the *Eye* needs to undertake these judicial high-risk skirmishes in the High Court in order to justify its existence. In the past, the magazine's shoe-string irreverence gave credibility to its savage and satirical attacks on the great and the good. Since the *Eye* had nothing, it had nothing to lose.

It is one thing for *Eye* readers to sympathise with an attack on Robert Maxwell, a millionaire, for which the impoverished magazine has to pay up for many thou-

Ian Hislop, new editor of *Private Eye*.

sands of pounds. But the *Eye* has now joined the ranks for the wealthy itself. Its turnover is £3m a year. What the *Eye* is already learning, under its new editor, is that big-league profitability means playing by the legal rules it has in the past always been able to ignore.

When the *Eye* is rich, as it is now, it is worth sueing. In future

no story which does not satisfy Fleet Street libel lawyers is likely to get into the magazine. Hunches and instincts will be a thing for the past. The *Eye* never be the *Eye* again.

(Jane Ellison used to work for Private Eye until she wrote a critical article on the magazine earlier this year).

agreed on a majority verdict. 'All right, let's call back the jury,' said the judge.

With the most perfect timing the usher responsible for guarding the jurors pushed open the door just as the judge completed his instruction. 'The jury are ready with a verdict, my lord,' she announced. There was a unanimous sigh of relief. It was 3.50 p.m. — five hours since the jury had departed.

A breathless Mr Maxwell returned to court as the jury filed into the seats they had come to know so well, not a glimmer in any eye betraying their decision. The bespectacled young man who had been the first name to be called on the opening day, rose to his feet as foreman. The Judge's Associate asked for a straight Yes or No answer to the first two questions.

'Do you find the words complained of defamatory?' Yes.

'Do you find the words are substantially true?' No.

'Do you award compensatory damages for the first article?' £3,500.

'For the second article?' £1,500.

'Exemplary damages?' £50,000.

Mr Maxwell smiled in his seat, barely a foot from the jury box. David Cash, in his usual seat behind his junior counsel, Desmond Browne, and wearing the same multi-striped jacket which had been a feature of the case, drummed his fingers and muttered: 'Bloody hell, it's worse than I expected.'

The judge granted an injunction which, with words slightly amended by Mr Bateson and with the agreement of Mr Hartley, banned *Private Eye* from publishing 'the said words or words of the like effect defamatory to the plaintiff'. Mr Justice Simon Brown thanked the jury and released them to return to the Old Bailey where they could well be called up for more work. Robert Maxwell vs Pressdram Ltd and Another was over. The costs of around £250,000 would have to be met by the defendants.

Mr Maxwell rose to his feet and told a throng of reporters: 'I am delighted that I have been able, with the jury's help, to nail *Private Eye* for the lying organ that it is, and thereby to help the thousands of people, their families and friends, who have suffered over the years by being targeted and recklessly attacked. We have exposed once and for all that they will publish anything for profit. They don't check their sources. They don't have the guts to apologise and when they finally do, they say in a court of law that some of their apologies are insincere. I had no alternative but to bring this case. I am glad that a jury of twelve men and women has upheld my case and supported my allegation that *Private Eye* are liars and peddlers of filth for profit. Anybody who now distributes *Private Eye* will know the risks to which they are exposing themselves. I would draw their attention to evidence given by the Chairman of *Private Eye*, Mr Wigwam, that they do not check their sources.'

Mr Maxwell said that, as a publisher, he had been reluctant to try to force *Private Eye* to disclose its sources. But the magazine had named Alex Kitson as a source, and had 'maligned' Dr John Reid, prospective Labour Parliamentary candidate for Motherwell North, in the same way.

Asked what he would do with the £55,000, Mr Maxwell said it would go to charity, for the benefit of children and possibly to help AIDS research — 'It comes from an infected organ, so it is appropriate it should go to AIDS.'

Outside the court Mr Maxwell repeated his comments for the benefit of TV and radio reporters, who had been barred from the precincts of the court, and had to duck one more meeting with a placard waving Stuart Holmes. Ian Hislop, the new editor of *Private Eye*, laughed away Mr Maxwell's words. 'Remember, it's only £3,500 to Maxwell, the other £51,500 is a slap on the wrist,' said Hislop.

The only man missing was Lord Gnome himself, alias Richard Ingrams, who lists litigation as a favourite recreation in Who's Who. He stayed at home in Berkshire — 'probably in his wife's bookshop,' volunteered David Cash — from where he commented later: 'I was amazed at the amount of damages, in particular the amount of punitive damages. In my experience, and that is extensive, the punitive damages are the highest ever. In comparison to other awards this is one totally over the top.' He talked of a possible appeal.

And so the Big Top came down and his circus cast dispersed about its business. Day Fifteen, and one of the most sensational libel actions of recent years, was over.

CHAPTER SIXTEEN
Epilogue

Private Eye was always a cheap champagne. Now it has finally gone flat. Although, paradoxically, its circulation is at an all-time high, its decline has set in, not because of a deterioration in its standards and competence - that would be difficult to achieve - but because there is a changing mood in the country.

The *Eye* was a product of the sixties, publishing a kind of anarchic humour which flourished in that decade in the public schools and universities from which its editor and its main contributors sprang. The public-school boys who ran the *Eye* never grew up. Instead they grew old. They still offer obscenity, scurrility and libel, which may appeal especially to the younger reader, but over twenty-five years there has been a surfeit of it. Enough is enough, as once was said in another circumstance.

Though the *Eye* has brought some public or political scandals to light, these did not justify and cannot justify its continued existence. If buckshot is fired indiscriminately at a football crowd, the pellets will no doubt injure a hooligan deserving of injury. That cannot excuse loosing off a shotgun at every football match. A great many innocent people will also be wounded. By its policy of publishing - but hardly ever checking - every rumour or piece of tittle-tattle which comes its way, the *Eye* is bound, on occasions, to print something with a grain of truth in it, bound to hit someone with something to hide. Even so, its articles rarely contain a whole truth.

The most revealing day in court during Maxwell v Pressdram and Another was the one in which the 'litany of lies' was put to Mr Ingrams by Mr Hartley. By its willingness to wreck reputations or to damage the relationship between a man and his wife - read, for example, the *Eye*'s monstrous defamation of Lady Havers - the *Eye* created genuine fear among those in public life, in business, in journalism, in public relations, in politics, and even in the law, the church and musical world. It relentlessly pursued its victims and the more it pursued them the more there were potential victims willing to ingratiate themselves with the *Eye* in the hope of protection from its beady gaze. The article in *The Listener* which I quoted in my opening chapter was written by me because others hesitated to do so.

The *Eye* had become the Joe McCarthy of British journalism.

Now those who took the *Eye* to the peak by destroying others are making enemies among themselves.

Jane Ellison, whose article in *The Independent* I quoted in the introduction to this book, has published a remarkable account of these divisions in *The Tatler* where she provides a penetrating portrait of Richard Ingrams and a hilarious account of the preparations for his retirement lunch at the Grand Hotel, Brighton.

Some members of the staff, apparently, favoured a night out in Chelsea dancing to the sounds of the sixties, which is understandable, seeing that the *Eye* is a product of that era.

But Mr Ingrams thought otherwise. 'With the autocracy that he has ruthlessly exercised for twenty-five years,' Ms Ellison writes, 'Ingrams got his own way.'

No expense was spared for the outing, says Ms Ellison - 'but then, the *Eye* has always been lavish in treating its employees to a good time.'

In a devastating judgment, she recalls: 'As they chewed their way through the lamb everyone knew it was the end of an era ... The *Eye* is a self-regarding, self-obsessed small society; almost everyone who works for the magazine hated everyone else.'

Ms Ellison has no doubts that Ingrams was a great editor, a 'man of improbable and irresistible charm.' He enjoyed nothing more, it seemed, than to read his own obituary and he was, she says, one of the funniest men one could meet.

But funny, too often, at someone else's expense.

Mr Ingrams may chuckle over his own obituary. But the real obituary of *Private Eye* is being written elsewhere. Since the trial ended, I have received hundreds of letters, postcards and phonecalls from those who are delighted that it has at last received its come-uppance, just as McCarthy eventually did.

The time has surely come when the tyranny which the *Eye* imposes - the threat that those who stand up to it will become its target or subject to 'the curse of Lord Gnome' - should be resisted and defeated.

How can any responsible journalist continue to feed the *Eye* with malicious gossip which he cannot prove to the standards set by his own newspaper? How can self-respecting politicians continue to supply the *Eye* with paragraphs about those whom they dislike or envy without becoming like the *Eye* itself?

How can wholesalers continue to distribute a magazine which, while it may offer an indemnity against libel, cannot offer indemnity against exemplary damages? W.H.Smith has discovered that, which is why it has apologised to me for rejecting my request of 24 July 1985 not to distribute the *Eye* containing its libel upon me, agreed to pay £5000 to a charity of my choice, and undertaken not to repeat the libel.

How can insurers continue to insure the *Eye* against libel or retailers continue to stock it?

Most of all, why should any of the *Eye*'s loyal readers continue to remain loyal? The *Eye* has no useful purpose left. It does not inform, it insinuates. It does not educate, it destroys. If it entertains, its entertainment is a kind of moral pornography. It failed in its defence of my case against it because it had no defence, any more than it had a defence in the 53 cases which were put to Mr Ingrams by Mr Hartley.

Over the years, the *Eye* has gravely injured many reputations. That those injuries were falsely based was no compensation to the injured. It makes enormous profits from its sales and about 30 per cent of those profits are devoted to paying legal expenses for the libels which it has published. Those who buy the *Eye* must pay a premium on its economic price for the lies which they read in it. Its response to the £300,000 in damages and costs it will have to pay for libelling me was typical. It is producing a special edition at a price of £1 in order that the readers should foot the bill for its recklessness.

Before readers do that, out of a loyalty to those who forfeited any right to it a long time ago, they might look again at what Ms Ellison says the *Eye* spends its money on - it is, she said, 'always lavish in treating its employees to a good time' - and then keep their money in their pockets.

The 'Litany of Lies'

Richard Ingrams admitted that during the last ten years he had published 53 apologies, many of which involved the payment of damages. This was the 'litany of lies' on which Mr Ingrams commented during cross examinations: 'I would say, very roughly, that 75 per cent are genuine, and the others slightly more questionable.'

1. Dec. 12, 1976
Damages for conductor André Previn for alleging he did not know the score of Tchaikovsky's Sixth Symphony when he conducted the Philadelphia Orchestra.

2. Mar. 23, 1977
Damages for Lord Weidenfeld for suggesting he had attempted to ingratiate himself with Mr Harold Wilson by paying him £250,000 for the right to publish his memoirs so as to secure a peerage.

BOTTOM LEFT: *March 1977. Damages for former Tory MP Harold Soref.*

BELOW: *June 20, 1978. Damages for film Director Blake Edwards, husband of Julie Andrews.*

LEFT:
*Feb. 2, 1979.
Damages for Sir
Arnold Weinstock.*

3. Mar. 1977
Damages for former Tory MP Harold Soref for suggestions that he and his company, of which he was chairman, were attempting to break government trading sanctions against Rhodesia.

4. Apr. 10, 1977
Apology for Sir James Goldsmith for an article which referred to the Lord Lucan affair.

5. June 20, 1977
Damages for freelance journalist Bennie Gray.

6. July 1977
Damages for Lord Foot and John Ennals, then respectively chairman and full-time director of the UK Immigrant Advisory Service.

7. June 20, 1978
Damages for film director Blake Edwards, husband of Julie Andrews, for offensive references which *Private Eye* admitted had "no basis whatever in fact".

8. Jan. 16, 1979
Damages for then *Sunday Times* editor Harold Evans who complained he had been libelled several times.

9. Feb. 2, 1979
Damages for Sir Arnold Weinstock for suggestion that as managing director of General Electric Company he tried to force the government to use an American nuclear reactor.

10. Apr. 9, 1979
Damages for Advanced SOS Security Group Ltd, for an article said to have impugned the honesty and integrity of the company, its directors and employees.

11. June 26, 1979
Damages for wine expert Allan Hall for suggestion he was an inefficient and incoherent writer and wrongly stated he was one of the authors of a colour supplement feature.

12. Oct. 9, 1979
Damages for ASTMS general secretary Clive Jenkins for 'utterly false' suggestion he had queue-jumped for hospital treatment.

13. Oct. 11, 1979
Damages for freelance fashion writer Valerie Wade for reference to her as a 'hookette'.

14. Oct. 6, 1980
Damages for Roddy Llewellyn, friend of Princess Margaret.

15. Feb. 27, 1981
Damages for Dr Vassos Lyssarides, Cypriot Socialist leader, for article referring to the assassination of Youssef Sabai and the subsequent attempted hijacking at Larnaca Airport.

16. Apr. 24, 1981
Damages for Lord Tanlaw for suggestion he frequented a well-publicised disorderly house.

17. Oct. 23, 1981

Damages for Lord Goodman for allegations said to be "scurrilous, vicious and totally false".

18. Nov. 20, 1981

Damages for public relations consultant Ian Coulter for suggesting he was guilty of scandalous and unprofessional conduct, and then publishing his private telephone number.

19. Dec. 4, 1981

Damages for actress Penelope Keith and husband Rodney Timson for implication they had obtained a large and expensive bracelet by dishonest means.

20. Mar. 4, 1982

Damages for then Army Minister Peter Blaker for claims he obstructed inquiries into a policeman's death in Hong Kong.

21. May 6, 1982

Damages for TV producer Desmond Wilcox for allegations he was involved in "sharp practice" with BBC money.

22. July 30, 1982

Damages for Rev. Kenneth Leech for totally untrue allegations.

23. Aug. 13, 1982

Damages for St Margaret's Insurance Ltd, over allegations of criminal offences under the Insurance Companies Act, 1974.

24. Feb. 25, 1983

Apology for Louis Freedman, deputy senior steward of the Jockey Club, for alleging a receiving order in bankruptcy had been issued against him.

25. Mar. 11, 1983

Apology for Robert Maxwell over Look-alike letter with photographs of Mr Maxwell and Ronald Kray.

26. July 1, 1983

Damages for Lady Havers, wife of the Attorney-General, for a "complete fabrication" that she was carrying on an adulterous affair with the general manager of the Lowndes Hotel, Belgravia.

27. July 1, 1983

Apology for Sir James Goldsmith for connecting him incorrectly with two Italians on currency charges.

28. Oct. 7, 1983

Damages for solicitor Michael Harris for a number of serious and unwarranted allegations.

29. Nov. 18, 1983

Apology for Jocelyn Stevens for a "pure invention" report that he had said the *Sunday Express Magazine* was making enormous losses.

30. Dec. 2, 1983

Damages for Edward Knight, Kenneth Livingstone and Matthew Warburton for suggestions that Colonel Gaddafi had been asked for, and had given, financial backing for weekly newspaper *Labour Herald*.

RIGHT:
Dec. 2, 1983. Damages for Kenneth Livingstone (and Edward Knight and Matthew Warburton).

31. Feb. 10, 1984
Apology for Lady Rothermere for alleging she was paying the rent of a young actor friend.
32. Feb. 24, 1984
Damages for Cyril Allgood, chief engineer (construction) of the West Midlands County Council, for a series of articles.
33. Mar. 9, 1984
Apology for Rio Centre Ltd, (Dalston) for certain allegations about the state of the Centre's account.
34. Mar. 9, 1984
Apology to Miss Sara Keays and Marcus Fox, MP, for suggestion they were having an improper relationship.
35. May 4, 1984
Damages for three senior officers of Nottingham Constabulary for allegation they acted improperly in preventing a prosecution.

ABOVE:
Mar. 9, 1984.
Apology to
Marcus Fox, MP
(and to Miss Sarah
Keays).

LEFT:
*July 11, 1984.
Damages for
Sir Larry Lamb,
then editor of*
Daily Express.
*(And Mar. 11,
1983. Apology for
Mr Robert
Maxwell!)*

36. Apr. 6, 1984
Apology for ASTMS General Secretary Clive Jenkins for allegation he had flown from London to Miami in middle of an official TGWU dispute at Heathrow, that he had ignored official pickets and that he was a scab and a strike breaker.

37. Apr. 20, 1984
Damages for Gordon Kirby, then Second Secretary in the British Embassy in Belgrade, for series of articles linking him with death of nurse Helen Smith in Jeddah in 1979.

38. May 18, 1984
Apology to Chief Adi Balogun for article wrongly linking the Chief to commissions paid to magazine *Africa Now*.

39. July 11, 1984
Damages for then *Daily Express* editor Sir Larry Lamb over allegations that he was known for "swilling expensive Burgundy and taking three-hour lunches".

LEFT:
*July 29, 1985.
Apology for Cecil
Parkinson (and
damages for his
secretary, Miss
Angela Matthew).*

FAR LEFT:
*July 27, 1984.
Damages for
former general
secretary of
the TGWU,
Moss Evans.*

40. July 27, 1984
Damages for former general secretary of the TGWU Moss Evans for suggestions he arranged departure from Gatwick of trade union delegates to a conference in Miami in order to circumvent TGWU pickets at Heathrow.

41. Aug. 10, 1984
Apology for publisher Jocelyn Stevens.

42. June 14, 1984
Apology for former Prime Minister Edward Heath for suggesting his air fare to New York was paid by Andrew Lloyd Webber.

43. July 29, 1985
Apology for Cecil Parkinson and damages for his secretary, Miss Angela Mathew, for allegation they had been carrying on an adulterous affair.

44. July 30, 1985
Damages for Sir Eldon Griffiths, MP, for allegation he had grossly abused his position as advisor to the Police Federation.

45. Aug. 6, 1985
Damages of £20,000 for solicitor David Roberts for allegation he had conspired to conceal a £500,000 fraud concerning the defunct Bob Hope British Golf Classic charity golf tournament.

46. Jan. 24, 1986
Damages for former American Ambassador Mark Austad for allegations of grave misconduct as to cause offence to the governments of Finland, Norway and the United States.

47. Feb. 7, 1986
Damages for the London Symphony Orchestra and its chairman, Anthony Camden, following a long and sustained campaign against them.

48. Feb. 26, 1986
Damages for Gloucestershire Chief Constable Leonard Soper over allegations he was a Freemason and conspired with other Freemasons to pervert the course of justice.

49. Apr. 4, 1986
Damages for John Morphew in connection with the Bob Hope Golf Classic alleged fraud.

50. May 16, 1986
Damages for Dr John Casey and James Tregear for "causing great distress and embarrassment" to both of them.

51. June 27, 1986
Damages for Gloucestershire Chief Superintendent Colin Eynon for allegations, as with Chief Constable Soper.

52. Sept. 19, 1986
Apology for Judge Callman for allegation of totally untrue improper behaviour.

53. Oct. 17, 1986
Apology for Mrs Carolyn Andrews for allegation of an improper domestic or personal relationship with David Simpson to influence her professional career.

Sept. 19, 1986. Damages for Judge Callman.

Feb. 7, 1986. Damages for the London Symphony Orchestra.

Mr Maxwell's Diary

It was business as usual in the hectic world of Robert Maxwell despite his determination to spend as much time in court as possible. His Rolls Royce became a focal point for passers-by, parked on the shortest of yellow lines outside the Law Courts at the top of Fleet Street. Secretaries and legal advisers continually tiptoed into court to pass him notes as he sat at the front alongside his solicitor. The notes were either answered and passed back through a chain of hands, neatly folded and placed in a jacket pocket, or they prompted Mr Maxwell to rise, give a long bow to the Judge, and take control of the situation by means of a portable telephone held for him in the corridor.

No message was more urgent than on the morning of the fourth day, shortly after he had completed his six hours in the witness box. A note ripped from a pad said: 'One of our helicopters is down in the North Sea. There are many people dead.'

Mr Maxwell left immediately to get a full report from the Shetlands of the tragic accident which had killed forty-five men. He volunteered to visit the scene, but it was not necessary. By afternoon he was back in court - keeping abreast of the latest developments via another flurry of notes.

He announced later he had launched an appeal for the crash victims' families with a personal cheque for £10,000.

After spending most of the first Wednesday in the witness box Mr Maxwell returned to the *Mirror* office in Holborn, where negotiations went on into the early hours in the take-over battle for control of McCorquodale, the Basingstoke printing and financial services concern.

It had been a busy year leading up to the trial. Away from big business the highlight came when Oxford United, the club of which Mr Maxwell is chairman, won the Milk Cup at Wembley.

A week in the summer was spent attending the Labour Party conference at Blackpool.

Business achievements were:

February. BPCC and Pergamon emerge as a significant shareholder in Extel, supporting a £180 million take-over bid from Demerger Corporation.

March. BPCC buys Pergamon Journals for £239 million in new shares.

August. Hollis pays Pergamon £30 million for a package of Pergamon companies and publishing rights.

BPCC pays £355 million for the Philip Hill Investment Trust, in its second disguised rights issue.

Maxwell buys British Airways' helicopter division for £12.5 million.

September. BPCC agrees to buy Webb, a US printing company, for $117 million cash.

BPCC sells almost all of the Philip Hill portfolio to Goldman Sachs for a reputed £330 million.

October. BPCC agrees to buy Providence Gravure, US printer of magazines and medical catalogues, for $152.5 million.

Hollis proposes to inject £4 million into crane manufacturer Stothert & Pitt for a 77 per cent stake.

Hollis offers £8.9 million for Grosvenor Group, the ailing electronics and engineering company which had previously agreed to an £8 million bid from BDA.

November. Maxwell asserts his 19 per cent stake in McCorquodale to Norton Opax and carries on buying shares.

Hollis makes a £265 million recommended bid for AE, the engineering company previously bid for by Turner & Newall.

The *Eye*

In the course of the *Private Eye* trial, lawyers for the *Eye* exploited an article written by columist John Smith in *The People,* one of the newspapers owned by Mr Maxwell.

The article appeared in Smith's 'Straight Talk' column on December 29th, 1985. Reminding readers that publication of the New Year's Honours list was only a few days away, Smith commented: 'I'm willing to bet it will be sprinkled with peerages and knighthoods for people who have done damn all to deserve them.

'Looking down the list in recent years, you can't help thinking that some folk have secured places on it not because of their services to the public but their contributions to political party funds. Every tycoon knows that the short cut to a title is to cough up cash to the party in power.'

The column went on to point out the existence of a little known Act of Parliament which was passed in 1925 following revelations that Prime Minister Lloyd George had a 'price list' for those seeking honours. Under this Act, anyone trying to buy his way to a title was liable to serve two years in jail.

'What a pity those powers aren't strictly applied,' wrote Smith.

The reference to Smith's column was not included in reports of the trial which appeared in British newspapers.

It was left to an American newspaper, *The New York Times*, to highlight this particular piece of evidence. A few days after the trial ended, they carried a feature article on Mr Maxwell in which they recalled how the John Smith column had been 'triumphantly wielded' in court by *Private Eye*'s counsel.

What Smith had said in his column, said the *New York Times* article, was 'the very contention *Private Eye* used in raking Mr Maxwell, and here it was in a Maxwell publication in a different, long-ago connotation.'

Describing what happened when Mr Maxwell was confronted with the column, the New York Times reported: 'With the smile of a player achieving checkmate, the opposing lawyer had asked Mr. Maxwell: "Is this a lie?"

'Mr Maxwell replied: "It is a star reporter exercising his right of freedom of expression in our free society. His column you cannot tangle with. It is subject only to the laws of libel."'

John Smith does indeed enjoy freedom of expression in his column. He writes what he thinks, and is not dictated to by his editor. But the idea for this topic in his column came from a surprising source.

The editor of *The People*, Ernie Burrington, said after the *Private Eye* trial: 'I have been asked by many people - including, naturally, Mr Maxwell - about this particular column which was referred to so pointedly by the *Eye*'s counsel.

'I was not in court during the trial and merely read what was reported in most British newspapers.'

Mr Maxwell learned from Mr Burrington after the trial that the idea for the New Year Honours piece came from Mr Oscar Beuselinck, *Private Eye*'s solicitor, who had the conduct of the *Eye* action under his management and control.

Beuselinck is a flamboyant entertainment industry lawyer whose clients have included the Beatles, and the Rolling Stones.

A blunt, down-to-earth character, he said in an interview with *Tatler* magazine: 'You don't need brains in this business, my boy, just cunning - animal cunning.'

The People editor knew Beuselinck through friends and as a leading show business lawyer. Indeed it was in this latter role that Beuselinck had represented an actress called Charlotte Cornwell who sued *The People* for libel in December, 1985, after the newspaper's TV critic described her as having a 'big bum'. The subsequent award of £10,000 libel damages to Miss Cornwell is now the subject of appeal.

The People editor recalls that Mr Beuselinck phoned him in late November or early December, 1985.

'Mr Beuselinck asked me if I had studied the law governing Honours awards which was enacted after the Lloyd George scandal,' said Mr Burrington. 'He said it was interesting because many people believed the Act had been flagrantly ignored by successive governments whenever it suited them.

'Mr Beuselinck read out relevant parts of the Act and offered to send me a copy. I said I would get it for myself, and perhaps consider the subject for comment before the New Year's Honours came up at the end of December.'

'Might be an idea for you,' Beuselinck suggested to Burrington. He did not mention the *Eye* libel action or that this attack on the Honours system would be put to Mr Maxwell in court without notice in an attempt to justify their libel of the Mirror Group publisher. A week or two later, discussing topical subjects with John Smith, Burrington mentioned the statute to John Smith,who genuinely considered it was a tenable and timely topic for his column.

Little did Smith or Burrington realise that, almost twelve months later, the column would be exploited by the *Eye* defence lawyers who were trying to discredit Mr Maxwell.

Those lawyers, of course, included Mr Oscar Beuselinck, the original source for the article which was used against Mr Maxwell in the libel action.

RIGHT: *Oscar Beuselinck.*